Jean-Pierre Cassely

Jonglez

Nyons
Bollène
ORANGE
Carpentras
84
AVIGNON
Uzès
NIMES
Beaucaire
Tarascon
St-Rémy-de-Provence
Cavaillon
Gordes
Les Baux-de-Provence
ARLES
Salon-de-Provence
13
Istres
Martigues
Marignane
Vitrolles
Port-de-Bouc
Stes-Maries-de-la-Mer
MARSE

Sisteron
04
DIGNE-LES-BAINS
Forcalquier
Manosque
Gréoux-les-Bains
Riez
Moustiers-Ste-Marie
Castellane
Draguignan
83
St-Maximin-la-Ste-Baume
Brignoles
Barjols
Aubagne
La Ciotat
Bandol
TOULON
La Seyne-sur-Mer
Hyères
Le Lavandou
Porquerolles
Île de Porquerolles
Île de Port-Cros (Parc National)
ÎLES D'HYÈRES
RADE D'HYÈRES
Corniche des Maures
Corniche Sublime
Cassis
Cavalaire-sur-Mer

ACKNOWLEDGMENTS

L'Alcazar, Bibliothèque municipale à vocation régionale de Marseille, Sylvie Allemand, Michèle Amar, Sandra Artore, Association des Chevaliers de la Tarasque (Christian Guiot), Mireille Astolfi, Madame Barrere-Ellul, Agnès Baruol, Christian Battle, Latifa Bennezzar (sté Ricard), Berceau de la pétanque (Monsieur Negro), Caroline Bernard, Sabine Bernicaud, André Berrutti, Micheline et Jacques Bersia, Martine Bertrand, Muriel Bertrand, Nathalie Betthaueser, Bibliothèque Méjannes (Gilles Eboli, M. Ferrand), Bibliothèque municipale d'Aubagne, Bibliothèque municipale de Cassis, Bijouterie Commeiras à Digne, Fabienne Bonsignour, Pierre Boujon, Colette Bouvier (sté Ricard), Frédéric Brouillard, Andrée Brunetti, Christophe Cachera, Gérard Caminale de la direction interrégionale chargée des anciens combattants (ainsi que M. Rodot et Madame Renucci), Maryse Candela, Nathalie Carbonne, Pierre Cardin, Carrières du Bestouan à Cassis, Raymond et Huguette Casile, Caroline Casta (sté Ricard), Pierre Cauvin, Centre des Archives d'Outre-Mer (Marie-Thérèse Weiss), Centre Hospitalier de Montfavet, Madame Charpentier, Château d'Ansouis (famille Geraud de Sabran Pontevès), Château de Lourmarin (Danielle Antonelli), Château des Creissauds, Chemins du Patrimoine et Raoul Décugis (remerciements spéciaux pour tout le temps accordé et ses précieux guidages et renseignements), DJE Chol auteur de "Secrets et décors des hôtels particuliers aixois", Paul Chovelon, Comité départemental du tourisme des Alpes-de-Haute-Provence, Comité départemental du tourisme des Bouches-du-Rhône, Comité départemental du tourisme du Var, Comité départemental du tourisme du Vaucluse, Comité régional du tourisme PACA, Conseil général des Bouches-du-Rhône, Conseil général du Var, Monsieur Decourt, Département des sciences de l'éducation à Lambesc, Direction des cimetières de la ville d'Aubagne (Madame Gaudio), Domaine de Château-Bas (Madame de Blanquet), DRAC PACA et ses bibliothécaires et documentalistes, Martine Droit créatrice du monument dédié à Camille Claudel à l'entrée du Centre Hospitalier de Montfavet, Écomusée des appeaux et de la faune de Saint-Didier, Aziz El Kharif, Ermitage de Saint-Gens au Beaucet (Jean-Gabriel Fally), Espace Lumière-Michel Simon (Monica Tixier), Nelly Esposito, Etbts Chauvin, Claude Famechon, Dominique Fenolio, Monsieur Fenouil, Michèle Establier, Madame Feynas, Christian Gazel , Eric Giarratana, Dominique Gosselin chef de gare de la Ciotat, Axel Graisely et la grotte de Gaspard de Besse, Groupe Militari Conservation, Monsieur Guercia, Véronique Guerin Pointbasson, Marc Heracle, Hostellerie de la Source à Saint-Pierre-lès-Aubagne, Hôtel Jules César à Arles (Michel Albagnac), Hôtellerie de la Sainte-Baume, Joël Jacobi (spécialement), Danielle Jacqui, Jardin d'Elie, JP Jaubert, Pierre Javelle, Christian Julia, Roberte Lentsch, Les amis de Jouques, Les amis du Beausset-Vieux (Monsieur Salicetti), Les amis du Dixmude (Monsieur Tissier), Les amis du Vieux Rognes, Hélène Maignan, Monsieur Démosthène Maillis, Mairie de Valayans et le musée de la Vieille École de Pernes-les-Fontaines, Maison du tourisme de la Provence Verte, Nicole Manera, Bernadette Marchand, Marché d'Intérêt National de Châteaurenard, Mas de la Brune, Monsieur Maubet, Roland Maurel, Lolo Mauron, Méhari-Club de Cassis, Gérard Melanie, Anne Ménard, Jean-François Michel, Marie-Edith Michiels, Daniel Molinari, Monsieur le curé de Cornillon-Confoux (abbé de Boisgelin), Monsieur le curé de Cuges-les-Pins, Monsieur le curé de l'église Saint-Vincent à Saint-Andiol, Monsieur le curé de la Basilique de Saint-Maximin-la-Sainte-Baume, Monsieur le curé de la cathédrale Saint-Siffrein à Carpentras (abbé Daniel Bréhier), Monsieur le Curé de la cathédrale Saint-Veran de Cavaillon, Monsieur le curé de la collégiale Saint-Laurent (Père Desplanches), Monsieur le curé de l'église de la Sainte-Famille d'Istres (Père Brice de Roux), Monsieur le curé de ND de la SEDS à Toulon, Monsieur le curé de Notre-Dame de l'Assomption à Cuers, Monsieur Pelissier, Musée brignolais, Musée de l'Arles et de la Provence antiques (Claude Sintes), Musée de la glace à Mazaugues, Musée de la mine à Gréasque, Musée de la plongée Frédéric Dumas et son Président tragiquement disparu l'été 2005 Yves Maucherat, Musée de la RN 7 à Piolenc, Musée de Vachères (Madame Keller), Musée des amis du Vieux-Toulon (tout à fait particulièrement Henri Bouvet), Musée des gueules rouges de Tourves, Musée du Vieil-Aix (Nicole Martin-Vigne), Musée Gassendi à Digne (Nadine Passamar-Gomez), Musée Georges Mazoyer à Ansouis, Musée Marc Deydier (Monsieur Muller), Musée Melik (Danièle Malis), Muséum d'histoire naturelle d'Aix (Yves Dutour), Raphaëlle Nicaise, Observatoire SIREN à Lagarde d'Apt, Office de tourisme de la vallée du Gapeau, Philippe Palvini, Iris Perben, Père Dominique Petit de l'église de la Madeleine à Aix, Père Magnan curé de Cassis, Pharmacie de la Rotonde à Aix, Michel Pichoud, Fernand Pouillon à titre posthume, Véronique Prat, R.M. fleurs Mathieu à Avignon, Léon Ravaux des 2G, RCT (Rugby Club Toulonnais), Réserve Géologique de Haute-Provence, Restaurant le parc des Cordes, Restaurant le Carillon, Raymond Reynaud, Yves Rousset-Rouard, Michel Roy, Bouzid Sabeg, Salon de coiffure Jo à Aix, Xénia et Bernard Saltiel, Céline Salvetat, Sanctuaire Notre-Dame des Anges (Père Antoine), Serge Sappino, Bruno Saunier, Max Sauze, Famille Schlagdenhauffen à Volonne, Sébastien Schmit (archéologue), Frédérique Segond, SIANPOU, Lilianne Sireta, SNCF (Philippe Peugnet, Marion Larroche), Michèle Soyer, Fabien Strak, Syndicat ND des Anges (Chantal Molinas), Bruno Tassan (pour ses visites de la Via Aurelia),The Camargo Foundation à Cassis, Théâtre Georges Galli à Sanary, Madame Torrese, Maxime Tissot, Karine Tramier, René et Gérard Truc, UDOTSI Var (Christian Gazel), Denis et Corrine Urvoy, Joëlle Valentini, Vidéothèque lyrique de la Cité du Livre d'Aix (Valérie Bedouk), Villes d'Evenos, Goult (et la Communauté Notre-Dame de Lumière), La Celle, La Penne-sur-Huveaune, Lacoste (et office de tourisme intercommunal du canton de Bonnieux), Lambesc, Meyreuil, Mollégès, Oppède-le-Vieux, Pélissanne (et office de tourisme du massif des Costes), Pourrières, Rougiers, Rustrel, Saint-Saturnin-les-Apt, Salin-de-Giraud, Sanary-sur-Mer (et Maison du tourisme), Velaux (et Musée de la Tour - Véronique Prat),Vernègues, Volonne, Villes et offices de tourisme d'Aix-en-Provence, Arles, Avignon, Bandol, Barjols, Baux-de-Provence, Berre-l'Etang, Besse-sur-Issole, Brignoles, Cadenet, Carpentras, Cassis, Cavaillon, Céreste, Charleval-en-Provence, Châteauneuf-les-Martigues, Châteaurenard, Cornillon-Confoux, Cucuron, Cuers, Cuges-les-Pins, Digne-les-Bains, Eguilles, Fontvieille, Istres, La Ciotat, La Roquebrussanne, Lamanon, La Seyne-sur-Mer (direction des cimetières - Christian Battle), Lourmarin, Maillane, Manosque, Marignane, Marseille, Ménerbes, Miramas, Pernes-les-Fontaines, Peyrolles, Pierrefeu-du-Var, Pignans, Rognes, Saint-Andiol, Saint-Chamas, Saint-Cyr-sur-Mer (Monsieur Maubet), Saint-Etienne du Grès, Saint-Mandrier, Saint-Maximin la Sainte-Baume, Saint-Remy de Provence, Salon-de-Provence, Sénas, Six-Fours-les-Plages, Solliès-Pont, Tarascon, Toulon, Tourves, Vitrolles, Saintes-Maries de la Mer, Les Taillades, Le Beausset, Plan-d'Aups la Sainte-Baume, pays de Forcalquier, Ville et point d'information touristique de Banon, Ville et point info-tourisme de Cabrières-d'Avignon, Ville et syndicat d'initiative de Grambois et Grans.

Photo credits: all photos by Jean-Pierre Cassely, **except:** the map of the Mur de la Peste, ("Document Pierre Sèche en Vaucluse" - map excerpted from La ligne dans le paysage, by Denis Lacaille eand Danièle Larcena with their kind permission), Les Milles internment camp (courtesy of the Direction interdépartementale chargée des Anciens Combattants), the tomb of Latouche-Treville (courtesy of the Direction interdépartementale chargée des Anciens Combattants), the ex-votos of Beausset-Vieux (courtesy of Les Amis du Beausset-Vieux), and the lime kilns (Association "Les Chemins du Patrimoine")

Cartography: Michelin - **Design:** Roland Deloi - **Layout:** Véronique Desanlis and Thomas Laurens - **Copy-editing/proof-reading (French text):** Thomas Laurens and Romaine Guérin - **English translation:** Thomas Clegg and Caroline Lawrence
Printed in Italy
Cover page: "Statue of the virgin of Cornillon-Confoux"

Secret Provence is the result of an observation: the guidebooks available to the inhabitants of Provence and frequent visitors to the region all seem to describe the same familiar places. There is nothing or very little in them that would surprise anyone who already knows the region fairly well.

This guide is aimed at such readers, although we hope it will also please the occasional visitor seeking to depart from the beaten tourist paths.

Comments about this guidebook and its contents, as well as information concerning places we may not have mentioned herein, are more than welcome. They will permit us to enrich future editions of this guidebook.

Don't hesitate to write us:

- By e-mail: infos@editionsjonglez.com
- By post: Éditions Jonglez, 3, rue Duban 75016 Paris, France.

CONTENTS

AIX AND AROUND

AROUND MARSEILLE

TOULON AND WEST VAR

PROVENCE VERTE AND CENTRAL VAR

AROUND L'ÉTANG DE BERRE AND SALON-DE-PROVENCE

CAMARGUE

ALPILLES

AVIGNON AND AROUND

LUBÉRON

HAUTE-PROVENCE

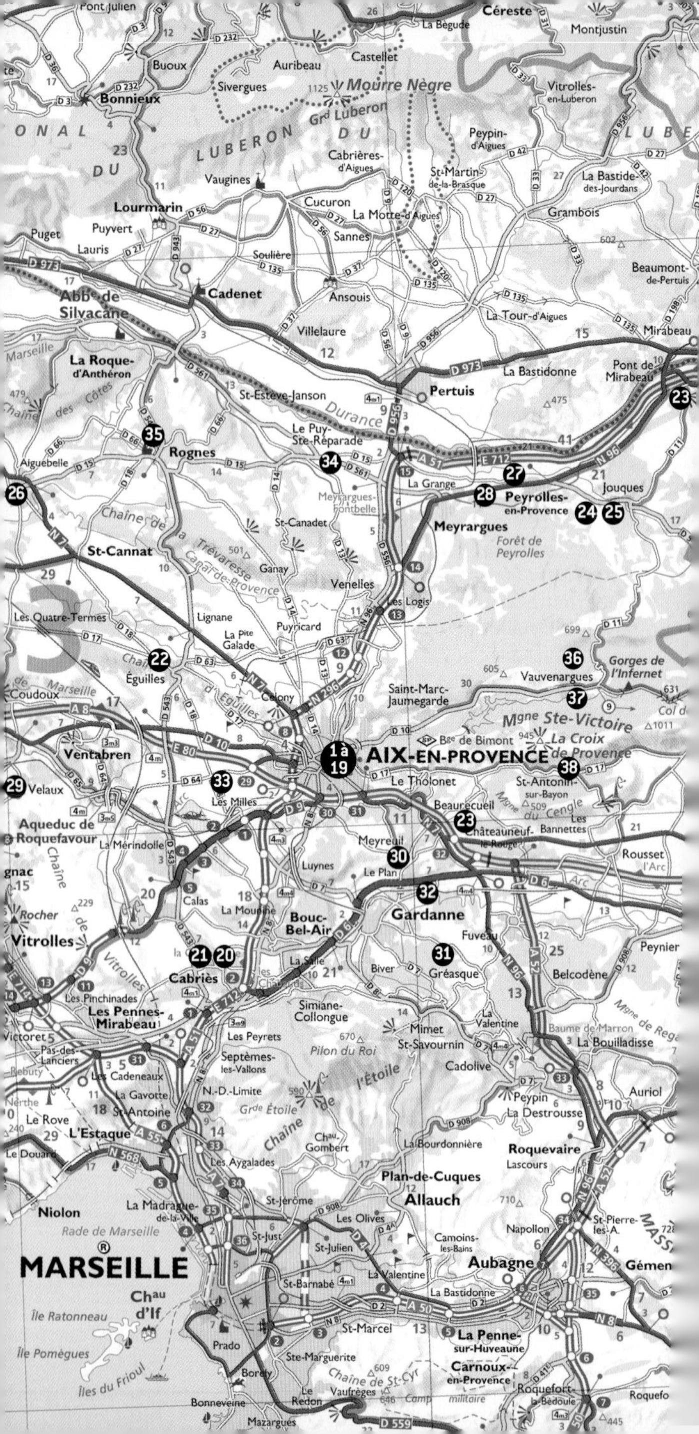

MARSEILLE
AIX-EN-PROVENCE
Mourre Nègre
Grd Luberon
Bonnieux
Lourmarin
Cadenet
Ansouis
Pertuis
La Tour-d'Aigues
Rognes
Meyrargues
Peyrolles-en-Provence
Jouques
Vauvenargues
Mgne Ste-Victoire
La Croix de Provence
Gardanne
Aubagne
Vitrolles
Les Pennes-Mirabeau
Cabriès
Bouc-Bel-Air
Allauch
Plan-de-Cuques
Roquevaire
La Penne-sur-Huveaune
Carnoux-en-Provence
L'Estaque
Niolon
Rade de Marseille
Chau d'If
Île Ratonneau
Île Pomègues
Îles du Frioul
Chaîne de l'Étoile
Pilon du Roi
Chaîne de St-Cyr
Durance
Aqueduc de Roquefavour
Ventabren
Velaux
Éguilles
St-Cannat
Venelles
Puyricard
Le Tholonet
Châteauneuf-le-Rouge
Fuveau
Gréasque
Mimet
St-Savournin
Septèmes-les-Vallons
Simiane-Collongue
Abbe de Silvacane
La Roque-d'Anthéron
St-Estève-Janson
Le Puy-Ste-Réparade
Mirabeau
Beaumont-de-Pertuis
Grambois
La Bastide-des-Jourdans
Vitrolles-en-Luberon
Céreste
Montjustin
Cucuron
Vaugines
Sannes
Villelaure
Gorges de l'Infernet
Forêt de Peyrolles
Rousset
Peynier
Belcodène
La Bouilladisse
Auriol
Gémenos
Roquefort-la-Bédoule

AIX-EN-PROVENCE AND AROUND

THE HIDDEN STATUE OF AIX'S REVOLUTIONARY LEADER

- Palais de Justice,
- Place de Verdun, 13605 Aix-en-Provence
- Open 8.00–17.00 weekdays

Mirabeau gives a helpful pointer...

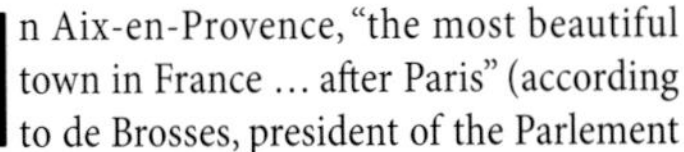

In Aix-en-Provence, "the most beautiful town in France … after Paris" (according to de Brosses, president of the Parlement de Bourgogne in the 18th century and a seasoned traveller), it is difficult to escape from the shadow of Gabriel-Honoré Riquetti, Count de Mirabeau (1749–91). But paradoxically, the statue of Mirabeau, one of the town's most emblematic figures, is much harder to find than the Cours (the broad boulevard in the town centre) that bears his name.

Most residents of Aix seem to believe that his statue is at the upper end of the Cours … when in fact that statue is of King Réné I d'Anjou, "The Good" (1409–80), who was King of Naples, Duke of Anjou and Count of Provence. Their ignorance is understandable, because the real statue is not only "hidden", but has been moved several times from its original site. Today, it is to be found in the waiting hall of the Palais of Justice [law courts], and represents Mirabeau making his reply to Marquis Henri-Evrard de Dreux-Brézé, who had just ordered the dissolution of the French National Assembly (23 June 1789), with this famous phrase: "Go tell your master that we are here by the will of the people and will yield only to the force of the bayonet."

The statue previously stood in the courtyard of the town hall (place de l'Hôtel de Ville) and its inauguration was marked by a rather comical incident. When, following the usual speech, the statue was finally unveiled, some of the people in the watching crowd began to laugh. Others, not understanding the reason for this hilarity, protested with indignant shushing noises. The next day, the mystery was resolved, thanks to a citizen who took the initiative of hanging a sign from the revolutionary orator's arm that read:

[Admire Mirabeau in his proud pose, / Upon a pedestal of marble he does repose. / Passer-by, do you feel an urgent need to piss? / The great man's finger points to the urinals, you can't miss …]

The outstretched hand did indeed point to the public lavatories of the town hall, and for this reason the statue was removed to another spot …

UNDER THE MIRABEAU BRIDGES

If the name of the Mirabeau bridge evokes the Seine and Apollinaire's poetry for Parisians, in Provence there are twin Mirabeau bridges spanning the River Durance. These bridges, which can be seen from the Autoroute des Alpes, lie just below the village of Mirabeau (Vaucluse), whose existing chateau was built on the ruins of that belonging to the Mirabeau family. The name Mirabeau is said to be derived from mira beü, the Provençal expression for "beautiful view", or "belvedere".

MIRABEAU, EROTIC WRITER

- Mirabeau's L'Errotika-Biblion in the Bibliothèque Méjannes
- Cité du Livre, 8–10, rue des Allumettes, 13100 Aix-en-Provence
- Tel: 04 42 91 98 88
- Open Tuesday, Thursday and Friday 12.00–18.00; Wednesday and Saturday 10.00–18.00

"Imprisoned, then banished to Hell...

Following his much publicized divorce from Émilie, daughter of the Count de Marignane, Mirabeau "eloped" with Sophie de Ruffey, the wife of the Marquis de Monnier, an act that earned him a death sentence. Prisoner in the Bastille fortress at the same time as the Marquis de Sade, Count Mirabeau wrote various libertine works for his mistress Sophie, including L'Errotika-Biblion, which surprisingly was published in 1783 by the Vatican's own printers. Why would the Vatican publish erotic books? It did so in order to control the publication and its distribution, limited to Roman Catholic confessors, the restricted sections of certain libraries, and the underground vaults of the Vatican itself. Still considered diabolical despite its outmoded style, and unavailable in bookshops, L'Errotika-Biblion can be consulted (though not borrowed) in the patrimonial section (salle Peiresc) at the Bibliothèque Méjanes, reference ENF (enfers)* 16 or 36. This work is divided into 10 chapters with very learned titles: L'Anagogie, L'Anélytroïde, L'Ischa, La Tropoïde, Le Thalaba, L'Anandrine, L'Akropodie, Le Kadesch, Béhémah and L'Anoscopie. Mirabeau demonstrated here with great erudition that ancient and biblical customs were even more depraved than the corrupt practices of his own times.

*The restricted sections of French libraries, with works forbidden to minors, are known as les enfers [hell].

MIRABEAU (1749–91), LIFE AND DEATH OF AN IDOL

Born with two teeth, an enormous head and a twisted foot, Gabriel-Honoré Riquetti, Count de Mirabeau, contracted smallpox at the age of 3. Very precocious in all matters, he ran up debts that his father refused to repay, for which the young Mirabeau was sent to prison several times. He wedded Émilie, daughter of the Marquis de Marignane, then divorced her and became famous for his numerous female conquests. Extremely cultivated and curious about everything, he wrote several works and impressed his contemporaries with his talents as an orator. At the onset of the French Revolution, he was elected deputy of the Third Estate by the voters of Aix and Marseille. But it was later discovered that he maintained correspondence with the French king, Louis XVI. When news of Mirabeau's death reached Aix, a banner was stretched across the Cours, reading: "Mirabeau is dead, Diogenes can extinguish his light." The funeral took place at Saint-Eustache church in Paris. 100,000 people followed the procession.

CEZANNE AT THE CATHEDRAL

• Rue Gaston de Saporta, 13100 Aix-en-Provence

Never too late for salvation…

Does anyone notice the plaque on the floor, just to the right of the main doors with Saint-Sauveur cathedral in Aix-en-Provence? Placed at the exact spot where Germain Nouveau, a poet better known by his pen name of Humilis, begged for money on Sundays before Mass, this commemorative plaque bears the following inscription: Saint-Sauveur cathedral, where Cézanne assiduously spent time at the end of his life. Does this imply that he wasn't so assiduous before …? Cézanne carefully prepared alms for his "paupers" before leaving for the cathedral on Sunday morning. He gave each of them a small cloth bag tied with a knot, containing the exact same sum of money.

Was it this attendance "late in life" to holy duties that caused Matisse to comment one day in 1925: *"You see, Cézanne is sort of the Good Lord of painting …"*?

SIGHTS NEARBY

CÉZANNE TOURS

Cézanne interested no one in his own time, to the point that Pontier, the curator of the Musée d'Aix, declared in 1901: "As long as I'm alive, not a single work of Cézanne will enter this museum." And he kept his word!

Today, there are several routes in or around the town of Aix that follow in Cézanne's footsteps, to places he lived or painted or was fond of, from the sign of his father's hat shop at 55 cours Mirabeau to his own artist's studio in Les Lauves (which is open to the public), and the Sainte-Victoire mountain, a hikers' paradise. And, lastly, a detour by the Saint-Pierre cemetery (in Aix, not the one in Marseille dedicated to the same saint) allows for a few moments reflection before his grave, arranged admirably so that it looks towards his favourite mistress: Sainte-Victoire.

ATELIER CÉZANNE
9, avenue Paul-Cézanne, 13100 Aix-en-Provence
• Tel: 04 42 21 06 53 • Fax: 04 42 21 90 34
• E-mail: infos@atelier-Cézanne.com • http://www.atelier-Cézanne.com

NUMBER ZERO, RUE PAUL DOUMER

5

Rue Paul Doumer, 13100 Aix-en-Provence

If you live at Number 0, do you still pay tax?

Strange but true: the numbering of the buildings along rue Paul Doumer in Aix start with the number 0. According to Roux-Alpheran, author of a work entitled *Les rues d'Aix* published in 1846, the spot bearing this unlikely number was previously a ditch where soldiers trained with crossbows in front of the ramparts of Aix. The day they filled in this ditch between "2" and nothingness, they thus had to create a … zero. The street used to be called rue du Trésor, because the town treasury was located here. One amusing detail is that Paul Doumer, whose name is now given to the street, was born in Aurillac to a relatively poor family. He later became the French Minister of Finance and invented … income tax.

Today, a real estate firm has its offices at number 0. As their name contains the word savon [soap], the managers have conjured up the image of a soap … bubble, rather than that unlikely zero. They also claim that a soap factory previously had premises here.

SIGHTS NEARBY

3, COURS MIRABEAU: BONAPARTE IN AIX

6

The Cours Mirabeau itself presents another anomaly (or rather, two anomalies) in its numbering. Impossible to find a number 1, or a 2: both these numbers belonged to posterns or sentry boxes that once stood against the first two buildings in this street.

Next to the green cross of the pharmacy at number 3 of the Cours, you'll see a plaque informing you that it was in this building (at the time, the Hôtel des Princes et des Quatre Nations) that Bonaparte, on returning from Egypt, announced his arrival in France to the Directoire which governed the country. He spent the evening and night of 18 Vendemiaire VIII (by the Revolutionary calendar – 10 October 1799) in this hotel and it's said that he received the relatives in Aix of soldiers who had taken part in the Egyptian campaign. Among them was a woman wearing laurel on her forehead and around her neck. She offered them to the future French emperor, who gave them to a young valet, saying, "Boy, take these bay leaves down to citizen Imbert in the kitchen, to put in the stew."

RESTAURANT LE CARILLON

- 10, rue Portalis, 13100 Aix-en-Provence
- Menus €10 and €13
- Closed Saturday evening, Sunday, and during August

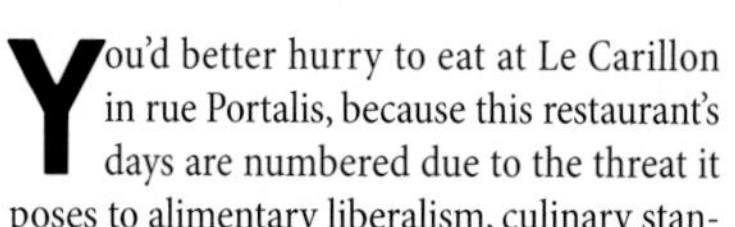

You'd better hurry to eat at Le Carillon in rue Portalis, because this restaurant's days are numbered due to the threat it poses to alimentary liberalism, culinary standardization, the dictates of nutritionists, and runaway globalization. The fact that a restaurant can survive by offering a complete fixed-price meal at €10 (assorted raw vegetables, fresh gnocchis à la tomate, foie d'agneau persillé, salad, apple compote and a quarter litre of good red wine) seems miraculous. It's easy to see why the restaurant has no phone, so don't bother trying to look it up in the Yellow Pages, it's simply not there … On the other hand, the queue that forms twice a day at its door at 10 rue Portalis, near the Palais de Justice, shows that it has no need to be in the directory to attract customers.

Le Carillon is so old-fashioned that it could almost set a style itself. The menu, typed out in two columns on an old Remington, is presented in an album with photos of the owner's travels round the world. You might have trouble reading this, depending on whether you get the original typed sheet or the fourth carbon copy, but no matter, the food is always good.

Like the prices, the two waiters seem to have stumbled out of another era, and that's not a criticism.

JEAN ÉTIENNE MARIE PORTALIS (1746–1807)

A famous Aix jurist born in the village of Beausset (Var), Portalis was one of the men who first drafted the French Civil Code. His statue stands in front of the Palais de Justice. To the right is a statue of Siméon, while Portalis is on the left. Unless it's the other way around: both statues are so worn by time that their features are unrecognizable.

SIGHTS NEARBY

LA PLACE DES TROIS ORMEAUX

The place des Trois Ormeaux [Three Elms] is one of those small squares that make walks in Aix an immense pleasure. The peculiar feature of this square is that today there remain only two-and-a-half trees, and two of them aren't elms … When the Connétable de Bourbon held a victory parade in Aix in 1524, the crowd was asked to yell *"Vive Bourbon!"* with enthusiasm … But in this square, one man refused to acclaim the victor. He was immediately hung by the neck from one of the three trees. It's said that, ever since that day, the third tree has always had problems growing …

MEMENTOES OF AIX'S FÊTE-DIEU

9

• Musée du Vieil Aix - Hôtel Estienne de Saint-Jean
17, rue Gaston de Saporta, 13100 Aix-en-Provence
• Tel: 04 42 21 43 55 • Open weekly except Monday and during October, 10.00 to 12.00 and 14.30 to 17.00 (winter), or 14.30 to 18.00 (summer)
• Admission: €4, reduced rate (students, unemployed, etc.) €2.50; free for children 14 and under

"Religious entertainment

In a room on the first floor, the Musée du Vieil Aix presents some interesting mementoes of the Fête-Dieu, which until the mid-19th century was the big annual festive occasion that drew people from all over Europe to Aix-en-Provence.

First of all, you'll come across a superb 18th-century screen that portrays in great detail the various processions and "games" held during this event. The "Devils' Game", the "Game of the Cat", or the "Game of the Massacre of the Innocents", were all intended to illustrate episodes from the Old and New Testaments, entertaining the common people while stimulating their religious fervour. The wealth of detail is such that you can linger awhile before this fascinating object from the past. In a display case close by, there are jointed marionettes that could replicate the festival with even greater realism because the operators added their voices and songs to the show. Along similar lines, the museum exhibits a "talking" Christmas crib.

THE FÊTE-DIEU

Born in 1192 near Liege in Belgium, St Juliana had a revelation at the age of 18 that would drastically change her life: God instructed her to establish within the Roman Catholic Church the feast of the Holy Sacrament or Fête-Dieu. After numerous difficulties, the first Fête-Dieu was finally celebrated at Liege in 1247, before becoming an official Catholic holiday in 1264. Falling on the Thursday following the first Sunday after Pentecost, the Fête-Dieu (called "Corpus Christi" in some countries), expresses gratitude to God for having offered to mankind the symbol of the Eucharist and the Host as the Body of Christ.

SIGHTS NEARBY

RUE ESQUICHO-COUDE, THE NARROWEST STREET IN AIX-EN-PROVENCE 10

Starting from the Musée du Vieil Aix, go down rue de Saporta for a few metres, then take rue Gibelin on your left, and rue Esquicho-coude is the first alleyway on the left. Esquicho is the Provençal term for "to crush" or "to squeeze", while coude is French for "elbow". Here's how Roux-Alpheran, author of the guidebook Les rues d'Aix [The Streets of Aix] explains the origins of this name: *"The rue Esquicho-coude is thus named because it is so narrow that those passing through it need to squeeze in their elbows if they want to avoid touching the rows of houses on either side."*

SALON DE COIFFURE JO 11

• Le Mirabeau, 3, avenue des Belges, 13100 Aix-en-Provence
• Tel: 04 42 27 67 64 • Open Tuesday to Friday, 8.00–12.00 and 14.00–18.00, Saturday 8.00–12.00

Room for just one Figaro...

On the ground floor of the Mirabeau building, a hundred metres from the place de la Rotonde, Jo provides service with a smile as a men's barber. He has no employees, and no intention of hiring any, as there simply isn't room for two figaros (the French nickname for barbers) in his salon. It's only 9 m2, although conveniently located by the entrance to the building. You might think that these premises were once a glass cabin to observe the comings and goings of residents and block access to any unwelcome visitors.

Jo likes doing women's hair, too, but as he himself admits, they may feel a little cramped in these premises ... So Jo mostly cuts men's hair. He thus reinforces the traditional image of Aix-en-Provence, a town where two operas dear to the hearts of "quality" barbers have triumphed although they are now seldom presented in France: Mozart's Marriage of Figaro and Rossini's Barber of Seville.

SIGHTS NEARBY

VIDÉOTHÈQUE D'ART LYRIQUE ET DE DANSE

Cité du Livre, 8–10, rue des Allumettes, 13100 Aix-en-Provence
• Tel: 04 42 91 90 89 • Open Tuesday to Friday, 13.00–18.00, Saturday 10.00–13.00 and 14.00–18.00 • Database and Minitel consultation: 04 42 26 62 15 • Group visits: mornings, by appointment • Closed August

The main complaint of Aix residents (and tourists) concerning their International Festival of Lyric Art is the price of tickets. Although you can find seats for €28 on the first day of booking, if you're willing to spend the previous night sleeping in front of the festival offices ... The other complaint is that outwith the festival, held in July, there is no opera in Aix.

There is, however, a means of seeing opera in Aix without emptying your wallet, 11 months out of 12: by settling yourself comfortably in a booth at this video library of lyric art, with headphones, you can enjoy over and over again most of the operas and concerts performed in Aix-en-Provence since 1950, almost as if you had been there. It's a unique chance to see and hear great voices first discovered at the Aix festival: the two Teresas (Berganza and Stitch-Randall), Renato Cappechi, Marcello Cortis, Gabriel Bacquier and many others.

There is also a collection of dance videos available and the festival archives are enriched each year with new productions. From the moment you enter this musical haven, the lyrical atmosphere is conducive to a moment of auditory bliss.

RÉSIDENCE FERNAND POUILLON

- 2, avenue Jean Moulin (route des Alpes)
13100 Aix-en-Provence
- http://www.culture.gouv.fr/culture/ paca/dossiers/xxeme/fiche11.pdf

Architect, convict, escapee, and medal-winner…

Despite the frenzy of postwar reconstruction, some architectural projects of the time are still noteworthy achievements today. This particular project in Aix called for a housing development on a human scale, whose flats would be sold with 25-year mortgages but no down payments, in order to give a larger part of the population the chance to become homeowners. The key factor in the project's success, however, was the fact that its design was entrusted to an architect who would later become famous for his talent (but also his imprisonment): Fernand Pouillon. The specifications for this assignment were daunting: 200 dwellings to be built for 200 million (old) francs, only 200 m from the town centre, in less than 200 days.

Started in 1951, the residence would in fact contain 159 dwellings costing 368 million francs and be finally delivered in 1953 … But never mind, the Pouillon residence is still very much a "des-res" today, with a queue of candidates seeking to acquire one of its flats. The architectural originality of this building project lies in its materials, with a stone façade and layered brick load-bearing walls, and the tidy arrangement of both the building's exterior and the communal areas inside.

One detail demonstrates the pains taken by Fernand Pouillon to integrate the building with its surroundings: he called for a fountain with a drinking trough to be installed by the side of the road dividing the residence, which forms part of the Alpine seasonal migration route (once called the Cours des Alpes, today avenue Jean-Jaurés), so that sheep could be watered there.

FERNAND POUILLON: MEDITERRANEAN ARCHITECT

Born in 1912 at Cancon (Lot-et-Garonne), Fernand Pouillon studied architecture in Marseille. Although his first building projects in Marseille and Aix date from before the Second World War, he is best known in Provence for having rebuilt the Vieux-Port of Marseille, devastated by the Nazi occupation. But following the bankruptcy of the property company, Le Comptoir du Logement, he was sent to jail, from whence he escaped Ɛ After living in hiding for three years in Italy, he gave himself up and was sentenced to three years' imprisonment. It was while serving this sentence that he would write two books, the best known of which is Les Pierres sauvages [The Wild Stones]. He then worked on a number of major urban projects in Algeria (including the 200 columns of "Climat de France") and finally received the French Légion d'Honneur from President François Mitterand. He passed away in 1986.

VENEZ HABITANTS DE LA TERR
NATIONS ECOVTEZ LA LOI

JOSEPH SEC MONUMENT

14

• 6, avenue Pasteur, 13100 Aix-en-Provence

A Revolutionary mausoleum for a wealthy merchant

Is this an esoteric folly, the eulogistic work of a sincere citizen moved by his recent experiences, a shamefaced rallying to the victory of the class enemy, a grand gesture by a repentant man of wealth, or simply a heartfelt artistic legacy? All these questions spring to mind on contemplating one of the first rare, private, secular monuments known to exist in France. It was on 20 February 1792 that this mausoleum was dedicated by Joseph Sec, wood merchant, to the "law-observing" town of Aix … Other inscriptions engraved on the stone are equally strange:[Freed from a cruel slavery

I have no other master but myself, / But of my freedom I wish no use, / Other than to obey the law.]

Located alongside the avenue Pasteur, and blending into its surroundings, the monument is surprising on a closer look: its imposing size, first of all, its interior garden filled with statues saved by Joseph Sec from the pillage of the nearby Jesuit church, and its ostentatious wealth, which must have attracted attention. Why would Joseph Sec have wanted to build such a mausoleum with inscriptions echoing revolutionary sentiments? Perhaps in order to rest in peace, protected from any subsequent outbreaks of popular wrath?

The observant will find any number of meanings in the rich symbolism, including both religious representations (particularly daring in those revolutionary times) and Masonic symbols (much more fashionable).

TO FIND OUT MORE

One invaluable source of aid in deciphering this monument is Michel Vovelle's book, Les folies d'Aix, ou la fin d'un monde [The Follies of Aix, or the End of a World], published by Éditions le Temps des Cerises, which devotes a whole chapter to the life (and death) of Joseph Sec.

SIGHTS NEARBY

FONTAINE DES NEUF-CANONS

15

The first fountain you come across going up the Cours Mirabeau in Aix-en-Provence is the Fontaine des Neuf-Canons [Nine Cannons Fountain]. The edge of its basin is very low and when the sun pierces through the plane trees, you often sees dogs having a dip and then shaking themselves off, spattering the delighted children of tourists. This fountain served as a drinking trough for flocks on the seasonal migration between Arles and the Alps. The edge had to be low enough to allow sheep to drink, as stipulated in a statutory right of way accorded by Aix to the town of Arles beginning in the 12th century!

THE ANNUNCIATION OF SAINTE-MADELEINE CHURCH

• Église Sainte-Madeleine
Place des Prêcheurs, 13100 Aix-en-Provence
• Fifth bay on the left, just before the rostrum

Wearing owl wings, Gabriel may not be so angelic...

Only the central panel of the Annunciation triptych remains in the Sainte-Madeleine church in Aix, the left panel (in two parts) and the right panel having been removed to Brussels, Rotterdam and Amsterdam. This work, the subject of numerous controversial interpretations, is attributed to Barthélemy d'Eyck, a relative of the much more famous Van Eyck, and was commissioned in the will of Pierre Corpici, a draper in Aix, on 9 December 1442.

In Guide de la Provence mystérieuse (Éditions Tchou), there is an analysis of the painting highlighting its wicked aspects, contrary to religious teachings. For example, the wings of the angel Gabriel are not at all "angelic", but composed of the feathers of an owl, a supposedly evil bird. There are other strange features: on top of the lectern in front of Mary there is a monkey who seems to be intercepting the breath of God; the columns rising above the archangel support two curious prophets; while the arch below is decorated with the figures of a devil and a bat. Émile Henriot, in his book, *Diable à l'hôtel* [Devil in the Hotel], also notes that the gesture of the Lord bestowing his blessing upon Mary, *"with the thumb folded over the index and middle fingers, has something obscene about it"*. And he adds, *"the flowers gathered in a vase next to Mary were regarded as evil in the Middle Ages: they are foxglove, belladonna and basil"*.

On the part of the Roman Catholic Church, these interpretations are refuted as tendentious. Concerning the owl wings, it is pointed out that this bird represented Athena in ancient times, while the monkey bathed by God's breath represents man, as the sinner who will be saved by the incarnation of Christ. The gesture bestowing God's blessing was commonly portrayed like this at the time of the painting, and as for the flowers in the vase, it is maintained that these are in fact roses and columbines.

We'll leave the final word to Yoshiaki Nishino, who for the first time was able to interpret the triptych in its entirety, having examined all four fragments. According to this expert, the painting is a representation of the two worlds, that of the Old Testament (sub lege – the realm of law) and that of the New Testament (sub gratia – the realm of grace), the first being superior to the second. He confirms that the two prophets portrayed are Jeremiah and Isaiah. He describes in detail the outdoor scene glimpsed through the opening behind the angel. You see a horseman on a white steed riding towards a town. Some people have recognized Sainte-Victoire mountain in the painting. In the background, behind the pillars, fragments depicting a Mass can be perceived. Lastly, the breath of God containing a homunculus (the Infant Jesus already holding his Cross) will purify Mary, who like any human being still bears original sin.

TO FIND OUT MORE

Guide de la Provence mystérieuse (Éditions Tchou).
Primitifs français, découvertes et redécouvertes, catalogue of the exhibition organized 27 February–17 May 2004 under the direction of Dominique Thiébaut (Réunion des Musées Nationaux).
Professor Yoshiaki Nishino, "Le triptyque de l'Annonciation d'Aix et son programme iconographique", Artibus et Historiae, No. 39, 1999.
The last two documents cited can be consulted in the library of the Direction Régionale des Affaires Culturelles (DRAC) 24, boulevard du Roi René, 13617 Aix-en-Provence Cédex. Tel: 04 42 16 19 75

SIGHTS NEARBY

DARET'S TROMPE-L'OEIL - GRAND STAIRWAY, HÔTEL DE CHÂTEAURENARD
19, rue Gaston de Saporta, 13100 Aix-en-Provence

This townhouse today houses the offices of the municipal cultural services. The trompe l'oeil can be viewed from the grand staircase during office hours. If this trompe l'œil by the local painter Daret is well known, it is rarely visited because you first need to enter this townhouse, then from the courtyard go through a second doorway on the right in order to discover one of the marvels of Aix-en-Provence. The figure drawing back the fictitious curtain to spy on you will haunt you until the evening, and even into the night. Louis XIV, who stayed in this townhouse during his time in Aix, was quick to take Daret into his entourage, making him a royal painter.

TO FIND OUT MORE ABOUT PRIVATE TOWNHOUSES IN AIX

D. J. E. Chol, Secrets des hôtels particuliers aixois

PHALLIC BALCONIES OF L'HÔTEL DE BOYER D'EGUILLES 

- Muséum d'histoire naturelle d'Aix-en-Provence
- 6, rue Espariat, 13090 Aix-en-Provence

> ***The wrought-iron railings on this 17th century façade display a curious motif***

The Museum of Natural History in Aix-en-Provence occupies the large townhouse at 6 rue Espariat, built in 1672 for Marquis Jean-Baptiste de Boyer d'Eguilles, a lawyer at the Parlement de Paris. On the part of this townhouse that faces rue Espariat itself, a curious pattern can be seen in the wrought ironwork of the balconies. You wonder whether someone as proper as the Marquis authorized this touch of erotic whimsy or whether he remained oblivious to what a slightly more salacious mind perceives there … We should add here that one of his grandsons was none other than the Marquis d'Argens, notorious for the erotic work (a speciality of Aix?), *Thérèse philosophe*, which he undoubtedly wrote, but never admitted to being the author.

SIGHTS NEARBY

CENTRE D'ARCHIVES D'OUTRE-MER 

29, chemin du Moulin Detesta, 13090 Aix-en-Provence,
Tel: 04 42 93 38 50 • Fax: 04 42 93 38 89 • E-mail: caom.aix@culture.fr
http://www.archivesnationales.culture.gouv.fr/caom/fr/

Created in 1966, the Centre des Archives d'Outre-Mer houses the archives of the French presence overseas. Put more bluntly, it is here that the record of French colonization has been preserved, with millions of documents concerning Africa, America (including both Canada and Louisiana), Asia (Indochina and Siam), the Indian Ocean and the Pacific Ocean stored in these austere, futuristic premises. Beyond the legal limit of 100 years, all these documents can be consulted by anyone, and the research and consultation room lets you look up documents on the online database.
Researchers as well as students, authors and a large number of both professional and amateur genealogists make use of the archive's consultation facilities every day. Concerning Algeria in particular, there is computer access to 1.3 million documents in the "European" civil registry, the originals of which remain in the former French colony. This number grows as the 100-year rule releases more documents into the public domain. For those whose ancestors were sent off to the infamous penal colony of Cayenne, a trace of their sufferings can also be found here …

MUSÉE EDGAR MELIK 

- Château de Cabriès, 13480 Cabriès
- Tel: 04 42 22 42 81 • Fax: 04 42 22 23 25
- E-mail: museemelik@melik.net
- http://www.musee-melik.com/
- Open 10.00–12.00 and 14.00–17.00. Closed Tuesday and Sunday morning, open Sunday afternoon 14.00–18.00

Admission: €4.60, reduced rate (students, unemployed, etc.) €1.50, children 12 and under free

> ***The fascinating works of an artist from beyond the art scene, in a chateau beyond time***

If Edgar Melik has not received the recognition his talent deserves it is because he himself cut his ties with the "system". This fascinating painter bought the Château de Cabriès which he restored and which now provides a home for his works.

Economical in his means, employing only two colours in his last period, one of which was a Provençal ochre, he refused to receive any "dealers" or art critics at his estate. Abbé Rey, the local priest in Cabriès, recounted how Melik, who had just sold three paintings to a rich collector, refused to sell him a fourth that formed part of the artist's "private museum", going so far as to tear up the buyer's cheque ...

Melik's chateau museum spreads into the painter's living quarters and into the 17th-century chapel where he painted the frescoes on the walls. The curator of the museum, Danièle Malis, has enthusiastically brought to life both the painter and his work, giving visitors a real insight into his peculiar universe. One of the most fascinating aspects was his admiration for Edith Piaf, to whom he dedicated the texts and drawings gathered together in a very beautiful album on sale at the museum.

From the chateau, the view of the countryside around Aix is magnificent.

SIGHTS NEARBY

CABRIÈS' MYSTERIOUS COAT OF ARMS 21

The name of the village comes from the word cabre, Provençal for "goat". The heraldic definition of the Cabriès coat of arms is as follows: "Gold, a sinople (green) oak tree, a gules (red) goat rampant at the foot of the tree." What is this tree-climbing goat trying to tell us? For your information, the name of the neighbouring village, Bouc-Bel-Air (bouc is a billy goat in French), is also inspired by goat-raising.

LE JARDIN D'ÉGUILLES 

- 7, rue Saint-Roch, 13510 Éguilles
- Tel: 04 42 92 51 80 - 06 03 77 67 40
- Open from 15 April to 15 October, by appointment
- Admission: €3
- Access on foot from the tourist office in Eguilles: walk up rue du Grand Logis, turn left on rue Saint-Antoine until you reach rue Saint-Roch on the right. Open the (ordinary) gate, cross the courtyard and open the second gate ...

“A fantastic bestiary occupies the garden created by Max Sauze

In Eguilles, a village to the west of Aix-en-Provence, there is an artist's garden, selected as "remarkable" by the French Ministry of Culture, where visits can be booked.

Max Sauze's garden is not easy to find, and the Eguilles tourist office doesn't do very much to promote it. With a little determination you'll discover its location, completely surrounded by more recent developments.

Max Sauze was born in Algiers in 1933 where he was first drawn to the fine arts. Further study at the Camondo school in Paris confirmed his chosen career as an artist. He did not limit himself to any single discipline and defined his approach in the following terms, *"My artistic research and the forms that flow from it are essentially the result of observing the natural mechanisms of life: multiplication, the propagation of primitive cells, their organization in space, the occupation of emptiness, the creation of interstices, vicinities, assemblies, and arrangements were the pilot elements that would lead me to aleatory vegetative forms."*

Max Sauze moved to Eguilles in 1963. At that time, his house lay outside the village and the present garden was a vegetable patch with concrete channels for watering. *"There were rabbit hutches and a hen house with broken wire fencing... There were two mean-looking green lizards. They later disappeared, no doubt to give me space."*

Max Sauze's garden is an evolving work with about a hundred different pieces of art spread over 950 m2. Sculptures in metal, wood, cement and paper mingle with the vegetation. There are also trees, most of them planted when the artist arrived in 1963: maples, pines, poplars, a palm tree, bamboo, and a single tree that was already there 40 years ago – an old lime.

The works of art imitate the plants and make use of natural materials such as snail shells, as well as recycled elements. Only 13 of the works are listed on the map supplied at the start of the visit. These include, for example, the bascine, the squirrel's library, the newspaper bas-relief, the brodules, and nutshells on the windshield of a Simca automobile or on anisette bottles.

Descriptions and photos can only give you a vague idea of Max Sauze's garden. You really need to go and see, feel, and enter into a dialogue with this work in order to apprehend it as the creation of an artist who wends his way through nature with respect and without confrontation.

THE BAS-RELIEFS OF SARTORIO

• Access from Aix: take the A51 motorway in the direction of Manosque and Sisteron.
Exit at Pertuis via the RN96 in the direction of Manosque and Sisteron. Just before the Mirabeau bridge, you'll come to the roundabout with the sculptures of the four adjacent départements by Sartorio.

An (almost) unique geographical peculiarity

At the junction of the four American states of Utah, New Mexico, Arizona and Colorado, whose borders were defined with a ruler during the conquest of the West, a symbolic pole declares that this point named "Four Corners" is the only place on Earth where four different states meet. But no doubt Americans are unaware that there is a similar geographical feature involving four Provençal départements.

Antoine Sartario, one of the major French sculptors of the early 20th century, was commissioned to represent these four départements near the point where their borders touch. He thus decided to sculpt, upon the arches of a bridge, four bas-reliefs symbolizing Bouches-du-Rhône, Basses-Alpes (before it was renamed Alpes-de-Haute-Provence), Vaucluse and Var. After the bridge was destroyed, they were transferred to the roundabout where the RN96 crosses the RD952 to Saint-Paul-lez-Durance.

All four of Sartorio's sculptures belong very much to the Symbolist school. Thus the representation of Vaucluse is a woman holding the Palais des Papes at Avignon in her hands. The other three are similar in style. How did this likeable artist win so many artistic commissions in this period? It's something of a mystery, but the list of his works speaks for itself. Following his Seven Deadly Sins for the Baumettes prison in Marseille (see Marseille insolite et secret, in the same collection as this guide), between the two world wars Sartorio produced L'Indépendance du Brésil in Santos, the high relief *L'Afrique* at the Palais de Chaillot à Paris, the façades of the Grand Théâtre, the new Palais de Justice and the monument to L'Armée d'Orient in Marseille, as well as the Palais de la Méditerranée in Nice.

SIGHTS NEARBY

VISIT TO SARTORIO'S STUDIO 
Les Amis de Jouques • Tel: 04 42 63 76 12

VISIT TO THE MUSÉE DES SILOS À GRAIN ㉕
Monsieur Yves Meyer • 39, rue Grande • Tel: 04 42 67 61 22

A magnificent village ignored by most guidebooks, Jouques perches on its heights. A museum devoted to grain silos, in a private home, adds to the charm of this place. It was here that Sartorio settled down during his rather active retirement, as he worked right up to his death in 1988 at the age of 103. You can visit his studio by appointment.

THE STATUE OF JOSEPH-ÉTIENNE ROULIN 

- Square Joseph-Étienne Roulin, 13410 Lambesc
- Lambesc is 22 km north-west of Aix-en-Provence on the RN7.

The postman who entered art history

Right next to the Lambesc post office (as you might expect!) in the square Joseph-Etienne Roulin, is a stele reminding us that this local postman was both a friend of the artist and the subject of several paintings by Vincent Van Gogh. Joseph-Etienne Roulin was born in the impasse du Castellas of Lambesc on 4 April 1841. His career in the postal service, starting as a rural postman, led him to Arles where he was assigned to the railway station with the rank of brigadier-chargeur. It was at the Café de la Gare that he met Vincent Van Gogh, with whom he came to share both friendship and a taste for absinthe. The painter lived nearby at the famous "yellow house" in place Lamartine.

What brought these two very different men together? At this time, Joseph Roulin lived with his wife and children, was politically active as an ardent socialist, and … a civil servant. It seems that in his home Van Gogh found the calm, warm family atmosphere missing from his own life, the disinterested company of a simple yet curious man and the unstinting assistance of a friend. During the mental crisis when Van Gogh cut off the lobe of his ear and tried to murder Gauguin, Joseph Roulin was at his side, resisting the efforts by neighbouring residents to have the artist committed, writing to Théo and his sister to keep them informed of their brother's state of health, and later succeeding in getting Van Gogh out of the asylum.

Joseph-Etienne Roulin appears, with his blue cap, in six paintings by Vincent Van Gogh. In December 1888, the artist wrote to Théo saying that he had just produced *"the portraits of an entire family, that of the postman whose head I previously painted – the man, his wife, the baby, the little boy and the 16-year-old son – all of them with very French features, although they look like Russians."*

LAMBESC: FRANCE'S FIRST UNIVERSITY VILLAGE

Since 1997, Lambesc has hosted the teacher training, health and social work sections of the Education Department of the Université de Provence. Depending on sessions, 250 to 300 students attend this establishment, housed in the former Hôtel-Dieu.
Université de Provence • Département des Sciences de l'Éducation
Ancien Hôtel-Dieu • 1, avenue de Verdun, 13410 Lambesc
Tel: 04 42 57 17 17 • Fax: 04 42 57 17 07
E-mail: educaix@romarin.univ-aix.fr

THE PALM TREE CAVE OF PEYROLLES 27

- Visits to the cave can be booked at the local tourist office
- Château du Roi René, Place de l'Hôtel de Ville
13860 Peyrolles-en-Provence

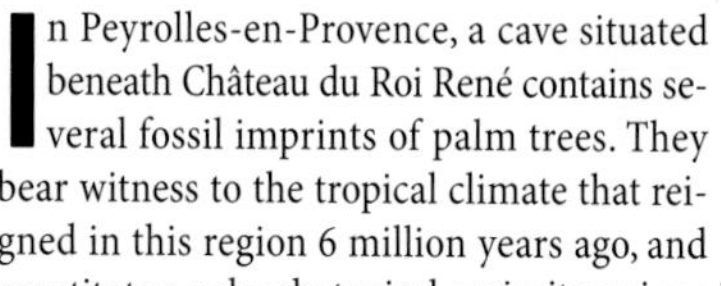

"Beneath the ramparts, a prehistoric beach…

In Peyrolles-en-Provence, a cave situated beneath Château du Roi René contains several fossil imprints of palm trees. They bear witness to the tropical climate that reigned in this region 6 million years ago, and constitute a palaeobotanical curiosity unique in Europe. The cave, 20 m long and 10 m wide, runs beneath the foundations of the chateau and ends under its courtyard.

It was accidentally rediscovered by children in 1979 after its entrance had been walled up. The inhabitants of the village knew of its existence, however, because it was used as a larder for food during the Middle Ages and a bomb shelter during the Second World War. But only a systematic exploration led to the major discovery: a series of fossilized imprints of palm trunks, hollowed into the ceiling of the cave.

The tufa rock that enveloped these palm trunks has been dated back to the Tertiary Period (Pliocene Epoch – 6 million years ago). At that time, it's thought that the Mediterranean reached as far north as the present course of the River Durance, which runs beneath the chateau walls. Fifteen imprints of palms have been identified, the biggest 1 m across and 2 m high. They belong to four different species. Note that the palm is not actually a tree but a monocotyledon: the trunks form from piled fibrous stalks of dead leaves.

Other fossils are also present in the cave: ferns, leaves and stems, but no animal fossils have been discovered there, although they are common elsewhere in the region. Well-adapted lighting gives a good view of the relief of the palm trunks in the ceiling, and at the far end of the cave you glimpse the escape route that communicated with the chateau in case of enemy invasion.

SIGHTS NEARBY

KING RENÉ'S CHATEAU 28

Open Monday to Friday 8.00–12.00 and 14.00–17.00

Above the palm tree cave, the town hall is today housed in the Château du Roi René whose main attraction is that it has preserved its former architectural environment. Inside, windows reveal the archaeological and palaeontological riches of the area. The existing buildings date for the most part from the 17th century, but there are some medieval remains including a defensive wall on the eastern terrace (this wall being 1.54 m thick, exceptional in Provence), a square tower on the western side, and the latrines that poured directly into the Durance.

THE SANCTUARY OF ROQUEPERTUSE 

- Site Archéologique de Roquepertuse, 13880 Velaux
- Musée de la Tour, 13880 Velaux
- Opening hours: Saturday 14.00–17.00 • Group visits: it is essential to enquire first at the municipal Service du Patrimoine
- Mairie de Velaux, Place de Verdun, 13880 Velaux • Tel: 04 42 87 73 59

"The objects found at Velaux show that this site was a Celto-Ligurian sanctuary

Roquepertuse (Provençal for "rock passage") is a strange place. A Celto-Ligurian archaeological site that was occupied between the 5th and 2nd centuries BC, it is still being explored. If the objects that have been found there are quite well known, the site itself is far less famous. A plan to post signs for visitors is being drawn up by the municipal service for archaeological and historical heritage.

The site is quite striking at first glance because of the way this rock mushroom emerges from the otherwise flat landscape. You'll soon notice the caves and holes, and walking round the rock, you'll come across the digs that have brought to light the walls of pre-Roman constructions.

It was the fortuitous discovery around 1860 of two statues representing human figures sitting cross-legged that launched the first digs at the Roquepertuse site. Current explorations have confirmed that they did indeed possess a sanctuary with its village around a fortified plateau. The objects found here are extraordinary and well worth a visit to the Musée de la Vieille Charité in Marseille where they are displayed, as well as to the Musée de la Tour, in the village of Velaux, where an entire floor is devoted to the digs at the Roquepertuse site, including castings of the most remarkable objects found there. There are examples of the cross-legged men, no doubt warriors, but also unique pieces such as the sculpture of a double head and two stone poles with hollows to hold the skulls of vanquished enemies or dead tribal heroes. This tends to confirm the idea that there was a sanctuary here, that is, a place of worship where complex rituals were carried out.

The site also gives a better idea of the lives of the peoples occupying Provence long after the arrival of the Phocaeans in Marseille: it was during the Second Iron Age that Roquepertuse was most active. Several attacks and a siege finally wiped out the inhabitants of the village at the beginning of the 2nd century BC, well before the Roman conquest.

Access by the RD20 linking Aix-en-Provence to Berre-l'Étang.
At Velaux, the RD20 passes below the old village to the south and an immense property to the north. There is no sign for the site itself, but follow signs for the wine-growing cooperative. At this cooperative, follow the road that runs alongside the railway line on the left. The site is announced by the sign: "Site archéologique de Roquepertuse". A large clearing lets you park a short distance from the rock.

THE TALLEST CHIMNEY IN EUROPE

30

MEYREUIL POWER PLANT

- From Aix-en-Provence, take the RN7 in the direction of Nice.
- At the roundabout, continue straight on towards Gardanne.
- http://www.ville-meyreuil.fr/

Almost as tall as the Eiffel Tower!

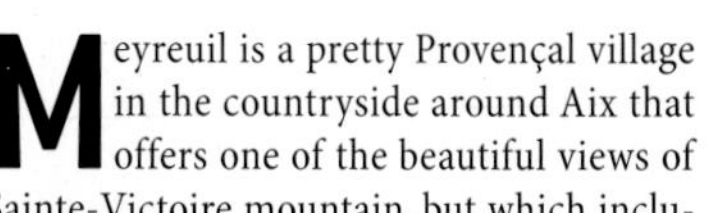

Meyreuil is a pretty Provençal village in the countryside around Aix that offers one of the beautiful views of Sainte-Victoire mountain, but which includes a thermal plant with the tallest chimney in Europe (300 m), also the second-tallest edifice in France next to the Eiffel Tower. Obviously, this spoils the landscape somewhat.

SIGHTS NEARBY

MUSEUM OF MINING AT GRÉASQUE 31

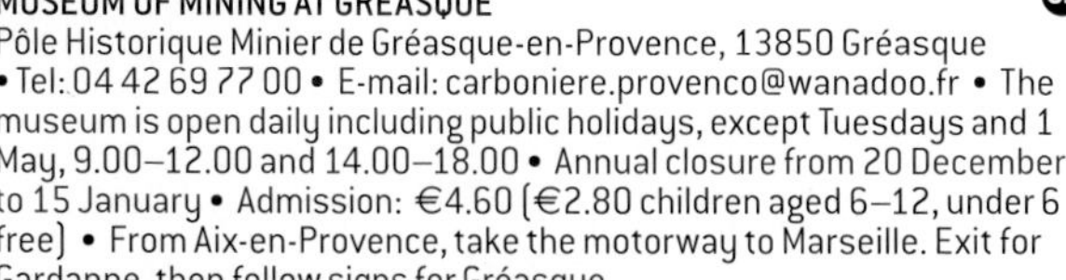

Pôle Historique Minier de Gréasque-en-Provence, 13850 Gréasque • Tel: 04 42 69 77 00 • E-mail: carboniere.provenco@wanadoo.fr • The museum is open daily including public holidays, except Tuesdays and 1 May, 9.00–12.00 and 14.00–18.00 • Annual closure from 20 December to 15 January • Admission: €4.60 (€2.80 children aged 6–12, under 6 free) • From Aix-en-Provence, take the motorway to Marseille. Exit for Gardanne, then follow signs for Gréasque.

South-east of Aix is a rich mining basin from which coal has been extracted since the 15th century. The last pit, at Gardanne, was closed in 2003, and the Hély d'Oissel pit at Gréasque, where you can visit the Musée de la Mine, ceased operations in 1962. A series of exhibits, along with machinery used in the past, evoke the hard labours carried out by miners at a depth of 450 m. The visit is quite impressive, but not recommended for claustrophobes.

CITÉS MINIÈRES

In Provence, mining villages are not called corons as in northern France, but cités minières. There were two such settlements in Gréasque: "Salonique Sud", just beneath the Hély d'Oissel pithead, and "La Cité Nord".

A SIGHT (TO AVOID) NEARBY

THE HOUSE OF DEAD DOLLS 32

Quartier Valabre, 13120 Gardanne • RD7 between Gardanne and Luynes

On the right coming from Gardanne you might be horrified to discover a house covered with the corpses (no other word for them ...) of teddy bears, dolls and marionettes, hanging on the shutters and walls. The owner, Monsieur Francis Barral, explains with implacable logic that he keeps hundreds of toys brought to him by the children and grandchildren ... Of whom? It's a nightmare. Above all, don't ever take children here.

LES MILLES INTERNMENT CAMP ㉝

THE FRESCOES IN THE CAMP GUARDS' REFECTORY

• Mémorial National des Milles
Lieu-dit la Tuilerie, Chemin de la Badesse, 13290 Les Milles
9 km south-west of Aix-en-Provence
• Open Monday to Friday 9.00–12.00 and 12.45–17.00
• Admission free • Tel: 04 42 24 33 02
• Groups, information: Direction Régionale des Anciens Combattants
11, rue Lafon, BP 6, 13251 Marseille Cedex 20
• Tel: 04 91 04 75 00

> **"*The road to Auschwitz also started in Provence***

A concentration camp near Aix-en-Provence? It seems so unreal, even impossible. But it's the truth. During the Second World War, thousands of victims of Nazism were interned in the camp at Les Milles.

In 1939, just after the outbreak of war, the climate of suspicion in France towards immigrants of German and Austrian origin sometimes led to their internment in camps like this one. Later it became a camp de regroupement, from whence foreign or stateless Jews living in France were sent away in sealed railway wagons, as the Vichy government had promised to Nazi occupation authorities. More than 2,000 Jews were thus regrouped at Les Milles before being transferred to Drancy and then Auschwitz.

Among the more famous internees at the camp were Max Ernst, Golo Mann (son of Thomas Mann), Hans Bellmer and Lion Feuchtwanger. Concerning the latter, the irony of fate was that his best known novel, Le Juif Süss, became the most notorious anti-Semitic propaganda film … It was a photo taken of Feuchtwanger as a prisoner in the camp at Les Milles that sparked a worldwide wave of protest and first revealed to the American public the reality of this sinister period.

The visit to the memorial at Les Milles is rendered even more moving by the frescoes in the refectory used by the camp guards, painted by the interned artists, which have been preserved and recently restored. The names of their creators remain unknown, but the frescoes are striking due to both their artistic merit and their sense of humour. One of them, for example, has a caption that reads: Puissent nos dessins vous calmer l'appétit [May our drawings cut your appetite].

Along the frieze, little characters dressed in blue carry grapes, a beetroot and a giant sausage. A brick blocks the path of the one carrying the artichoke, no doubt an allusion to the fact that the camp was previously a brick factory, but also that the prisoners' forced sojourn in this place represented a brutal constraint. Another astonishing fresco shows a banquet with caricatures of people from all corners of the globe, in a way recalling Leonardo da Vinci's Last Supper.

PROVENÇAL COOKING LESSONS AT CHÂTEAU D'ARNAJON

- Domaine d'Arnajon , 13610 Le Puy Sainte-Réparade
- Tel: 04 42 61 87 47 • Fax: 04 42 61 82 27
- E-mail: marc.heracle@free.fr
- Access map and fees available on request.

Recipes fit for a Sun King

In the middle of grey winter, we sometimes feel a desperate need to prepare one of those dishes that can only come from the south of France: daube à la provençale, aïado d'agneau, gardianne, alouettes à l'orange amère, tian de légumes, tarte aux épinards …

The Domaine d'Arnajon in Puy Sainte-Réparade is probably one of the most interesting places there is to learn how to cook. Chef Marc Heracle gives lessons in tradition Provençal cooking in the extraordinary setting of the ancient kitchen in the métairie [farm] belonging to the estate of the Château d'Arnajon. We are still in the Grand Siècle here: most of the recipes taught were first elaborated in the 17th and 18th centuries, and Louis XIV even slept here. After the lesson and a visit of the listed gardens, the only regret is that you can't be like the Sun King and stay here for the night …

LE REBOUL: BIBLE OF CUISINE PROVENÇALE

It's no big secret because most people who love Provence and its cuisine have long since acquired a copy of La Cuisinière provençale by J.-B. Reboul (Éditions Tacussel). In Provence, it's simply known as Le Reboul. This classic work presenting 1,120 recipes and 365 menus (one for each day of the year) is now in its 27th printing! But beware, this bible of Provençal cooking does contain a number of pitfalls:

– It's out of the question today of respecting these recipes to the letter, our modern bodies are no longer used to ingesting so much cholesterol.

– When you plan to follow a recipe, you'll need to read it at least a week in advance. In the margin of many recipes, you'll see the phrase, d'autre part. This *"side dish"* is presented in the following manner: *"On the side, prepare some ordinary quenelles, some foie gras escalopes, or instead some chicken livers browned in butter, some heads of mushrooms and as many sliced truffles, some cockscombs and kidneys."* You'll need to plan ahead, especially for those cockscombs … There are other traps at the ends of recipes: *"If, as you're putting this in the oven, you have some of that special gravy you prepared the night before* (grrr!), *and described on page 99 ..."* The gravy in question requires no less than six hours to cook …

THE VIRGIN OF LE FOUSSA AT ROGNES

35

• Colline du Foussa, 13840 Rognes

This giant ex-voto thanks the Virgin for having spared the village during World War II

Rognes is a village with a little over 4,000 inhabitants that has preserved its traditional Provençal charm, full of trees and flowers despite the still visible wounds caused by the 1909 earthquake. The name of Rognes is often used in Provence to designate the soft, warm, honey-coloured stone extracted from the nearby quarries. It is found particularly in cours Mirabeau at Aix-en-Provence, where most of the townhouses, whether 17th- or 18th-century, have been built in Rognes stone.

Strolling through the streets of the village, you'll notice that the upper neighbourhood has no inhabitants or any actual buildings, only the remnants of cellar vaults that lay underneath the houses destroyed in the earthquake. Le Foussa was formerly the oppidum [hill-fort] that surrounded the chateau (the name of Foussa might have referred to the dry moat once separating the chateau from the village).

Following rue des Pénitents and then avenue du Cégarès, you end up on a footpath. After scrambling up some rough steps carved into the hill, you emerge in front of the immense Virgin of Le Foussa. This is an ex-voto 6 m in diameter sculpted in the side of the cliff, and offered by the inhabitants of Rognes in thanks to the Virgin Mary for having protected the village during the Second World War.

When you approach from the direction of Aix you can see this Virgin of Le Foussa from a great distance, amidst holes in the cliff that betray the presence of an abandoned troglodyte dwelling.

In walking around the village you should also stop before the Notre-Dame-de-l'Assomption church. It was built in 1607 using part of the village ramparts for its northern wall and one of the seven watchtowers as the base for its belfry. Inscribed on the lintel of the church's main door, since the Revolution, is the name of the present owner of this property: the French Republic.

OFFICE DE TOURISME DE ROGNES
5, cours Saint-Étienne, 13840 Rognes • Tel: 04 42 50 13 36
• e-mail : office.tourisme.rognes@wanadoo.fr • www.ville-rognes.fr

PABLO PICASSO'S TOMB

• Château de Vauvenargues
Vauvenargues is 15 km east of Aix-en-Provence on the RD10
• http://www.picasso.fr/

Here lies Picasso, in the park of his chateau

Contrary to ordinary mortals, Pablo Picasso was granted the privilege of burial in the park of his private dwelling. It was out of admiration for his "one and only master", Paul Cézanne, that in 1958 Picasso bought the Château de Vauvenargues at the foot of Sainte-Victoire mountain. The chateau belongs to the family of Picasso's last wife, and is not open to visitors. If you'd nevertheless like at least a glimpse of his tomb, follow the RD10 above the village. Depending on the season and the amount of greenery, you can see the bronze piece that the master cast himself: the sculpture is entitled La Femme au vase and was presented at the Exposition Universelle of 1937 in Paris, at the same time as the famous painting, Guernica.

EXCEPTION TO THE GENERAL RULE ON BURIALS

Burial on private land is an exception to the general rule on interments in the communal cemetery: in application of the general code of local government *"any person can be buried on private property, as long as this body is outside the limits of cities and towns and at the prescribed distance"*. For more information, enquire at the local prefecture, which is empowered to decide on this matter.

SIGHTS NEARBY

A DRIVE AROUND SAINTE-VICTOIRE

The drive starts from Aix-en-Provence in the direction of Vauvenargues. 8 km from Aix on the RD10, a road on the right leads to the Bimont dam, a facility that now supplies Aix with water since the capacity of the preceding dam, constructed by François Zola, father of Émile, proved insufficient. The Zola dam, the first vaulted dam ever built, was constructed using uncut stones between 1843 and 1852. At Vauvenargues, you drive in the shadow (literally) of Sainte-Victoire mountain. For the next 18 km, the road crosses wild, craggy scenery, and then emerges *"in front"* of Sainte-Victoire. At Pourrières, a monument recalls the fact that here, Marius vanquished the Teutone in a battle that *"left so many dead that the River Arc turned away from its channel, tired of carrying so much blood"*. The name Pourrières is derived from the Latin campi putridi [putrid fields] ... It's also where the poet Germain Nouveau was born.

GEOLOGICAL RESERVE OF ROQUES-HAUTES

Route du Tholonet, CD 17, 13100 Beaurecueil
2, place du Général-de-Gaulle, BP 160, 13605 Aix-en-Provence Cedex 1
Tel: 04 42 161 161 • Fax: 04 42 161 162
• E-mail: infos@aixenprovencetourism.com
• http://www.aixenprovencetourism.com
• Access by car from Aix, via the CD17. After Le Tholonet, head for Puyloubier. 400 m beyond the crossroads at Beaurecueil, take the concrete track on your left, marked by an illegible wooden sign by a rusted windmill. Leave your vehicle in the car park where there are some picnic tables. The path that starts on the right leads to the Roques-Hautes farm that lends its name to the deposit and the red marl that contains the eggs. Remember that all digging is strictly prohibited. To reach the geological reserve, take the path to the left that passes the quarries of Le Tholonet, now abandoned, but whose marble was often used to make Provençal furnishings in the 17th and 18th centuries. Beyond the crête de marbre [marble ridge], this path gives you a magnificent view of Sainte-Victoire mountain.

Eggs in Provence

On 2 July 1992, a 70 million-year-old dinosaur egg from Aix-en-Provence was sold at an auction at Christie's in London and fetched $5,550 (about €5,000).

The site of Roques-Hautes, where lies one of the largest and richest deposits of dinosaur eggs in the world, is only a few kilometres from Aix-en-Provence, below the Sainte-Victoire mountain, and was discovered in the 1940s. It was some facetious American scientists studying the site who rebaptized the Roques-Hautes deposit "Eggs en Provence". During the Upper Cretaceous Period (between 80 and 65 million years ago), when the climate was tropical, a vast river ran between the Esterel massif and L'Étang de Berre, to which fauna straight out of "Jurassic Park" came to graze, hunt and lay their eggs. Today, despite measures to protect the deposit (guards on horseback, the listing of the site as a geological reserve, and a prohibition on straying from the marked paths), fossil poaching continues to flourish.

Thousands of eggs have already been extracted by palaeontologists (and poachers) but none of them contain embryos. The reason remains a mystery. It is by studying the shell and the mode of nesting that experts have deduced which type of dinosaur laid eggs. They include a Taracosaurus, a carrion-feeding carnivore related to Tyrannosaurus rex. One amusing detail recounted by Yves Dutor, a palaeontologist at the natural history museum in Aix is: *"Dinosaurs covered their eggs with earth and foliage because they couldn't sit on them ... given their weight ... without making gigantic omelettes ..."*

Be warned, on windy days in summer, access to the Saint-Victoire massif may be restricted. Details from: Office de Tourisme d'Aix-en-Provence	MUSÉE D'HISTOIRE NATURELLE 6, rue Espariat, 13100 Aix-en-Provence Tel: 04 42 27 91 27 http://www.museumaix.fr.st Open daily 10.00–12.00 and 13.00–17.00

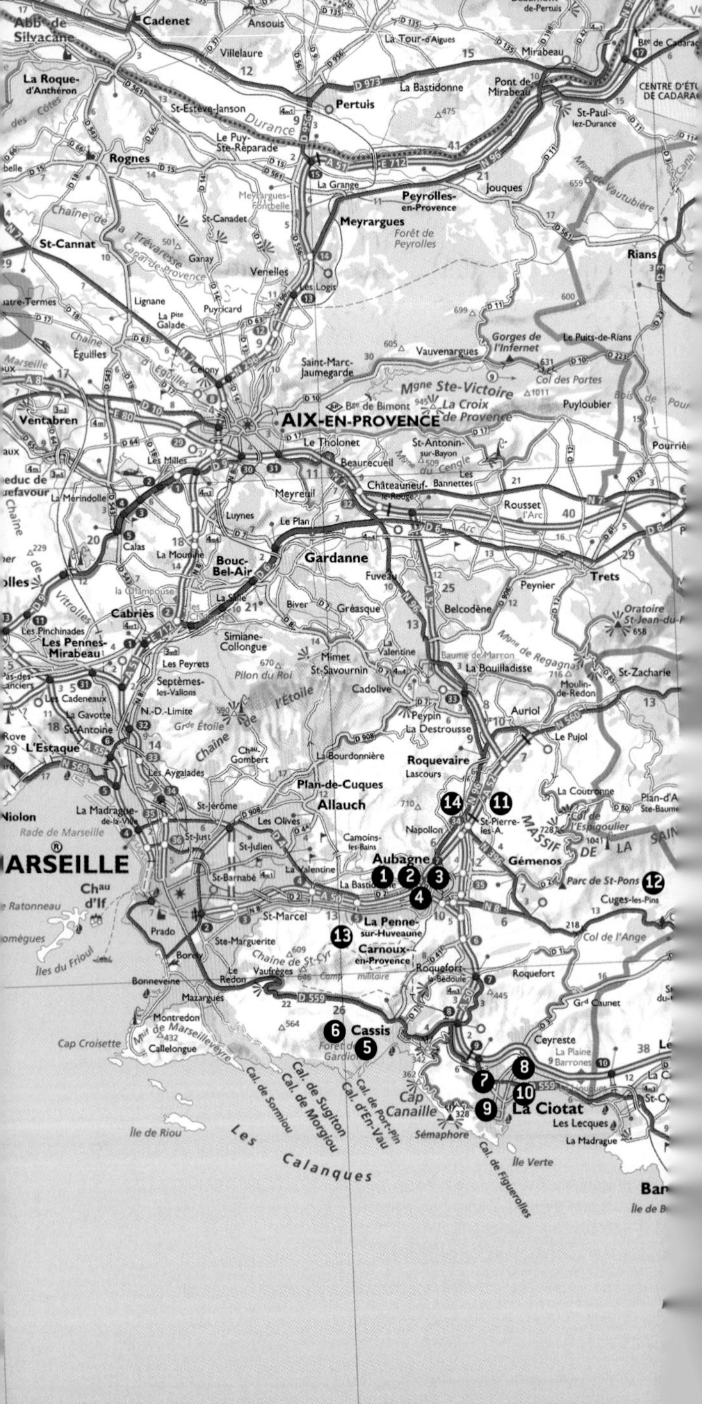

AIX-EN-PROVENCE
MARSEILLE
Aubagne
Cassis
La Ciotat
Gardanne
Pertuis
Meyrargues
Peyrolles-en-Provence
Jouques
Rians
Trets
Gémenos
Roquevaire
Allauch
Plan-de-Cuques
Bouc-Bel-Air
Cabriès
Les Pennes-Mirabeau
L'Estaque
Mgne Ste-Victoire
Chaîne de l'Étoile
Massif de la Sainte-Baume
Les Calanques
Cap Canaille
Carnoux-en-Provence
La Penne-sur-Huveaune
Parc de St-Pons

AROUND MARSEILLE

CHÂTEAU DES CREISSAUDS

- Clos Rufisque, 13400 Aubagne
- Tel: 04 91 24 84 45
- E-mail: contact@chateaudescreissauds.com
- http://www.maisonperchee.com
- €60–€120 per night, depending on the season
- From the A50 motorway (direction Marseille-Aubagne), exit at La Penne-sur-Huveaune, drive through the village and take the RN8 in the direction of Aubagne. When you leave the commune of La Penne-sur-Huveaune, turn right (pharmacy on the corner) and follow signs for Clinique la Casamance. About 100 m before the Clinique la Casamance (place des Farigoules), turn left on boulevard des Tamaris and follow the signs to the main entrance to the chateau. If coming from Aubagne, take the RN8 in the direction of Marseille until you reach the sign for Clinique la Casamance on your left; then follow the directions above.

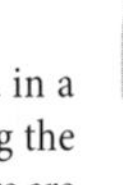

Sleep in a treehouse

This is a real wooden hut, perched in a plane tree in the park surrounding the Château des Creissauds. Inside, there are all mod cons in a very tiny space: air conditioning, bathroom, toilet. On the ground floor is a living room with a kitchen space and a little terrace for breakfast. Upstairs, the bedroom ringed by windows offers a 360° view. Let's be frank here, it's a treehouse for lovers. On the other hand, if you suffer from dizziness or are allergic to heights, you had better seek more classic lodgings.

From the treehouse, you can see the Château des Creissauds, a 19th-century dwelling with tourelles, a park of 80 hectares planted with century-old trees and fountains, a sports club with its various activities, and the sky through the leaves of the plane tree. For those of you who never got to play in a treehouse when you were little or regret never having spent the night in one …

SIGHTS NEARBY

THE STATUE OF JEAN-BAPTISTE CHAULAN

WHO SAID VIRTUE IS ITS OWN REWARD?

A couple of steps from rue de la République, the main street of Aubagne, you'll discover in the maze of little streets various curiosities such as the statue of Jean-Baptiste Chaulan, at the end of rue Frédéric Mistral. Born in Marseille and very soon an orphan, Chaulan was raised by his aunt and uncle in Aubagne and went on to make his fortune as a joiner in the Canary Islands. In his last will and testament, dated 25 April 1864, he bequeathed 40,000 francs to the town with the stipulation that the annual interest accruing to this capital should be granted as a dowry to a virtuous girl of Aubagne without means of her own, whose wedding should take place on the feast day of St John the Baptist. The first "Rosière"* to win the prize in 1875 was Baptistine Magdeleine Dupont. This tradition lasted until 1948. Could it be because the nearby rue Vive la Joie [Long Live Joy] finally proved more inspiring to young women than virtue?

***Rosière:** a virtuous young woman who, in some localities, was solemnly given a crown of roses accompanied by a reward.

CHAMBRES D'HÔTES LA ROYANTE ❸

• Xénia and Bernard Saltiel
Chemin de la Royante, 13400 Aubagne
• Tel/Fax: 33 (0)4 42 03 83 42 / 33 (0)6 09 47 19 51 / 33 (0)6 12 80 36 28
• E-mail: xbsaltiel@aol.com • http://www.laroyante.com
• Rooms €115–€137, depending on the season and the room.
Breakfast is served on the terrace in summer. A large dining-room with fully equipped kitchen is reserved for the exclusive use of visitors.

> ***"Saint Thomas doubts whether you washed behind your ears...***

La Royante is a very beautiful Provençal bastide [fortified village] surrounded by a vast park with an overflow pool, only five minutes from the centre of Aubagne. A summer residence for the bishops of Marseille, it has a large chapel consecrated by Pope Pius IX. Dedicated to the four Evangelists and decorated with stained glass windows, this chapel possesses a sacristy that is today occupied by one of La Royante's four guest rooms. With their traditional furnishings, these four rooms have a very unusual atmosphere.

The sacristy, with white linen and fresh atmosphere, is one of the two most original rooms, with its private terrace and proximity to the chapel.

The St Thomas room is decorated in papal blue and also communicates with the chapel through its bathroom, separated from the place of worship by the original stained-glass window portraying the apostle. When you tell people that you took a bath under the gaze of St Thomas, they may doubt your word ...

Xénia and Bernard Saltiel have managed to give the bastide function rooms a 19th-century atmosphere without falling into the clichés of conventional decor. In the lobby, the sofa on which you may be lucky enough to be seated comes from the Jas de Bouffan in Aix-en-Provence, the dwelling of Paul Cézanne's parents.

Finally, the visitors' book contains messages that echo the peculiar vibrations felt in this establishment. For those who want their diviner to perform a long-distance analysis of its telluric impact, here are its GPS coordinates: 5°33'02" E / 43°18'06" N.

Among the recommended excursions in the vicinity of La Royante, the first to spring to mind is a pilgrimage to La Sainte-Baume and to the Basilica of Saint-Maximin where Mary Magdalene, the patron saint of Provence, reposes (see page 125).

ACCESS

From Marseille, take the A50 motorway in the direction of Aubagne/Toulon, exit for Aubagne centre, and at the roundabout take the direction marked "Marché de gros", then D44 in the direction of Éoures, and take the first right after the small bridge. La Royante is at the end of this road. **From Nice or Aix-en-Provence,** take the direction of Aubagne/Toulon, then the direction of Marseille, exit at La Penne/Huveaune (exit 5), take the D2 towards Le Charrel, Camp Major, then the D44 towards Éoures, and turn first right after the small bridge. La Royante is at the end of the road.

THE TOMB OF PIERRE BLANCARD

4

• Cimetière des Passons
Quartier des Passons (east of Aubagne), 13400 Aubagne

"Because of a flower, we remember him."

In the Passons cemetery of Aubagne, a singular tomb draws the eye. Permanently decked in chrysanthemums, it marks the memory of Pierre Blancard, who brought back the first chrysanthemum plants to France from a trip to China in the 19th century.

Born in 1741 in Marseille, but buried in Aubagne in 1826, Blancard became a navigator and explored the world. One day in Canton, he spotted a plant in a pagoda that was unknown in France. How should what he did be described? Borrowing? Stealing? Or a disinterested contribution to European botany? Whatever the case, the plant he introduced to France soon multiplied, because chrysanthemums are today the flowers that the French most like to put on the graves of those who have passed on: 25 million pots are sold each year …

A flower that's resistant to frost, the chrysanthemum blossoms at a time of year when competitors are rare, and hence its success around the beginning of November and Toussaint (All Saints' Day), when people honour their dead in the cemeteries. In 1980 a French gardener cultivated a chrysanthemum that produced 1,028 blooms, which is still far from the Chinese record of 3,200.

By the way, Pierre Blancard's notebook recording his travels was discovered by chance in 2003 in a cupboard at the Académie de Marseille.

His epitaph is moving: À cause d'une fleur, on se souvient de lui [Because of a flower, we remember him].

THE FRESCO IN CASSIS CHURCH 

From avenue Victor Hugo (the main street) and going towards the port, take one of the two streets that climb to the right, rue du Docteur Séverin Icard or rue Adolphe Thiers. Both of them lead to the church.

> ***Two improbable soldiers bear witness to the debacle of 1940***

For the visitor who takes the time to examine it carefully, the fresco in this parish church will not fail to surprise.

In 1940, following France's collapse before the German onslaught, the country found itself divided into two. There was the occupied zone in the north and the "free" zone in the south, to where all those who had reason to fear the Nazis fled. For a while, both Marseille and Cassis thus became centres to which thinkers, artists and musicians gravitated. It was in this strange climate that the painter Jean Lair proposed to redo the fresco in this church, which was in very poor shape. Inspired by the spirit of the times, he gave a major role to Joan of Arc, who in another age wished to liberate her country from foreign occupation. He used villagers as models and placed two French civil defence soldiers in their kit (including one wearing a helmet) to the right of the Virgin Mary. This tableau is strange enough to justify a visit to the Cassis church, standing in a shady square and prettily illuminated at night. Jean Lair had already carried out some frescoes in 1933 for the law courts in Marseille, rue Émile Pollak, which represented justice and its consequences, including torture on the roue [wheel] painted on the staircase leading to the courtroom, which immediately put things into perspective …

CASSIS STONE

The church of Cassis, like most monuments in the area, was built using local stone. This was limestone from the calanques [creeks], containing fossils of rudistes (primitive oysters) and of a light beige colour. Extracted from the shore, Cassis stone is exported by boat all around the Mediterranean. The quarries of Cassis have supplied stone for the quays of Alexandria, Port Said, the banks of the Suez Canal, the doors of the famous Campo Santo cemetery in Genoa, and for the pedestal of the Statue of Liberty in New York. Cassis stone continues to be exported today by the Tierno family from the Bestouan quarry: Carrières du Bestouan.
Avenue Amiral Ganteaume,13260 Cassis - Tel: 04 42 01 03 42.

OFFICE DE TOURISME DE CASSIS
Oustau Calendal, Quai des Moulins, 13260 Cassis
• Tel: 0892 259 892 (0.34 HT/min) • Fax: 04 42 01 28 31 • E-mail: omt@cassis.fr

THE CAMARGO FOUNDATION

Avenue Amiral Ganteaume
13260 Cassis
• Tel: 04 42 01 11 57
• http://www.camargofoundation.org

A Provençal Villa Médicis

Located on the way to the calanques and the Plage du Bestouan, the Camargo Foundation is a private American establishment founded by Jerome Hill.

Born in 1905 and heir to an extremely rich family that had made its fortune in railways, Hill developed a passion for art and became a painter of some renown. He also dabbled in cinema, musical composition, competitive swimming, artistic diving, classical dance, and flying fighter aircraft. He spoke five languages, learned Chinese, was a gourmet, and never slept … like a certain Bonaparte. Having fallen in love with Cassis in the 1930s, he in fact bought the very same cabin where Bonaparte is supposed to have reorganized the fishing port defences, and made it his home. He named it "La Batterie" in honour of the emperor who had placed cannons at this very spot.

In 1967, he created the Camargo Foundation, which operates rather like a private Villa Medici: its vocation is to help academics and artists whose projects are connected to French-speaking culture. The foundation provides free of charge 13 furnished apartments as well as a library, a photo laboratory, an artist's studio and a music studio. The apartments are accompanied by a grant of $3,500 attributed automatically to residents.

Each year, during the Printemps du Livre (spring book festival) in April, the foundation opens its doors to the public, meetings with writers taking place in the splendid amphitheatre which enjoys an extraordinary view of the breakwater and the lighthouse, the sea and Cap Canaille.

VIRGINIA WOOLF IN CASSIS

The English novelist Virginia Woolf also liked to visit Cassis in the 1930s: along with her sister, her painter friends and her husband, she appreciated the light, the climate, the white wine, and the freedom to do as she pleased, far from the stuffy constraints of England in the early 20th century. During her four stays here, she took rooms at the Hotel Cendrillon (now called Cassitel) when she wasn't a guest at the Château de Fontcreuse, property in those days of Colonel Teed of the Bengal Lancer corps in the army of the British Raj (who had forgotten to bring his wife back with him from India...). Virginia Woolf wrote that Cassis was the only place in the world where she had experienced true moments of happiness. It was, she said, "a voyage out".
To find out more, read Virginia Woolf à Cassis (Éditions Images en Manœuvres).

THE TRAIN ARRIVES AT LA CIOTAT STATION 7

Chemin du Pareyraou, 13600 La Ciotat
• Tel: 08 92 35 35 35
La Ciotat railway station is quite a distance from the town itself. You can get there by car or bus. By car, follow the signs. The bus station is in front of the local tourist office.

During the Lumière brothers' first projections, the audience screamed in terror!

Even if Salvador Dali once declared the Perpignan railway station to be the centre of the world, it hasn't diminished the renown of La Ciotat station.

It was in 1893 that the Lumière family first took its summer quarters at the Château du Clos des Plages, a dwelling constructed by Antoine Lumière, father of the two famous brothers. This palace consisted of forty rooms (including three painters' studios) on 90 hectares of land. During the summer of 1895, Louis and Auguste would shoot a series of films at La Ciotat: Baignade sur la plage, Le Repas de bébé, L'Arroseur arrosé, and above all, L'Arrivée du train en gare de La Ciotat [Train Arriving at La Ciotat Station]. These films would be projected before 150 guests in the Lumière residence at La Ciotat, on 22 September 1895. Three months later, the official screening took place in Paris, in the Salon Indien of the Grand Café of boulevard des Capucines, on 28 December 1895.

L'Arrivée du train en gare de La Ciotat has often been considered to be the first film in the history of cinema. That's not quite correct, because the subject of their very first film was a shot of workers leaving their factory in Lyon. But it was this film, where the train is seen being pulled by its very large locomotive into La Ciotat station, which provoked scenes of panic during the first screenings: people screamed in fright and some fainted, believing that the train had actually penetrated into the screening room.

SIGHTS NEARBY

LUMIÈRES' PALACE

The Château du Clos des Plages, the summer residence of the Lumière family, is situated at the end of allée Lumière. If you walk along the beach up to the Lumière monument, allée Lumière is the first on the left. The palace was converted into a hotel in the 1930s, and then became a jointly owned private residence that is closed to the public. The exterior can be viewed, however, from avenue Émile Ripert on the other side of the building.

MICHEL SIMON'S HOUSE

From the town centre of La Ciotat, take the direction of the calanques (Le Mugel and Figuerolles). Then follow the signs for Notre-Dame-de-la-Garde (a hill chapel). Chemin de la Garde becomes chemin du Sémaphore. The house is then on the left, identifiable by the tower that was added by the actor, covered with pebbles and built without a plumb line at his request. Although you can't visit the inside, you can go up to the terrace in front of the entrance. The actor bought this house in 1946. He liked to show guests, particularly those of the opposite sex, the fabulous collection of erotic objects he had gathered and which were dispersed following his death in 1975 ... The masterpiece in this collection was an 18th-century figurine representing Cardinal de Richelieu, with his cassock raised, revealing the least religious aspect of his person.

MICHEL SIMON

"I was born in 1895, and since misery loves company, that very same year the Lumière brothers invented the cinematograph." Michel Simon grew up in Geneva with a father who wanted him to become a pork butcher. But he went off to Paris instead, and after a period of bohemian life, he entered Georges Pittoëff's theatre troupe, where he started his vast career as an actor. As a partner to Louis Jouvet and Gérard Philippe he appeared in plays of Shakespeare, Bernard Shaw, Pirandello, Oscar Wilde, Gorky, Bourdet and Bernstein.

But it was in cinema, above all, that the actor became a familiar face. In fact he used to say: "Better to have an ugly face than no face at all." His films included Dreyer's La Passion de Jeanne d'Arc, Jean Renoir's On purge bébé and Boudu sauvé des eaux, Marcel Carné's Drôle de drame and Abel Gance's Austerlitz.

To find out more about the Lumière brothers at La Ciotat, visit the Espace Lumière Simon, in the town centre, a former shop transformed into a homage to cinema, to the Lumière brothers, and to French actor Michel Simon.

OFFICE DE TOURISME DE LA CIOTAT	ESPACE LUMIÈRE – MICHEL SIMON
Bd Anatole France, 13600 La Ciotat	20, rue Maréchal Foch, 13600 La Ciotat
• Tel: 04 42 08 61 32 • Fax: 04 42 08 17 88	• Tel/Fax: 04 42 08 94 56
• E-mail: tourismeciotat@wanadoo.fr	• Opening hours: October to May, 15.00–18.00; June–September, 16.00–19.00
• http://www.laciotatourisme.com	

LE BERCEAU DE LA PÉTANQUE

• Avenue de la Pétanque, 13600 La Ciotat
• Tel: 04 42 08 08 88

La Ciotat, birthplace of la pétanque

The game of boules has long been a special passion in Provence. In La Ciotat, a municipal ordinance dated 22 Pluviôse VII (10 February 1799) provides some proof of this: "The municipal administration [of La Ciotat] has been informed that various persons have taken the liberty of playing boules in public places and passageways. A citizen was struck yesterday by a boule in front of her door on the Tasse [today boulevard Anatole France]. The municipal adminstration therefore prohibits any person from playing boules in public passages on pain of a fine of 12 francs."

Until the 20th century, the traditional game was the la longue or jeu provençal (similar to the jeu lyonnais). This was played at a distance of 15–20 m (hence its name) by teams of three: the pointeur [pointer], the milieu [middle-man] and the tireur [shooter]. To point, the player takes a large sidestep to either right or left, depending on the configuration of the terrain. To shoot, you make three running leaps in succession before releasing the ball. Without being an extremely athletic game, la longue does require being in fairly good physical shape.

In 1910, at the Jeu de Boules Beraud (which would later become the "Berceau de la Pétanque" [cradle of pétanque], Jules Lenoir, crippled by rheumatism, could no longer play la longue. He spent his time sitting in his chair, forlornly watching other players. One day, Ernest Pitiot, one of the brothers who owned this boulodrome, took pity on poor old Jules and offered to play a short match with him, les pieds tanqués. In Provençal, tanca means to stand up straight, and pieds tanqués thus means keeping your feet immobile on the ground. The first part of what would become la pétanque was thus born. This "girls' game" (as players of la longue scornfully called it) turned out to be an enormous success. And because La Ciotat was a port and shipyard, the entire world, or almost, was introduced to the game within the space of a few years.

On the boules pitch at the Berceau de la Pétanque [Cradle of pétanque], there is a plaque commemorating the "invention", and in the adjoining bar, you can have a drink and take a look at the display case explaining the evolution of the elements in la longue and pétanque versions of the game. Above all, armed with a copy of the fixtures, you can watch matches of la longue, which really are much more spectacular than the doddering pétanque matches you see being played in the main squares of Provençal villages. Some people even say that la longue is to pétanque what tennis is to ping-pong …

THE SPRING AT SAINT-PIERRE-LÈS-AUBAGNE ⓫

• Hostellerie de la Source
Saint Pierre-lès-Aubagne, 13400 Aubagne
• Tel: 04 42 04 09 19 • Fax: 04 42 04 58 72
• http://www.lcm.fr/lasource.htm
The taps to the spring are in front of the entrance to the Hostellerie de la Source. Access from Aubagne or from the Pont-de-l'Étoile motorway exit, via the RN396.

Enthusiasts can fill up for free at the spring

The Hostellerie de la Source is one of those traditional Provençal hotels that are a pleasure to frequent. A 17th-century bastide surrounded by a splendid garden in which some of the box trees are over 800 years old, with a shaded terrace looking out over the swimming pool where meals are served when the season allows. There is even an underground Roman aqueduct on the property. At the beginning of the 1920s, the aide-de-camp to the last Tsar of Russia, Nicholas II, lived here with his family. Having fled their country, the Séménoffs stayed several years in Saint-Pierre-lès-Aubagne and even transformed what is now room No. 16 into a Russian Orthodox chapel.

The name of the hotel comes from the spring that runs through the property, whose water is said to have exceptional qualities. Its principal component is barium, an alkaline-earth metal with anti-acid properties that is rarely found in such concentrations. Not very gassy, the spring water is particularly light, rich in calcium and magnesium, and contains no nitrates. The spring, whose age has been determined by carbon-14 dating at between 2,500 and 7,000 years, could well be, who knows, an elixir of youth …

The tradition of thermal baths in the area is attested to by the discovery of Roman baths, identified as the Baths of Gargarius, at Saint-Jean-de-Garguier, which in Roman times encompassed both hamlets under the name of Gargaria Locus and had a population of 60,000. Caesar installed his wheat granaries here during the siege of Massalia (Marseille), while his troops were bivouacked at "Campus Majorem", today known as Camp-Major.

The extraordinary properties of this water has given the owners of the spring (and the hotel) the idea of creating a thermal bathing complex with a casino, while at the same time commercializing the mineral water. While awaiting these developments, which seem to have run into some administrative setbacks, they have decided to offer their water to the public. At the gate to the Hostellerie, a very busy car park allows enthusiasts of this free mineral water to come and fill jerrycans and demijohns. It is rare to find yourself alone at this spring, given its popularity in the region.

THE CADE OVEN AT CUGES-LES-PINS

• Association "Les Chemins du Patrimoine"
348 chemin des Gais Coteaux, 83190 Ollioules
• Tel: 04 94 63 16 93
NB: Raoul Décugis, of the association, is very happy to accompany visitors interested in local rural heritage.

> ***"In a simple drystone hut, juniper branches are "sweated" to produce oil***

In the Provençal countryside, the abundance of juniper trees in some places was an incentive to the construction of drystone ovens to extract precious oil of cade (juniper tar oil) from their wood.

A cade oven resembles a little drystone hut, except that inside this rustic structure is a hearth lined with baked earth bricks that will "sweat" the juniper (known as cade in Provençal) branches and trunks with an intense heat of about 250 °C in order to extract the oil (rather than the sap) from them.

The oil appears as a blackish liquid, thick and tarry, with an intense characteristic odour that still persists today in most commercial shampoos.

Traces remain of nearly 200 cade ovens in Provence, some of which have been restored but are found on private property. One of the rare intact ovens both visible and on public land is that of Cuges-les-Pins, restored with great dedication by the Chemins du Patrimoine association, as the nearby sign indicates. The ovens were situated close to the raw material, the junipers, and after being meticulously built, required constant attention. At the heart of the oven is the fabi [jar], covered with briquettes, surrounded by the wood for firing and, below, a type of still collecting the juniper nectar: oil of cade.

It was shepherds, noting that this product was helpful in treating the feet of their sheep, who first popularized its use. It was also used in medications for human skin ailments, as well as in soap and shampoo. French people over the age of 50 will recall "Cadum" soap and "Cadolive" shampoo, both products derived from this "essential" oil.

Today, oil of cade is produced commercially at Claret (Hérault) and in certain shops specializing in natural products, you can find sections of juniper branches sold as moth repellent.

Gin, the well-known alcoholic drink, is a distillation of the same plant.

When you come to the OK Corral amusement park, take the RD1, which leads to the little village of Riboux. Once you go through a small "pass" in the hills and start to descend again, just before the marker indicating 0.7 km to Riboux, you'll see a track suitable for vehicles on the left, marked "SB 110". This track links the village of Riboux to La Sainte-Baume. Park at the side and count on a 35–45 minute walk on an easy route to reach the cade oven.
At the first fork in the wide path, take the right path rather than that on the left marked "SB 209". At the second fork, take the left-hand path marked "SB 110" and "Le Poulet" (the small valley of Le Poulet is the final destination). After a long straight stretch and a cistern on the left, turn right on the path marked "SB 110". Another long stretch and you'll pass a barrier and a sign reading "Forêt Domaniale de Cuges-les-Pins". Keep watch on the left for trail markers with a red stripe on a large white background, sometimes on piles of stones. When your path crosses these, take the right-hand trail and continue to follow these markers. At the end of the trail, you'll see your well-earned cade oven ...

THE OTHER CADE

"Cade" is also the name given to pancakes made from chickpea flour, cooked over a wood fire and sold in Toulon from ovens that are also called fours à cade. This terminology comes from Italian immigrants who promoted their produce by shouting in their mother tongue, caldo or calda, meaning hot. If the mode of cooking or the thickness of portions varies somewhat, the composition is practically the same as socca, enjoyed in the region between Nice and San Remo, or the panisses widely served in Marseille.

The association asks that all those who come to see these treasures of the past spare a thought for Doctor Laurent Porte, who was the first to make an inventory and describe the fours à cade [cade ovens] in this part of Provence.

OFFICE DE TOURISME DE CUGES-LES-PINS
25, route Nationale, 13780 Cuges-les-Pins
• Tel: 04 42 73 84 18 • Fax: 04 42 73 81 10
E-mail: mairie.cuges-les-pins@wanadoo.fr

A ROMAN TOMB AT LA PENNE-SUR-HUVEAUNE 

• Montée Charles Paya
13821 La Penne-sur-Huveaune
On the A50 motorway between Marseille and Aubagne, take exit 5: La Penne-sur-Huveaune. Follow directions to the village and park as close as possible to the church. The pedestrian path that ascends to Le Pennelus starts just behind this church.

> ***This strange monument may be related to the siege of Marseille by Julius Caesar's legions***

Visible from the train, a strange pyramid protrudes from the top of the church at La Penne-sur-Huveaune, a small village in the Huveaune valley. Development in the valley has begun to affect the village, which was one of 111 communes forming the Marseille agglomération, itself now swallowed up by the métropole Marseille-Aubagne.

Known for its tendency to overflow its banks, the River Huveaune has its source in the Sainte-Baume massif.

Le Pennelus, according to the more learned appellation, or La Pennelle, as local inhabitants call it, is a Roman tomb dating from the end of the 1st century BC. Officially listed as a historic monument since 1886, this pyramid of hollow stones is of impressive size, 6.10 m by 5.35 m and 8 m high. Its presence here is somewhat surreal, like some kind of casting error in the midst of this industrial environment.

It's easy to gain access to the monument, and a pity to see it in this state, without protection or any surveillance. We don't advise trying to climb inside, but imagine that it has been used as a living shelter at times. The egg-shaped chamber within is 3 m in diameter and 5.40 m high.

Different theses have been put forward to explain the presence of this unusual monument. The hypotheses of a look-out post or a monument commemorating a battle (but which one?) have been suggested. Today it is generally accepted that it is the tomb of one of Julius Caesar's generals who died during the siege of Marseille. It's certainly plausible, although no inscription has been found to validate this claim. It should be recalled, however, that La Penne-sur-Huveaune is on the route to La Sainte-Baume and that it was there that Caesar procured the trees that would serve to build his counter-fortifications. He himself cut down the first tree in the forest, which at the time was considered to be sacred, the local woodcutters not wanting to touch it for fear of a curse. The assassination of Caesar, shortly afterwards, was in fact attributed to this sacrilege by the inhabitants of Provence.

As for the name of the village, which was also the origin of the monument's, it doesn't come from Latin and has no penile connotation. The word existed before the Ligurians, and then the Romans, occupied this territory.

14

THE HOUSE OF "SHE WHO PAINTS" 

• RN96, 13360 Pont-de-l'Étoile
• Free visits by appointment• Tel: 04 42 04 25 32
From Aubagne take the RN96 towards Roquevaire. From Marseille, take the motorway towards Aubagne/Toulon, exit at "Centre Commercial" and follow the signs for the Centre Commercial, then Aix and Roquevaire.
• For more information: http://www.icem-freinet.info/

Naive art with a feminine touch

Pont-de-L'Étoile owes its name to its bridge that lets travellers cross the River Huveaune and thus reach L'Étoile [Star] massif. But just opposite the bridge there shines the most astonishing maison de celle qui peint [house of she who paints]. If you have any children in the car with you, the stop is a must. They'll love it. Danielle Jacqui, the "painter woman", readily recounts how she came to devote herself to art, even if, as she admits, she started to express herself in this fashion without wondering whether she was creating art or not. When she was small, she was placed in a "special school" that grouped together children traumatized by war: children of Resistance members (her own mother was one), children of deportees, of Spanish Republicans, or people shot during the Occupation. Then she attended another unusual institution, La République des Enfants [Republic of Children], a school based on the same principles as the "Freinet method" (see box below).

Next she wanted to become a jeweller, but women were discouraged from taking up that sort of work, so she finally opened a second-hand shop and livened up her boutique with what we now call "installations". And she painted. One day, an art lover bought a first painting from her. And she continued to paint, and to decorate. Not a single square centimetre of virgin space eluded her. Until finally, by the 1980s, this house had almost become as famous as the Facteur Cheval's Palais Idéal (Drôme). Visits to the house, whose rooms are as surprising as the façade, are free. Furthermore, Danielle offers visitors a series of postcards and poems. You can support her work by buying a painting, if she decides she wants to sell it to you (!), or by joining her association.

On leaving Pont-de-L'Étoile, it may seem that in comparison the other houses look a little sad ...

THE FREINET METHOD

Célestin Freinet (1896–1966) experimented in the early 1920s at his school in Bar-sur-Loup (Alpes-Maritimes), with what would become the core of his pedagogical method. He refused the use of textbooks and other forms of educational "brainwashing", made his initiatives known through the press, and built up a network of correspondents. His school was organized as a veritable community in which the children called Freinet and his wife papa and maman. Manual activities, participation in drawing up timetables, and editing a class newspaper were some of the innovations that formed part of the method: "We prepare tomorrow's democracy by democracy in the school."

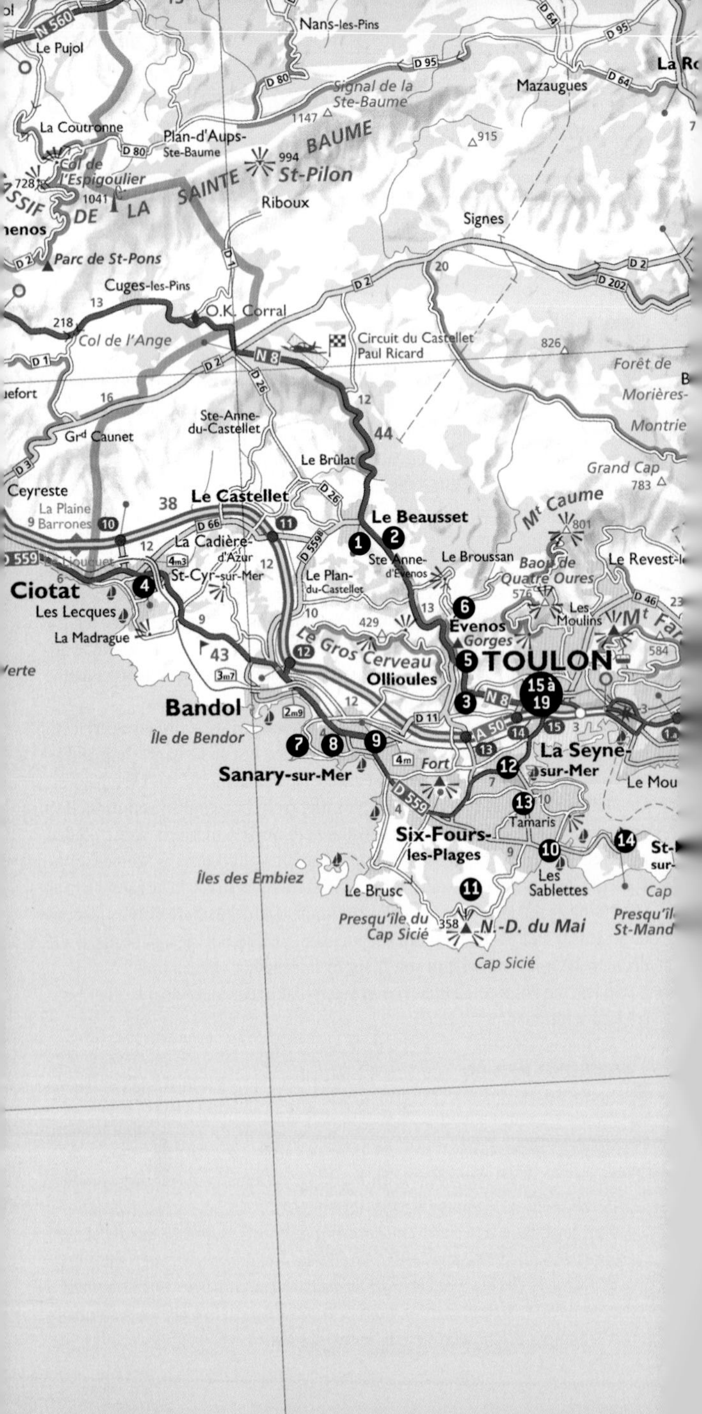

Nans-les-Pins
Le Pujol
Mazaugues
Signal de la Ste-Baume
La Coutronne
Plan-d'Aups-Ste-Baume
MASSIF DE LA SAINTE BAUME
St-Pilon
Col de l'Espigoulier
Riboux
Signes
Parc de St-Pons
Cuges-les-Pins
O.K. Corral
Col de l'Ange
Circuit du Castellet Paul Ricard
Forêt de Morières-Montrieux
Ste-Anne-du-Castellet
Grd Caunet
Le Brûlat
Grand Cap
Ceyreste
Le Castellet
Le Beausset
Mt Caume
La Plaine Barrones
La Cadière-d'Azur
Ste Anne-d'Évenos
Le Broussan
Baou de Quatre Oures
Le Revest-les-Eaux
Ciotat
St-Cyr-sur-Mer
Le Plan-du-Castellet
Les Lecques
La Madrague
Évenos
Gorges
Les Moulins
Mt Faron
Le Gros Cerveau
TOULON
Ollioules
Bandol
Île de Bendor
Sanary-sur-Mer
Fort
La Seyne-sur-Mer
Le Mourillon
Tamaris
Six-Fours-les-Plages
Îles des Embiez
Le Brusc
Les Sablettes
St-Mandrier-sur-Mer
Presqu'île du Cap Sicié
N.-D. du Mai
Presqu'île de St-Mandrier
Cap Sicié

TOULON AND WEST VAR

THE EX-VOTOS OF THE BEAUSSET-VIEUX CHAPEL

1

• Notre Dame du Beausset-Vieux
Le Beausset-Vieu, 83330 Le Beausset
From Le Beausset, drive towards Toulon on the RN8. After about 1.5 km, take the signposted road on the right.
• Open afternoons, 15.00–19.00 in summer and 14.00–17.00 the rest of the year
• Information at the sanctuary (Tel: 04 94 98 61 53) or at the parish (Tel: 04 94 98 70 49)

"Poetic, naive, and precise, the ex-votos of Le Beausset are a window into the past

If at Beausset-Vieux the panorama from the belvedere is stunning, don't forget to have a look inside the building which opens into a chapel and a gallery: its walls are covered with an exceptional collection of ex-votos wonderfully presented and lovingly restored by Les Amis du Beausset-Vieux.

The ex-voto is a mark of gratitude addressed to a male or female saint (often the Holy Virgin) after a "miracle" has been performed. These may involve shipwrecks, domestic accidents, or illnesses, where a request for intercession by a saint has been followed by a positive outcome. Sometimes the ex-voto consists of an object relating to the event: a crutch, a lifesaver, or quite often, a painting by a local artist, very descriptive and done in a naive style. Because of this, ex-votos reveal a great deal about daily life in past centuries.

Some fifteen of the ex-votos in Beausset-Vieux bear the signature of Eusèbe Nicolas, born in Beausset in 1828. Deaf and dumb, he became a joiner and expressed his difficulty in communicating by means of the ex-voto. If his works are naive, they are at the same time both poetic and meticulously detailed. On each painting you find the abbreviation "Sd. M." (sourd et muet – deaf and dumb).

The most unusual of all is the sculpture carved in olive wood, entitled Saumeto (Provençal for "she-ass"). This ex-voto represents the flight into Egypt, and St Joseph is depicted as well as Mary, holding the Infant Jesus in her arms, seated upon an ass. Note Joseph's bowler hat, similar to those worn by workers in their Sunday best until the 18th century. Experts believe that the sculpture was placed in this niche dug into the rock as a reminder on the part of those who left their hilltop refuges to go and live in the plain at the beginning of the 16th century.

OFFICE DE TOURISME DU BEAUSSET
Place Général-de-Gaulle, 83330 Le Beausset • Tel: 04 94 90 55 10 • Fax: 04 94 98 51 83

SIGHTS NEARBY

2

At the entrance to the village of Sainte-Anne-d'Evenos, be careful to respect the speed limit painted on the side of a house on the right but impossible to see from the road. You can park in the place de l'Église and go back to the edge of the road to take a picture of this historic traffic sign, very restrictive (8 km per hour) and difficult to observe literally …

THE TOMBSTONE OF LA MARTELLE

3

• Chemin du Kiosque, 83190 Ollioules

From Ollioules, take the RN8 in the direction of Toulon. Pass by the Bénéventi establishments on your right, then the Colombani vehicle body shop and the "kiosk" bus stop. At the kiosk, recently restored, turn right onto chemin du Kiosque. At the fork, take the left branch towards La Burelle, leaving chemin de Brignac, a private road, on your right. At the end of the road, when you reach the gate to La Burelle, look to the right and you'll see the La Martelle stone, beneath the three cypresses.

This tombstone is that of a 17th century rabbi

In 1927, while restoring a ruin in the countryside near Ollioules, Tercissius Esope (a mason of Greek origin) discovered one day a curious stone which, after he cleaned it, revealed a text written in Hebrew. The stone would later serve as a bench and as a surface for washing and drying clothes, until an erudite ecclesiastic, Abbé Boyer, came to hear of it. He translated the text and asked, without success, that the "discoverer" let him place the stone in a museum. Weary of visits from archaeologists and historians to study the object, Tercissius Esope finally decided to put it off his land so that visitors could read it without bothering him. This was to be the same place where it can be found today, even if, the stone's inscriptions being completely indecipherable to Tercissius Esope, it seems that he set it upside down …

A tombstone, found on this land where a synagogue once stood, the stele is dedicated to rabbi Jinah Duran, who died on 2 Nisan 5385 (9 April 1625). The text in seven verses of four lines reads:

Here is hidden and buried
A faithful pastor
And wise as Héman
Judge of his community.

Redoubling his efforts
And living rich in high deeds
Descendant of eminent ancestors
Who were known and illustrious.

He read and reread
"Gemara" and "Mishuah";
This in his mouth was always ready
Like a man with bread in his basket.

He had for name Rab Jonah
Duran chief of his people
And guide of his nation
By his faith and intelligence.

He was struck by an ordeal
And his pain did not recede
Until he died and passed away,
Broken by his suffering.

On 2 Nisan, towards the celestial dwelling
He rose, for the eternal sharing
In the year of the Hash-Shekinah,
Its light and its splendour.

May God in His mercy,
Invigorate his bones,
In the rivers of His waters
That flow in Eden.

Cited in the text, the Duran family lived since at least the 13th century in Tarascon. They turn up later in Algiers and Venice. It would seem that rabbi Duran was the chief of the Jewish community that was expelled from Provence in the year 1500 but had begun to resettle here at the beginning of the 17th century.

In the 1990s, the actor Henri Tisot published a book about his spiritual quest, Le Petit livre du Grand Livre, in which he wrote: *"I was so taken with the message on the stone that I am convinced today that this book would not have been born if I had not encountered the stone at La Martelle."*

BIBLIOGRAPHICAL REFERENCES:
- Le Petit livre du Grand Livre, by Henri Tisot (Éditions Fayard)
"Les monuments religieux de l'Ouest-Toulonnais",
- Cahiers du patrimoine Ouest-Varois, No. 5/6

THE STATUE OF LIBERTY OF SAINT-CYR-SUR-MER 

• Place Portalis, 83270 Saint-Cyr-sur-Mer

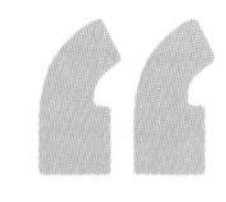

Yes, Cyr...

Saint-Cyr-sur-Mer possesses an astonishing replica of the Statue of Liberty. Signed by Bartholdi himself, it is made from cast iron and supposedly served as the model for the one in New York. Its dimensions, 2.50 m from tip to toe, are the equivalent of the index finger of the American statue.

When the first piped water distribution network in the commune was about to come into service, the idea was conceived of commemorating this event. It was decided that a subscription would be launched to fund this prestigious operation. But Anatole Ducros, a generous donor and landowner in Saint-Cyr, offended the population by insisting on paying the entire amount. Despite the protests of those who weren't able to participate, the statue was inaugurated in 1913.

In 1990, the statue was re-gilded and almost taken hostage by striking workers at La Ciotat, upset by the closure of the shipyards. Forewarned by mysterious sources, the authorities in Saint-Cyr were able to put the statue in a safe place until tempers cooled.

As for the water, the two streams passing through Saint-Cyr have unusual and amusing nicknames: "Dirty" and "Disgusting" (the latter is in fact a wadi that only flows when it rains).

OFFICE DE TOURISME DE SAINT-CYR-SUR-MER
Place de l'Appel du 18 juin, 83270 Saint-Cyr-sur-Mer • Tel: 04 94 26 73 73
Fax: 04 94 26 73 74 • http://www.saintcyrsurmer.com (The tourist office is on the seafront in the beach area of the commune, known as Les Leques.)

HOW MANY COPIES OF THE STATUE OF LIBERTY ARE THERE IN FRANCE?

Answer: at least seven. Two in Paris (in the Jardin du Luxembourg and on the Île des Cygnes), two others at Roybon in Isère and at Barentin near Rouen (glimpsed in the film The Billion Dollar Brain, directed by Gérard Oury, with Bourvil and Jean-Paul Belmondo), another in place de la Liberté at Poitiers, and finally one in Colmar, in addition to the one at Saint-Cyr-sur-Mer. The original statue is in New York and was a gift from France (or to be more precise from a private subscription by French people) in 1886. It was carried out by Frédéric-Auguste Bartholdi and by Gustave Eiffel as far as the metallic framework was concerned. The statue is in fact hollow and covered by sheets of riveted copper. It symbolizes "Liberty lighting up the world".

AN UNUSUAL WALK AT EVENOS

5

• Association "Les Chemins du Patrimoine"
348 chemin des Gais Coteaux, 83190 Ollioules
• Tel: 04 94 63 16 93

Carved into the rock, a graffitti preserves the memory of the plague of the 1720's

At the place where the lime kilns can be seen (page 82), several paths let you discover a series of spots that are unusual both in appearance and because of their history.

At the confluence of La Reppe and the Gorges d'Ollioules, you cross the valley of Le Destel by following the yellow markers and then climb the corner spur before you reach the ruins of the former hamlet of Saint-Estève, inhabited since antiquity. You can see the hollows in the rock that supported the beams of dwellings, and on the ground, a large number of ancient Roman tiles. Next to a medieval chapel in ruins there is the "watchman's seat", an anatomical armchair carved in the rock that lets you observe the defile comfortably. The inscription, "Pesto, 1721", on the side of the cliff, dates from the period when Saint-Estève was a cordon sanitaire: it prevented strangers from entering Ollioules to preserve the village from plague. Having arrived in Marseille in 1720 on the Grand Saint-Antoine, a vessel that brought a cargo of contaminated fabrics from Syria, the plague ravaged Provence between 1720 and 1722, taking more than 50,000 lives. Ollioules was not spared and lost half of its population at the time (2,800 inhabitants). According to historians, the authors of this testimony carved in the rock would have been inhabitants of Le Beausset fleeing the epidemic and stopped here by the quarantine guards, to stop them from infecting Ollioules.

Penetrating a little further into the Gorges du Destel, on the same hillside, you soon reach a cave that bears an inscription in red to the left of the entrance: grotte de la béate [cave of the saintly one]. It was inside this cave, 30 m deep, that the "Saint" of Le Destel lived. In 1735, Marie, a young girl from La Ciotat, came to live here as hermit to repent from her past errors. She had refused to marry Jean, the son of a rich shipowner who went to sea and never returned. She lived on roots, wild berries and river water. Every Sunday she came to the village of Evenos, kneeled for an hour on the front porch of the church, praying in silence, and then left with a little bread given to her by the villagers. Thirty years later she returned to die at La Ciotat.

You can find more details concerning the caves in the Gorges du Destel (the "Christianized" cave, the cave of "Ferrandin", Gaspard de Besse's hole) in bulletin No. 2 of Chroniques du patrimoine, dated September 2001, available from the association mentioned above.

GORGES AND LIME KILNS

6

A WALK FROM EVENOS TO OLLIOULES

Association "Les Chemins du Patrimoine"
348 chemin des Gais Coteaux, 83190 Ollioules • Tel: 04 94 63 16 93
• La Voûte, Bar-restaurant, 83330 Evenos-Village • Tel: 04 94 90 37 63
17 € for the dish of the day with vegetables, salad and cheese

The Gorges of Ollioules have always attracted robbers

The commune of Evenos, a truly astounding mineral spectacle, is composed of two main villages: Sainte-Anne-d'Evenos and Evenos. The road between the two villages plunges into a small valley from which rise stone spires, cut by quarrymen, and winds its way through a chaos of rocks suggestive of recent earthquakes.

The village of Evenos rests on a flow of basalt, a dark volcanic rock.* At the entrance to the village a viewpoint indicator puts some names to the spectacular panorama. But it is at the La Voûte restaurant, owned by Madame Hernandez, that the village truly reveals itself. From Evenos, set off for Toulon by way of famous Gorges d'Ollioules. Just before arriving at these gorges, stop off at the bakery of the Evenos mill: the view of the Saint-Anne sandstones, as they are called, is superb. Unfortunately, access to the sandstones themselves has become impossible, the owners having fenced off the passage after suffering for years the damage caused by negligent hikers.

The gorges are one of those legendary places of historical criminality. Not simply because Gaspard de Besse liked to attack stagecoaches here, but above all because the gigantic, looming, sinister aspect of this spot has always attracted the region's highwaymen.

Shortly after the gorges begin, and just beyond the roche coupée (a rocky overhang undercut by the road), you can leave your car on the right, in the parking space of a former quarry.

Cross the road, then walk a hundred metres towards Ollioules in order to traverse the bed of La Reppe river. Be careful, because La Reppe is sometimes dry and then becomes an unpredictable torrent if a big storm brews up. Coming back, on the far side of the river, you'll reach the site of the old lime kilns restored by an association called Les Chemins du Patrimoine [Heritage Roads] and the commune of Ollioules. A small sign with an arrow points to the first of these kilns. This one has the particularity of having been reduced in size three times. The kiln served to make lime (the concrete of its time) by heating limestone gathered locally to a temperature of 1,000 °C. At the end of the cycle, 56% of the heated mass was obtained in the form of quicklime, very useful for disposing of bodies in times of epidemics, and once it was slaked this became binding lime for construction purposes. This type of kiln had been conceived in Roman times and was used in the region until the end of the 19th century. Several hundred of them were in operation for nearly 2,000 years.

*Curiously, this flow emerges again near the sea, on the road to Brusc, after Six-Fours, near the Cap Nègre battery.

THÉÂTRE GEORGES-GALLI

• 1, rue Raoul Henry, BP 24, 83110 Sanary-sur-Mer
• Tel: 04 94 88 53 90 • http://www.mairie-sanary.fr/theatre.htm

A church in a theatre

In summer, when the church at Sanary-sur-Mur proves to be too small, Mass is said at the Théâtre Galli instead. It has 1,200 comfortable seats and the village priest on stage, all because Father Galli struck a deal with the local council. He offered his Cité de la Jeunesse [Youth City] to the commune, on condition that Mass could be said there when the need was felt.

Georges Henri Nicolas Galli was born in Aix-les-Bains on 24 Novembre 1902. He went to Paris to study law. One day, he was watching a film shoot (silent at the time), when director Julien Duvivier noticed him and got him to do a screen test. That was how the career of actor Georges Galli got started. He was as big a success in his day as Alain Delon 40 years later. L'Homme à l'Hispano was the film that turned this young man into a big star. In 1930, he was 28 years old, idolized, fulfilled and rich, when suddenly he underwent an existential crisis. He said that he felt that his life was empty and that he needed to "do something else". On 13 February 1938 he was ordained as a Roman Catholic priest. At first, he officiated in Esparron-sur-Verdon in Haut Var, then he became vicar at Morillon, a nice neighbourhood in Toulon on the seaside, and in the end he was put in charge of the parish at Sanary-sur-Mer.

This passionate man, friend of painters and actors, "confessor" of Paul Ricard (who furnished him with convertibles), devoted himself to his flock, and in particular, young people, for whom he conceived the Cité de la Jeunesse. This building hosted sporting events, concerts, variety shows, and Sunday Mass, when the village church became too crowded in summer. The priest took collection with a butterfly net whose mesh was too wide to retain anything but bills, letting coins fall to the ground, in order to embarrass small donators …

Once he retired, the Cité became the Théâtre Georges-Galli with his blessing. The ceremony took place without him on 9 July 1982: he died on 3 July that same year. Today the Théâtre Galli is a very beautiful auditorium. Around the stage trompe-l'oeil paintings represent emblematic figures who once lived in Sanary-sur-Mer, including Georges Galli, but also Cécile Sorel, Thomas Mann, Anna and Franz Werfel (*Jules et Jim,* see page 84), and the French painter of Polish birth Moise Kisling.

MEMORIAL TOUR OF SANARY-SUR-MER

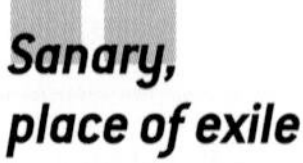

Sanary, place of exile

This tour starts from the tourist office where you can pick up a booklet (€3) with itinerary, explanations and commentaries about each stop along the way. It can be done on foot or bicycle. Some of the places are quite a distance from the village, and in certain instances the present owners have refused to allow a plaque to be erected on their properties.

Before the Second World War, Sanary-sur-Mer became a place of exile for hundreds of refugees, including German and Austrian writers persecuted by the Nazis and forced to flee their countries. A memorial tour today lets you look at some of the houses where they lived.

In 1933, the Nazis ordered that books written by opponents of the new regime or by Jews should be burned. These first autos-da-fé had an appalling effect and the German writer Thomas Mann was one of the first to draw the obvious conclusions. Although protected by his international celebrity (he had won the Nobel Prize in 1929), he opted for exile and on the advice of Jean Cocteau he chose the Var coast. After a stay at the Grand Hôtel in Bandol, he settled in Sanary. He showed the way for others and the entire German and Austrian intelligentsia, threatened by the madness of Nazism, soon followed his example. Almost 800 exiles came to live in Sanary between 1933 and 1942. If the village offered plenty of advantages (good train services, a low cost of living, and an exceptional climate), the defeat of the Allied armies in 1940 would precipitate another forced departure for these unfortunate people who had believed they would be safe in France.

The tour starts with the plaque in honour of these exiles on the wall of the Maison du Tourisme. Among the names listed there is Thomas Mann, of course, along with Bertolt Brecht, Wilhelm Herzog, Arthur Koestler, Stefan Zweig, Franz Werfel (who was the second husband of Alma Mahler, the widow of Gustav), as well as Lion Feuchtwanger. The latter, author of the popular novel, JudSüss [Süss the Jew], which was used for twisted ends by Nazi propaganda, was interned in the camp at Les Milles (see page 45). It was a picture of him wearing a prisoner's uniform that appeared in the international press which sparked action on the part of the United States to allow all these exiles to flee Europe. Thomas Mann lived in the La Tranquille villa at the end of the chemin de la Colline. A plaque recalls his stay there, but the original house no longer exists and has been replaced by postwar construction. It was German artillery officers who ordered this villa to be destroyed. Not because Thomas Mann had been there, but because it hampered the installation of guns intended to repel an Allied landing.

In the impasse Lou Cimaï, at the Mas de la Carreirado, Hélène and Franz Hessel would undertake a human experiment (with a third party …) that would be the point of departure for the novel Jules et Jim by Henri-Pierre Roché.

Along the chemin de la Colline, between Alma Mahler's "Moulin Gris" and Thomas Mann's "La Tranquille", a haunting musical air springs to mind: the adagietto of the Fifth Symphony by Mahler, the late husband of Alma and composer of the music that director Luchino Visconti used in his film, Death in Venice, adapted from a short story by … Thomas Mann.

MAISON DU TOURISME DE SANARY-SUR-MER
Les Jardins de la Ville, BP 24, 83110 Sanary-sur-Mer • Tel: 04 94 74 01 04
• www.sanarysurmer.com • e-mail : maison.tourisme.sanary.sur.mer@wanadoo.fr

BRAVE NEW WORLD IN SANARY

Although Aldous Huxley, a British citizen, is not included in the brochure about writers in exile [he was in Sanary-sur-Mer as a willing expatriate], he and his wife did spend time with the German writers. Several of them became close friends of the couple, as did the painter Kisling, the psycho-analyst Charlotte Wolff, Drieu la Rochelle and Paul Valéry.

In 1930, Aldous Huxley and his wife bought a house in allée Thérèse, part of the hamlet of La Gorguette, which they found while visiting D.H. Lawrence [who was staying at Bandol]. They spent several months each year there between 1930 and 1941. If the house is called Villa Huley, due to an error by a craftsman who forgot the "X", Huxley decided to keep this name that permitted him to gently deride Provençal workmanship. It was in 1931 in this Villa Huley that Huxley wrote Brave New World, published in London in 1932.

Aldous Huxley's death passed totally unnoticed, he expired on 22 November 1963, the same day that JFK was assassinated …

THE BIGGEST BOUILLABAISSE IN THE WORLD

On 24 June 1990 a bailiff from Toulon was sent to Sanary-sur-Mer to officially register the biggest bouillabaisse in the world, which is now included in Guinness World Records. Here are the ingredients to feed 1,300 persons:

– A cauldron 3 m wide and 60 cm high – 950 kilos of fish
– 300 kilos of potatoes – 2 magnums of pastis
– 2 bags of bouquets garnis

All this while still respecting the most basic instructions for this Provençal speciality: quand ça bouille, tu baisses … [when it starts to boil, turn down the heat …].

Since 1990, the giant bouillabaisse is prepared in Sanary-sur-Mer on the last Sunday of June in even-numbered years.

LE MUSÉE DE LA PLONGÉE FRÉDÉRIC DUMAS 

- La Tour Romane , Quai Charles-de-Gaulle, 83110 Sanary-sur-Mer
- Open weekends, public holidays and school vacations, 10.00–12.30 and 15.00–18.30. In summer, open daily, 10.00–12.30 and 16.00–19.30
- Admission free
- Access to the terrace of the tower, with a panoramic view of the port, the village and the bay of Sanary-sur-Mer

> ***The museum of the "Mousquemers", the inventers of modern deep-sea diving***

From the top of the Tour Romane, the oldest monument in Sanary-sur-Mer, you get a superb vista of the village and the port. Down below, it houses the interesting Frédéric Dumas diving museum which is all the more enticing to visit because admission is free.

A companion of Commander Cousteau, Frédéric Dumas was one of the three "Mousquemers", who invented the most essential items of equipment still used in deep-sea diving today. If Fréderic's parents originally moved to Sanary in response to medical advice on improving the health of their child, who suffered from respiratory problems, then subsequent events proved they did right by him. His problems not only cleared up, but little "Didi" became an ace at holding his breath and even one of the world's foremost underwater hunters. His first harpoon, made from a curtain rod, worked wonders. His meeting with Philippe Tailliez, the third Mousquemer, led to the pressure-reducing valve, the diving mask, and a passion for making underwater films.

It was Frédéric Dumas who swam with Jojo the grouper in the sequence that appears in Monde du Silence, a film that came out of the book he co-authored. The film itself was a big success and won the Palme d'Or at the 1956 Cannes film festival. Later, Frédéric Dumas distanced himself from the whole Cousteau adventure and became interested in underwater archaeology.

The museum presents materials that retrace the history of deep-sea diving, from diving costumes with helmets and lead soles to the lightweight suits now in use, and including flippers, masks and bottles, as well as photographic and cinematographic equipment. Some of this equipment comes from the very first factory to make "Squale" masks and flippers, established right here in Sanary-sur-Mer.

One of the most spectacular exhibits in the museum is the "Trunk Costume: project for equipping a diver", created by Pierre de Rémy de Beauve, a naval officer from Brest, in 1715. Considered to be the inventor of the diving helmet, the Chevalier de Beauve experimented with this equipment in the port of Brest down to a depth of 10 m. The model presented in the museum is a replica used in the shooting of the film Ridicule, directed by Patrice Leconte.

HOTEL
PROVENCE
PLAGE
C. FERNANDEZ

THE HAMLET OF LES SABLETTES

Fernand Pouillon's ideal seaside resort

Situated in the commune of La Seyne-sur-Mer, the seaside resort of Les Sablettes is an astonishing creation by the emblematic architect of the postwar years, Fernand Pouillon (see page 25).

In spring 1944 the Nazi occupying forces, foreseeing an imminent landing of Allied forces, strengthened the coastal defences, implanting blockhouses and installing artillery guns all along the shore. Anything that might prove a hindrance within the firing angles of these guns was destroyed. That was why the fishing village of Les Sablettes was razed and its population evacuated without any consideration.

In November 1944, after the Liberation, the French Ministry of Reconstruction and Urban Planning gave Fernand Pouillon carte blanche to create an entirely new seaside resort on this site. Started in 1950, the project was delivered 18 months later and became the archetype of the Mediterranean holiday villages that began to spring up during the 1950s. Pouillon imagined the traditional village coexisting with holiday-makers, where the stricken fishermen would be able to find a bigger dwelling at a lower cost. The pre-cut stones used for the outer walls came from the construction site at the Vieux-Port in Marseille, the floors are made from reinforced concrete, and brick vaults have replaced more traditional wooden frameworks.

The hamlet includes 35 dwellings, 28 boutiques, a family boarding house, one hotel-restaurant (now converted into more accommodation), five café-restaurants, public baths, a casino and a port.

Even the slightest detail contributes to the overall concept, and art plays a role in this project. Artists from Aix and the rest of Provence, who in this period of reconstruction worked and created in a team spirit focused around Fernand Pouillon's various projects, participated in the building of Les Sablettes. Jean Amado created the ceramic fountain. Louis Arnaud sculpted a monumental crouching naiad (nymph), Philippe Sourdive baked ceramic panels, and Carlos Fernandez encrusted earthenware plates into the hotel façade.

Of course, you'll need to do some visual filtering to reconstitute the original 1950s project, because other than the demolition of some elements such as the landing stage and boarding house, the anarchic proliferation of signs has confused the legibility of the ensemble. Since 1988, the local authorities and the French state have made efforts to preserve the essence of this harmonious and timeless village, witness to an age when holiday hotels were still simply called Hôtel de la Plage …

LA BATTERIE DE PEYRAS

• Visits by appointment from the "Militari Conservation" group
T• el: 04 94 06 42 64 / 06 76 30 25 28
• Admission: €3 (free during Journées du Patrimoine)
• Information on the closure of the massifs: 04 98 10 55 41

We advise you to travel to this battery from La Seyne-sur-Mer out of season, because in summer the road is closed practically every day. Follow the signs posted for the quartier de Fabregas, Notre-Dame-de-Mai and Cap Sicié. Once you've reached the corniche merveilleuse, which deserves its name, you'll find a route, closed to vehicles, 2 km beyond the barrier that blocks all traffic in case of fires. A small sign announces, very discreetly, "Peyras".

You can also reach Peyras by a pedestrian path, Sentier du Peyras (30 minutes) that runs from the forest of Janas (next to the Buffalo camping site). An itinerary is available from the Six-Fours-les-Plages tourist office.

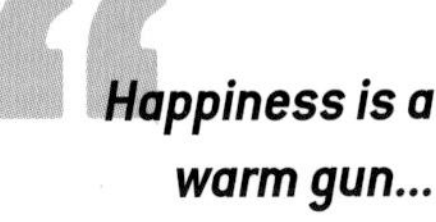

The battery of Peyras (Peyras means "stone") is a pretty fort built in the scrub land on top of Cap Sicié, and looks out over Toulon harbour from a height of 200 m. The association "Militari Conservation" whose object is to safeguard, maintain and highlight military heritage sites, proposes visits to this little-known fort constructed with red stone from the cape itself, with Vauban-style arrises and an atmosphere worthy of Schoendoerffer (director of the French film Le Crabe Tambour).

When it was constructed in 1879, the battery's mission was to control the western approach to the military port of Toulon. It was a "bombardment battery" with large-calibre guns, its height allowing it to subject enemy vessels to plunging fire, increasing both its effectiveness and range.

After the Liberation, the French Navy converted the site into an anti-aircraft training school, installing four German 105 mm guns recovered near Lorient. Today, Peyras remains the only flak (i.e. German AA) battery in existence in Europe, the rest of the equipment from the Germans' Atlantic Wall and Mediterranean defences in the Second World War having been sold to scrap merchants.

The stars at this site are, of course, these big guns, that you can still pivot and aim by turning the adjustment wheels. The only thing missing are the munitions to fire them. Here are some technical details that may be useful to know when you are under the cupola: the barrels each weigh 1,760 kg, the turret itself weighs 15 tonnes and the guns' range is 15 km.

Another item you must see during this visit is the telemeter, which lets you calculate the distance to the target with the instruments of the time, which would seem almost laughably clunky and outmoded in our computerized age if it weren't for the fact that these were deadly weapons.

The "alveoles" of the fort, that is to say, its vaulted chambers, have been fitted out by the association as exhibition rooms full of weapons, equipment and military uniforms, both French and foreign, ranging from the Second World War to more recent conflicts.

THE COUNTESS'S RESURRECTION 

• Cimetière de La Seyne-sur-Mer
Place du Souvenir français, 83500 La Seyne-sur-Mer
• Directions signposted from centre of town. Parking is a problem but walking there only takes 10 minutes.
• Source: http://perso.wanadoo.fr/marius.autran/glossaire/tome7/memoires_entre_tombes.html

When diamonds really were a girl's best friends...

La Seyne-sur-Mer cemetery even holds the graves of those miraculously saved from death: go in through the main gates, turn right at the far end, then walk down to the end of the row. The Countess of Pézenas's tomb lies against the boundary wall to the right: allée 10 Sud, 33rd place.

A plaque leaning on the wall explains: "Here lies Rose Louise Marguerite Vallavieille, wife of the late Monsieur de Pézenas de Bernardy, royal ship's captain, born 22 June 1754, died 22 June 1829, pray for her. A model among wives and mothers, she always supported the unfortunate."

What this plaque does not tell you is that the Countess of Pézanas died, in a manner of speaking, twice ... At the age of 20, she choked on an apricot stone and was therefore buried in Toulon cemetery. Her husband, whose distress you can imagine, wanted her dressed for her coffin just as she was on the day of her wedding, in her beautiful white dress with a splendid rivière [necklace] of diamonds. The following night, the gravedigger with the help of accomplices broke into the tomb in order to seize the necklace. But his brutal gestures woke the deceased who had in fact suffered no more than a prolonged faint. Her cries of relief caused the criminals to flee in panic.

She lived on for more than 55 years, and shortly after this incident gave birth to a beautiful baby, thus giving rise to the oft-told Provençal legend concerning the Pézenas child, "who died before it was born".

You can also see in the cemetery at La Seyne-sur-Mer the tomb of André Igual (1950–2000), the writer and humorist to whom his friends dedicated a newspaper in 2001: "The Andre Igual, that appears each time Igual dies ..."

OFFICE DE TOURISME INTERCOMMUNAL DE L'OUEST-VAROIS
Bureau d'accueil de La Seyne-sur-Mer, parc Fernand-Braudel,
corniche Georges-Pompidou, Les Sablettes, 83500 La Seyne-sur-Mer
• Tel: 04 98 00 25 70 • Fax : 04 98 00 25 71
• e-mail : info@ot-la-seyne-sur-mer.fr • www.ot-la-seyne-sur-mer.fr

THE POST OFFICE AT TAMARIS-SUR-MER ⑬

• La Poste, Corniche Michel Pacha, Tamaris, 83500 La Seyne-sur-Mer
• Villa Tamaris, av. de la Grande Maison, Tamaris, 83500 La Seyne-sur-Mer
• Open Tuesday to Sunday, 14.00–18.00 • Tél: 04 94 06 84 00
• Admission free

The Tamaris post office is by the sea, on the Michel Pacha corniche, opposite the landing stage for boat shuttles to the port of Toulon, at the corner of avenue Auguste Plane.

"The town whose mayor was a pacha

Blaise Jean Marius Michel was born in Sanary in 1819. Cabin boy on a ship, he distinguished himself during the French conquest of Algeria, when all on his own he seized the town of Djidjelli. It's said that, finding himself aboard a warship in this port, he swam to the shore in the middle of the night, a French flag tied to his belt. He then unfurled the flag from the top of the town minaret, so that in the morning the population thought that the French had already entered the town and opposed no resistance.

Later, when he became a captain of trading vessels, he ran his ship, L'Eurotas, aground in front of the lazaret* of Alexandria. He disembarked everyone aboard and was the last to leave the ship. In just a few hours, his hair had turned completely white. After this incident he wrote a monograph on navigation, emphasizing the need to build lighthouses along dangerous shores. Napoleon III, seeking better relations with the Ottoman Empire, next sent him to Turkey, where the sultan took a liking to him and made him a pacha. Thereafter he changed his name to Michel Pacha.

He then obtained the concession for the quays, docks and warehouses of Constantinople and created a maritime freight company. His fortune made, he returned to France and was thrice elected mayor of Sanary. It was at this point that he became interested in the section of shoreline in the Toulon harbour between the town of La Seyne-sur-Mer and the Plage des Sablettes. He bought 400 hectares in 1880 and constructed hotels, casino, 60 villas, in an eastern, neo-Moorish style or a mix of Italian, English and colonial. Although Tamaris would have its moments of glory, graced by the presence of figures such as Gabriel D'Annunzio, Camille Saint-Saëns, Auguste Renoir, the children of Victor Hugo, Georges Sand and the Lumière brothers, the bubble had burst by the 1920s and Tamaris fell into a slumber.

Today, you can visit Villa Tamaris which houses exhibitions of contemporary art, stroll by some of the other strange private villas, and post a card in the pretty mailbox at the Tamaris post office.

*Lazaret: an isolated port facility, used to passengers, crews and merchandise suspected of being contaminated. A place of quarantine. The word lazaret comes from Latin and means "patchy" or "leprous".

THE MAUSOLEUM OF ADMIRAL LATOUCHE-TRÉVILLE 14

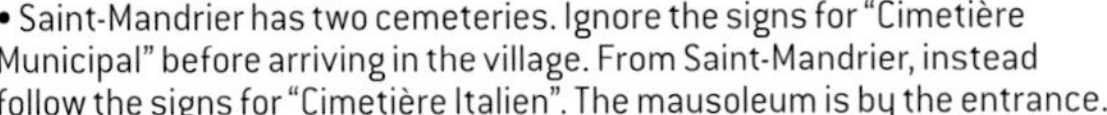

• Nécropole du Cap Capet, Chemin du Sémaphore, 83430 Saint-Mandrier

• Saint-Mandrier has two cemeteries. Ignore the signs for "Cimetière Municipal" before arriving in the village. From Saint-Mandrier, instead follow the signs for "Cimetière Italien". The mausoleum is by the entrance.

"A travelling pyramid for the "Terror of the English"

On the tip of the Saint-Mandrier peninsula, by the entrance to the nécropole nationale (the appellation given to a cemetery that only has tombs with the epitaph "mort pour la France" [died for France]), visitors come across the mausoleum of Admiral Latouche-Tréville, in the form of an enigmatic pyramid 7.25 m high.

Born in Rochefort in 1745, Louis René Madeleine Levassor de Latouche-Tréville joined the French Navy at the age of 13. Receiving promotion upon promotion, notably for having frustrated Admiral Nelson's attack with the British fleet on Boulogne in 1801, he was highly thought of by Napoleon who considered him to be the best of his admirals. In fact he was one of the first officers to receive the Légion d'Honneur from the hands of the Emperor.

Admiral and commander of the Mediterranean squadron, it was aboard his ship Bucentaure that he would again encounter Nelson, waiting in ambush before Toulon, but the British admiral declined battle. It was then that yellow fever, contracted during a journey to Santo Domingo, struck down Latouche-Tréville, on 1 Fructidor XII (19 August 1804). The death of the admiral, regarded as the terror of the English, France's hereditary enemies at the time, was at first kept secret.

It was only six years later that the mausoleum was erected in proximity to the Croix des Signaux semaphore, a place chosen to allow the admiral to be buried where he could see the English coming from all four points of the compass, as he had vowed to do. The naval officers from his squadron each contributed a day's pay towards the construction of the stone pyramid. In 1817, reports by the Navy pointed out the strategic inconvenience posed by this pyramid. Enemy fleets were in fact using it as a landmark to determine the position of the defensive batteries implanted on the Saint-Mandrier peninsula. But the decision to move the mausoleum was not taken until 1899 and this transfer was finally carried out in 1902. When the admiral's coffin was removed from the crypt, it was observed that the French flag had been reduced to dust, but remarkably, the three national colours could still be distinguished. On 29 April 1903, having been moved twice, Admiral Latouche-Tréville was at last laid to his final rest.

Portrait of the admiral: http://perso.wanadoo.fr/marine-imperiale/amiraux/latouche.htm

OFFICE DE TOURISME DE SAINT-MANDRIER
Place des Résistants, 83430 Saint-Mandrier • Tel: 04 94 63 61 69

THE CANNONBALL IN COURS LAFAYETTE ⑮

• 89, cours Lafayette, 83000 Toulon

A cannonball left behind from one of the many sieges endured by this military port

At 89 cours Lafayette, where the market is held (daily, except Monday), at a certain height you can see a cannonball stuck in the side of the building. To highlight the fact, it even has pretty stone collar around it.

This cannonball is a souvenir of the siege of 1707, when France was allied with Spain against a coalition (England, Holland, Austria, Savoy and Portugal) in the War of Spanish Succession. The enemy wanted to seize Toulon, fortified by Vauban, in order to cut off France's commercial routes. Hundreds of cannonballs were fired by the besieging ships and the streets were filled with them. It is sometimes said that the cannonball in cours Lafayette was left where its trajectory had sent it, but it's more plausible to think that it was "lifted" from the ground to this spot, as a memorial to those bellicose times.

BONAPARTE AIMS AND FIRES

Toulon has known other sieges besides that of 1707. In 1793, it was a certain Bonaparte who ordered his gunners to blast away at the British and Spanish fleets protecting Toulon, last bastion of the monarchist cause.

Toulon would see Bonaparte twice more. In 1798, it was the military port from where he embarked on the expedition to Egypt, with Joséphine waving her handkerchief from the Tour Royal to be certain that he was really gone. And lastly, on 7 July 1840, the frigate La Belle Poule departed with a funeral urn to collect the ashes of the former French emperor on Saint Helena in order to return them to Paris. For details of the Belle Poule's arrival in Corbevoie, near Paris, see the guide Banlieue de Paris insolite et secrète in this collection.

OFFICE DE TOURISME DE TOULON
334, avenue de la République, 83000 Toulon • Tel: 3265 ou 04 94 18 53 00
• Fax: 04 94 18 53 09 • e-mail : info@toulontourisme.com • www.toulontourisme.com

SIGHTS NEARBY

LE MUSÉE DU VIEUX TOULON 16

• 69, cours Lafayette, 83000 Toulon • Tel: 04 94 92 29 23
Open afternoons, 14.00–18.00 except Sundays and public holidays
• Admission free • Bibliothèque du Musée du Vieux Toulon
Open Monday, Wednesday and Saturday, 14.00–18.00

The museum of the Society of Friends of Old Toulon is very interesting. Paintings, objects (many of them made by prison convicts), and exhibits give you a better understanding of this port town that does not reveal its true nature at a brief glance. But in addition to these collections, the museum library offers a surprising wealth of material. There is an extremely large Provençal section and you can also consult the regional press, classified by subject since 1990.

SACRILEGE IN THE NOTRE DAME-DE-LA-SEDS CATHEDRAL 17

Place de la Cathédrale • Access: by the side entrance of the cathedral, on the left, just after the cannonball as you walk up cours Lafayette.

There isn't enough room to stand back from the façade of Toulon cathedral. The street is fairly narrow and the shop opposite is a constant temptation to chastity ... To the left of the façade, rather too near a drainpipe, some curious stones set in the wall draw your attention. These bear the epitaph of Dame Sibille, a 13th-century resident of Toulon, along with some mysterious symbolic drawings. A very sexual wolf is seen pursuing a rabbit and two comets.

Inside the cathedral, in the chapel on the left, a Virgin with Child in sculpted wood gazes at a Jesus with an arm broken off. It was in 1793, when the destruction of the cathedral was decided, that one man a little more daring than the rest committed this sacrilege with a hammer, a chisel and a ladder. As soon as he broke the holy arm, he fell from the ladder and broke his own arm in exactly the same spot. The crowd of miscreants saw in this a sign of divine protection and withdrew, abandoning their disastrous raid.

ÉLÉGANCE MARINE

18

27, rue Victor Micholet, 83000 Toulon • Tel/Fax: 04 94 92 74 17
Open Monday to Friday, 8.30–21.00

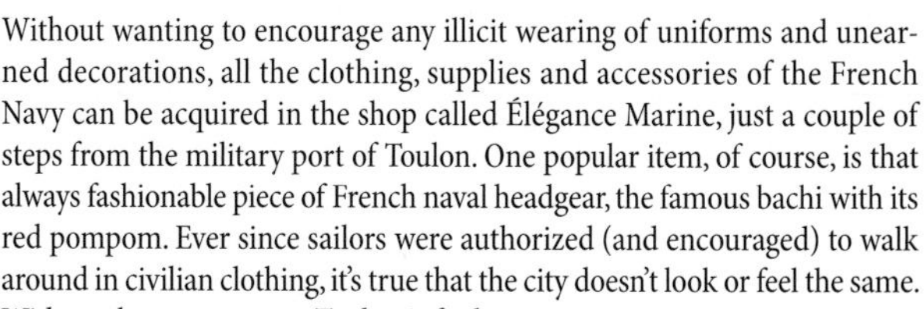

Without wanting to encourage any illicit wearing of uniforms and unearned decorations, all the clothing, supplies and accessories of the French Navy can be acquired in the shop called Élégance Marine, just a couple of steps from the military port of Toulon. One popular item, of course, is that always fashionable piece of French naval headgear, the famous bachi with its red pompom. Ever since sailors were authorized (and encouraged) to walk around in civilian clothing, it's true that the city doesn't look or feel the same. Without those pompoms, Toulon is far less quaint.
Élégance Marine also sells decorations, all kinds of military decorations. No point in bringing along your official document, there are no questions asked with the notable exception of the aeronautics medal, for which you must show your authorization and identity papers. For the Légion d'Honneur, no need to prove that you're entitled. If you want the grade of chevalier, you can procure the medal and the ribbon for €76, but the rosette awarded only to officiers can be had for the reasonable price of €9.

THE BUST IN THE STADE MAYOL

Avenue de la République, 83000 Toulon

The bust of Mayol is to be found at the top of the staircase at the Lafontan entrance to the stadium, but if the gate is locked, you can use the south entrance.
The Mayol stadium was inaugurated on 20 March 1920 in the presence of its sponsor, the singer Félix Mayol (1872–1941), accompanied by the enthusiastic applause of a roaring crowd. The singer had been hit on the head by a ball as he was out driving in a horse-and-carriage near the old velodrome stadium. One thing led to another, and he ended up sponsoring the Rugby Club Toulonnais (RCT), and financing the construction of the stadium. The players called him "godfather" and appreciated the "third halves" with plenty to drink at his home …
Félix Mayol enjoyed unbelievable success at the beginning of the 20th century. Born in Toulon in 1872, he made his debut as a singer in 1895 in Paris, where he adopted a Tintin-like quiff and a sprig of lily of the valley in his buttonhole. Hence the RCT emblem is a lily of the valley, too. Mayol sang over 500 songs, which made his fortune. He retired in 1932, living in a house (the Clos Mayol, boulevard du Docteur Amouretti) on whose gate you can read: La chanson a bâti cet asile champêtre, vous qui passez, merci, je vous le dois peut-être [Song has built this country retreat, but you who pass, thank you, I owe it to you, perhaps].

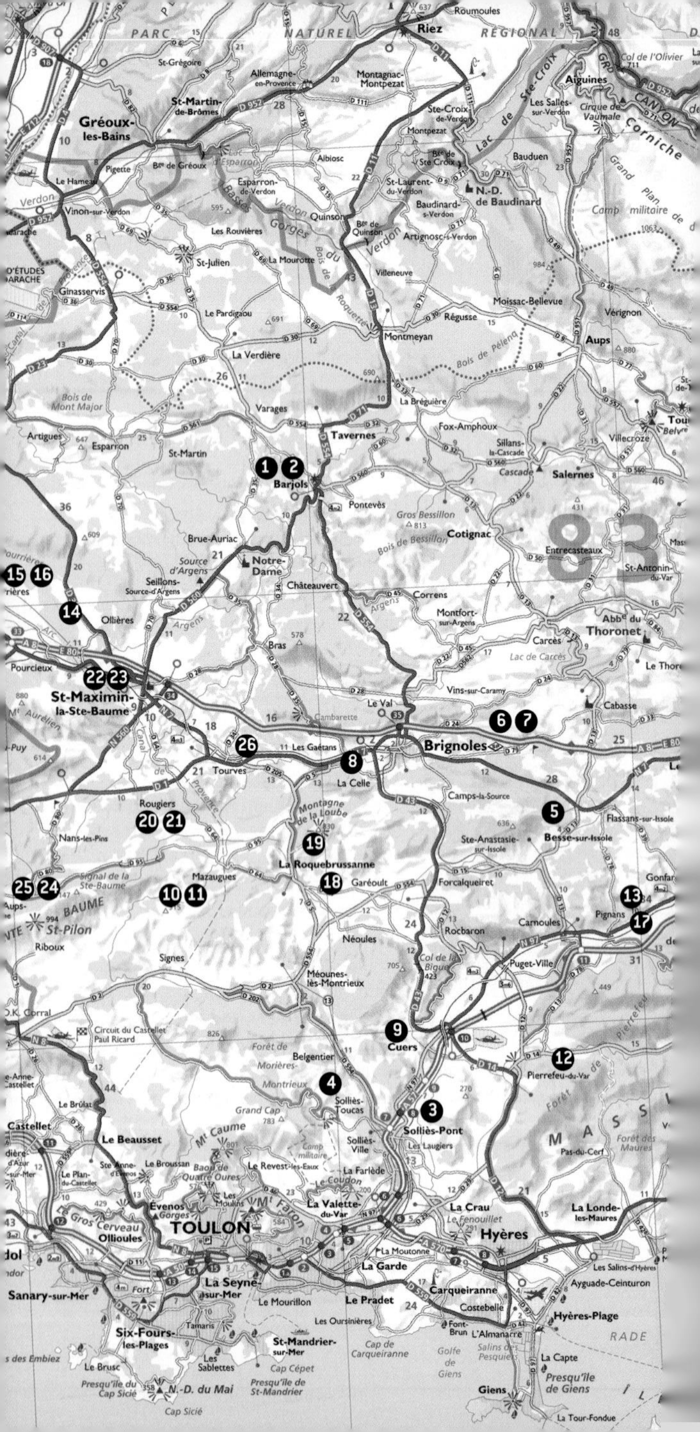
PARC
NATUREL
RÉGIONAL
Riez
Roumoules
St-Grégoire
Allemagne-en-Provence
Montagnac-Montpezat
Col de l'Olivier
Aiguines
Les Salles-sur-Verdon
Cirque de Vaumale
CANYON
Corniche
Lac de Ste-Croix
Ste-Croix-de-Verdon
Montpezat
Bge de Ste Croix
Bauduen
Grand Plan de
Camp militaire de
St-Martin-de-Brômes
Gréoux-les-Bains
Bge de Gréoux
Lac d'Esparron
Albiosc
Pigette
Le Hameau
Esparron-de-Verdon
St-Laurent-du-Verdon
N.-D. de Baudinard
Baudinard-s-Verdon
Verdon
Vinon-sur-Verdon
Basses Gorges du Verdon
Quinson
Bge de Quinson
Artignosc-s-Verdon
Les Rouvières
St-Julien
La Mourotte
Bois de Roquette
Villeneuve
D'ÉTUDES
DARACHE
Ginasservis
Le Pardigaou
Moissac-Bellevue
Vérignon
Régusse
Montmeyan
Aups
La Verdière
Bois de Pélenq
Bois de Mont Major
La Bréguière
Varages
Tavernes
Fox-Amphoux
Villecroze
Artigues
Esparron
St-Martin
Sillans-la-Cascade
Cascade
Salernes
1
2
Barjols
Pontevès
Gros Bessillon
Bois de Bessillon
Cotignac
83
Entrecasteaux
Brue-Auriac
Source d'Argens
Notre-Dame
Seillons-Source-d'Argens
Châteauvert
Correns
St-Antonin-du-Var
15
16
Ollières
14
Argens
Montfort-sur-Argens
Abbe du Thoronet
Bras
Carcès
Lac de Carcès
Le Thoronet
Pourcieux
22
23
St-Maximin-la-Ste-Baume
Vins-sur-Caramy
Cabasse
Mt Aurélien
Le Val
Cambarette
6
7
Les Gaëtans
Brignoles
26
Tourves
8
La Celle
Camps-la-Source
Canal de Provence
Rougiers
20
21
Montagne de la Loube
5
Flassans-sur-Issole
Nans-les-Pins
19
Ste-Anastasie-sur-Issole
Besse-sur-Issole
La Roquebrussanne
Signal de la Ste-Baume
18
Garéoult
Forcalqueiret
25
24
Mazaugues
10
11
Gonfaron
13
BAUME
St-Pilon
Pignans
17
Carnoules
Riboux
Néoules
Rocbaron
Signes
Col de la Bigue
Puget-Ville
Méounes-lès-Montrieux
O.K. Corral
Circuit du Castellet Paul Ricard
9
Cuers
Forêt de Morières-Montrieux
Belgentier
12
Pierrefeu-du-Var
Forêt de Pierrefeu
4
Solliès-Toucas
Grand Cap
3
Solliès-Pont
Le Brûlat
Castellet
Le Beausset
Mt Caume
Solliès-Ville
Camp militaire
Les Laugiers
MASSIF
Forêt des Maures
Pas-du-Cerf
Le Plan-du-Castellet
Ste Anne-d'Evenos
Le Broussan
Baou de Quatre Oures
Le Revest-les-Eaux
La Farlède
Le Coudon
Evenos
Gorges
Les Moulins
Mt Faron
La Valette-du-Var
La Crau
Le Fenouillet
La Londe-les-Maures
Le Gros Cerveau
Ollioules
TOULON
Hyères
La Moutonne
La Garde
Les Salins-d'Hyères
Sanary-sur-Mer
Fort
La Seyne-sur-Mer
Le Mourillon
Le Pradet
Carqueiranne
Ayguade-Ceinturon
Costebelle
Hyères-Plage
Six-Fours-les-Plages
Tamaris
St-Mandrier-sur-Mer
Les Oursinières
Font-Brun
L'Almanarre
RADE
Cap de Carqueiranne
Golfe de Giens
Salins des Pesquiers
La Capte
Les Embiez
Le Brusc
Les Sablettes
Cap Cépet
Presqu'île de Giens
Presqu'île du Cap Sicié
N.-D. du Mai
Presqu'île de St-Mandrier
Giens
Cap Sicié
La Tour-Fondue

PROVENCE VERTE AND CENTRAL VAR

ALLEE
FONTAINE
DU
BOEUF

THE BULLOCK'S FOUNTAIN 

THE FESTIVAL OF SAINT MARCEL

• Place Martin Ferdinand, 83670 Barjols

> ***"It's we who have them, the tripettes of St Marcel!"***

St Marcel was born in Avignon at the beginning of the 5th century and was the bishop of Die. One day, tired by his return journey from Rome to see the Pope, he stopped at the Saint-Maurice monastery in Montmeyan, between Aups and Barjols. He died there, was buried there, and was subsequently canonized. In 1349, by which time the abbey was falling into ruins, its last remaining monk had a dream in which St Marcel appeared, asking this monk to bear his remains to a more suitable place.

On learning this, the inhabitants of the towns of Aups and Barjols both demanded the right to adopt the saint. The Count of Provence ruled that the dispute should be decided by measuring the distance between each town and the ruined monastery, with the closer of the two acquiring the saint's tomb. Without waiting for the results, however, the men of Barjols went to Saint-Maurice on 17 January 1350 and returned home with the body of St Marcel, just when the women were cleaning the guts [tripettes] from a bullock. Several years later, on another 17 January when Barjols was under siege and short of provisions, a hitherto undiscovered bullock was found within the town. This unexpected source of meat saved the population. The fact that both events fell on the same date provoked a joyous procession to the church in a happy mix of the sacred and the profane, with the townspeople dancing, leaping and singing (in Provençal, of course), "It's we who have them, the tripettes of St Marcel!" And in later years, this gave rise to an annual feast where a bullock is roasted in the main square.

The feast of Les Tripettes now takes place each year on the Sunday closest to 17 January, but only once every three years with a bullock. The next time this will occur is in 2009. The ceremony proceeds as follows: the bullock is walked through the town and taken to the famous Fontaine du Bœuf [Bullock's Fountain] where it drinks for the last time before being led before the church to be blessed by the priest. It is then butchered and in the evening everyone takes part in the danse des tripettes in front of the church again, including the priest and his curates. The next day, a solemn High Mass is said, followed by another dance, and then the bullock is roasted and eaten when evening comes.

SIGHTS NEARBY

PLANE TREE OF BARJOLS 2

Place de l'Hôtel de Ville, 83670 Barjols

Often described as the biggest plane tree in Provence, the specimen in Barjols is in fact smaller than that of Lamanon: its declared circumference of 12 m includes visible roots that give it this measurement at ground level.

THE TWO CHAPELS OF SAINT CHRISTINE ❸

• Chemin de Sainte-Christine, 83210 Solliès-Pont

Exit the A57 motorway at Solliès-Pont (exit 7). At the end of the slip road, take a left towards Solliès-Toucas. At the first roundabout turn right, where you'll see a small sign mentioning Sainte-Christine and other directions. After a further 300 m, turn left onto the chemin de Sainte-Christine. When you reach the barrier blocking access to vehicles, park your car and expect a 20 minute climb on foot.

Parochial quarrel

There's a curious sight on the hill overlooking the two villages of Solliès-Toucas and Cuers: the two chapels, both dedicated to St Christine, turn their backs to one another, separated by only a few centimetres across the border between their respective communes.

How did this happen? As the official legend has it, a Greek prince sailing off the shore from Toulon was caught in a storm and swore that if he survived, he would build a chapel to St Christine on the first hill that he glimpsed in the squall. Let us make clear right now that there are two St Christines, one from Tyre who underwent atrocious tortures and always emerged unscathed and smiling, while the other, from Rome, was pierced by arrows near the lake of Bolsena.

The prince survived and the chapel, which was to be built on the hill where the "border" between the two villages passed, provoked a dispute: the two communes could not reach an agreement, so each built a chapel on its territory, thus illustrating the ordinary foibles of mankind. Even today, the subject is not mentioned in tourist brochures and there are no signs to the chapels.

Both of them are closed more often than not and it is practically impossible to visit them and admire their numerous ex-votos. But the view alone from the top of the hill makes it worth a trip.

OFFICE DE TOURISME DE CUERS	OFFICE DE TOURISME DE LA VALLÉE DU GAPEAU
18, place de la Convention, 83390 Cuers	5, rue Gabriel-Péri, 83210 Solliès-Pont
• Tel: 04 94 48 56 27	• Tel: 04 94 28 92 35
• Fax: 04 94 28 03 56	• Fax: 04 94 33 63 55
• e-mail : odt.de.cuers@wanadoo.fr	

SIGHTS NEARBY

On the marble pediment of the church in the village of Solliès-Toucas is written in gold letters the following curious phrase in Latin: Sol iste jam ipso bis cruce ligatis aut ecce solis aedes jam veri cruce fulgens [The sun is already tied twice to the cross; here is the temple of the sun now lit by the true cross]. Above the inscription, a representation of the sol invictus makes you daydream of standing before a temple of the sun, waiting for Tintin and the eclipse ...

Opposite the church, on the wall of the town hall, is another plaque, not religious in character but still in gold letters on white marble, which commemorates the liberation of the commune from "Germanic hordes" ... What a way to prepare for Europe and welcome our neighbours from across the Rhine!

THE PROVENÇAL ROBIN HOOD

5

- La Grotte de Gaspard
- Rue Pasteur, 83890 Besse-sur-Issole • Tel: 04 94 69 83 69
- Open afternoons, hours vary according to season

"He walked to his death as if it were a feast"

Gaspard Bouis was born in Besse-sur-Issole on 9 February 1757. It was during a visit to the village by recruiting sergeants that Gaspard, no doubt under the influence of alcohol typically employed by the military in those times, signed up for the French army. The following day, once the effects of the drink had worn off, he realized that he had made a huge mistake. But as he had already signed the contract, either he joined his unit or became an outlaw. He chose the latter course of action and thus entered history.

To protest against the methods of justice applied in this pre-revolutionary period, Gaspard Bouis, nicknamed Gaspard de Besse by the people of Provence, decided to organize a raid to free Joseph Augias, found guilty of fraud with respect to the gabelle [salt tax]. Augias would become one of Gaspard's lieutenants, as would Jacques Bouilly, who also escaped during this raid.

The band organized itself and specialized in attacks on stagecoaches. A few anecdotes soon forged the reputation of this bandit: whenever he robbed a tax collector, the highwayman returned the money to those who had been taxed. And if his motto was, "Frighten, but never kill", when one of his men cut off the finger of a lady to steal her ring, Gaspard did not hesitate to shoot him dead with his pistol.

While these adventures were taking place, the French were building up to their Revolution and generally supported this defender of the poor. Gaspard de Besse found refuge everywhere from the authorities and also seemed to be everywhere. There was not an inn, not a ravine, not a cave in the region that had not seen the passage of Gaspard and his band. The man was both brilliant and elegant, pleasing to… women, but less so to their cuckolded husbands… Was he finally denounced out of jealousy? Whatever the case, Gaspard and his two lieutenants were arrested at Valette-du-Var and sentenced to death by the Parlement de Provence. The execution took place in Aix. Elise Malherbe, niece of the French poet, was in the crowd and witnessed this event. "He walked to his death as if it were a feast, replying with graceful salutes to the kisses blown to him by the crowd. He asked to be allowed to wear his town finery for the occasion. I did not want to see any more …" Gaspard and his two friends were put to death by means of the roue [wheel] on 25 October 1781. None of them had reached the age of 30 …

At the Grotte de Gaspard, an exhibit on the life and times of Gaspard de Besse offers a further insight into his character.

THE STATUE OF ST SUMIAN – J.-L. LAMBOT'S BOAT 6

• Musée du Pays Brignolais, Place du Palais des Comtes de Provence 83170 Brignoles • Tel/Fax: 04 94 69 45 18
• Admission: 4, reduced rate (children aged 6–12, students) 2; children under 6 free • Open Wednesday to Sunday, 1 April to 30 September: 9.00–12.00 and 14.30–18.00 (Sunday 9.00–12.00 and 15.00–18.00). From 1 October to 31 March: 10.00–12.00 and 14.30–17.00 (Sunday 10.00–12.00 and 15.00–17.00)
• E-mail: contact@museebrignolais.com
• http://www.museebrignolais.com

A boat made of reinforced concrete

A roughly carved block of stone, the statue of St Sumian has long been an object of fixation for women of Brignoles longing for children. But its long exposure to the elements (it once stood outside the town ramparts) has made it difficult to "read". It represents an androgynous figure whose two hands join together at the navel (l'embouligo in Provençal: in Brignoles the statue is in fact known as the embouligue). The custom is to kiss the part of the statue just below the navel in order to stimulate fecundity. This practice was forbidden by the Church, but the constant shower of erotic kisses has eroded the statue to the point that today you can see a cupule (cup-shaped hollow) caused by the mouths of those worshipping this slightly pagan but decidedly Gallic saint …

Joseph-Louis Lambot's reinforced-concrete boat is the other bizarre curiosity in this museum. Born at Montfort-sur-Argens (Var) in 1814, the young Lambot pursued his studies in Paris, he devoted himself to agriculture on his family's estate. Where did he get the idea of "reinforcing" concrete? Nobody knows. But he employed this technique (inserting a steel framework in the cement) to make fruit crates and shelves, and so can be regarded as the true inventor of reinforced concrete. One fine day, he even decided to build a boat using this material. To everyone's surprise, it floated.

If you visit the museum, don't miss its real treasure, the sarcophagus of La Gayole, the oldest known sarcophagus of Gaulish origin and one of the oldest sculpted sarcophagi in the world (2nd century AD).

SIGHTS NEARBY

LANCERS' HOUSE 7

Quite close to the museum, the house at 10 rue des Lanciers was once the home of the guards serving the counts of Provence. At the level of the first storey of this building, hook-shaped stones protrude from the façade. When the lancers finished their guard duties, they would come back to this house to rest. Navigating the narrow spiral staircases with halberd was not very easy, so they used to lean their lance on one of these stones when they arrived. Then, from the first-storey windows, they could take hold of the upper half and lay it down flat, resting on two of these stone hooks, safe from any thieves.

INRI

ABBAYE ROYALE DE LA CELLE

- Place des Ormeaux, 83170 La Celle
- Visits: enquire at the Information Centre in La Celle
- 9, place des Ormeaux • Tel/Fax: 04 94 59 19 05
- E-mail: la-celle@wanadoo.fr • http://www.la-celle.fr

The abbey was once home to some very naughty nuns

In the 11th century, the monks of the Abbaye Saint-Victor in Marseille established the Abbaye de la Celle, composed of two Benedictine priories, one for the monks and the other for nuns. Two centuries later, Garsende de Sabran, who had just lost her husband, King Alfonso II of Aragon, came to La Celle in order to take the veil and was elected abbess of the convent, which thereby became "royal". She abandoned Aix-en-Provence and public life, reserving her bewitching beauty for God.

But beginning in the 17th century, a certain decline in moral standards set in: although still bound by their vows of chastity, some sisters obtained "exemptions" and the abbey soon came to resemble a bawdy house: its boudoirs and padded leather cells attracted more and more gentlemen and it's said that, come evening, there could be heard more rustling of silk than prayers ... As one chronicler reported, "These nuns could only be distinguished by the colour of their skirts and the first name of their lover ...

Once brought to light, the scandal caused the convent to be closed. The abbey was sold as national property during the Revolution and turned into a farm before being bought in 1938 by Sylvia Fournier, owner of the island of Porquerolles. Since 1990; the priory belongs to the Conseil Général du Var which is continuing restoration of the monument. You can visit the magnificent ambulatory, the chapter and the cellar. In the garden of the cloister, some ancient mulberry trees have been saved by treatment of their hollow trunks and sap flows within their bark.

The Sainte-Perpétue church, which was one of the convent chapels, shelters the marble sarcophagus of Garsende de Sabran, whose presence in this place is close to being miraculous. For a long time, it was used as a drinking trough for animals in the village square before sold by its purported owner. Several years later, an antique dealer in Draguignan spotted it at an auction and informed the Musée du Louvre, who blocked the sale. The Conseil Général was able to buy back this property, which should never have left the abbey.

"AS THIN AS THE GOOD LORD OF LA CELLE"

In the church, the 14th-century crucifix represents a Christ of corpse-like thinness. Today visitors are told that a local saying "As thin as the Good Lord of La Celle" is used to speak of a slender person. In fact, the more frequent expression used in the region is even crueller: "As ugly as the Good Lord of La Celle".

ST PETER'S ARM

9

- Notre-Dame-de-l'Assomption
- Place Bernard, 83390 Cuers

To see St Peter's arm, you'll need to book at the local tourist office.

A prestigious religious relic brought from Rome in the 14th century by Gantès le Brave, born at Cuers in 1328

In Cuers, St Peter is very present in a most peculiar fashion.

Although the village church is today called Notre-Dame-de-l'Assomption, it was Collégiale Saint-Pierre before the Revolution. Its lateral (and yet main) door is surmounted by a niche in which you can see a statue of St Peter lifting his head.

From the ground, it's difficult to grasp that he's looking at heaven with an angry expression. Nonetheless, it happens to be the case, even if no one can explain why … On the lintel of the door, but here again you'd need to know it was there, you can see the arm of St Peter. This is a stone replica of the extraordinary relic to be found inside the church, in the Saint-Pierre chapel, protected by a wooden door with yet another representation of the saint's arm. The peculiar feature here is that this arm is missing two fingers. If by chance or having booked a visit, this door is opened for you, you'll see behind a tightly meshed iron grill, an arm in vermeil (gilded silver) containing part of the saint's arm.

It was Jean de Gantès ("Gantès the Brave"), born in Cuers in 1328, who brought back from Rome this gift of Pope Clement VI in thanks for his courage and his loyalty to Queen Jeanne of Naples, Countess of Provence.

OFFICE DE TOURISME DE CUERS
Place de la Convention, 83390 Cuers • Tel: 04 94 48 56 27
• Fax: 04 94 28 03 56 • e-mail : odt.de.cuers@wanadoo.fr

NICKNAMES GIVEN TO CUERS VILLAGERS

The manja sauma means *"eaters of she-asses"*. This nickname comes from the siege of the village in 1383 by an army from Toulon that forced the inhabitants to eat she-asses in order to survive. It is also said that it was during the bloody repression of the villagers in Cuers by the soldiers of Louis Napoléon Bonaparte that a blacksmith was forced to eat his apron made from the hide of a she-ass.

The brulo frema means the "women burners". This nickname recalls the fact that in 1779 a woman was burnt at the stake in Cuers, the last woman accused of witchcraft to suffer this fate in Provence.

THE PIVAUT ICE HOUSE

• RD95, 83136 Mazaugues
From Mazaugues, leave the village in the direction of Marseille. At the fork in the road, take the direction of La Sainte-Baume. The Glacière [ice house] is signposted on the left. You can walk there in 5 minutes from the car park.
• Visiting hours: from July to September, there are guided tours of the ice house daily (except Monday) at 15.30 (starting at the Musée de la Glace, admission €4, including the museum).
• For further information tel: 04 94 86 89 47 or 04 94 86 39 24.

When ice was buried treasure

The next time you open your fridge, keep this thought in mind: how did our ancestors manage to conserve food or have cool drinks in summer when this aspect of basic comfort did not exist? Only a few years ago, ice boxes still contained blocks of ice that had to be replenished regularly. Historically, ice houses were where ice was manufactured.

This required constructing a building in an area that was as cold as possible and close to a water source. La Saint-Baume massif, which met these criteria, was selected for this purpose in the 17th and 18th centuries and came to have the biggest concentration of ice houses in the entire Mediterranean basin. The ice produced was used to preserve fish and other foods in general, to keep drinks cool in summer, and was also needed in hospitals.

The technique used was not very elaborate but required plenty of manpower in difficult working conditions. Each winter, for obvious reasons, a new "crop" was prepared for the following summer. Water was poured into freezing basins, then when the weather grew cold enough to convert it into ice, it was stocked up to the ceiling in the ice houses, which were in fact nothing but ice storage chambers. Once the ice house was full, the triple doors were shut until the following summer. Often half-buried in the ground, the ice house also had very thick walls to preserve the cold and thus the ice. When the weather grew warm, the workers cut the ice into blocks and loaded them into carts protected from the heat by blankets, which supplied Toulon or Marseille during the night, using mule trails.

At the beginning of the 19th century, the development of the railways allowed the natural ice of the Alps to be shipped easily. Then industrial ice finally sealed the fate of La Sainte-Baume ice houses.

The Pivaut ice house has a diameter of 18 m and a height of 25 m, but two-thirds of this height was underground.

SIGHTS NEARBY

MUSÉE DE LA GLACE, 83136 MAZAUGUES

Open from 1 June to 30 September, daily (except Monday) 9.00–12.00 and 14.00–18.00 • From 1 October to 31 May, open Sunday 9.00–12.00 and 14.00–17.00 • http://www.museeglace.fr.st/

The Musée de la Glace, close to the Pivaut ice house, is an ideal introduction before visiting the site. A model of the ice house showing a cross-section of its interior gives an insight into its workings.

THE DIXMUDE MONUMENT

- Boulevard Henri Guérin, 83390 Pierrefeu-du-Var
- Les Amis du Dixmude - Maison des Associations, 83390 Pierrefeu-du-Var
- Contact: Monsieur Tissier (Tél.: 04 94 28 23 27)
- Link for a history of dirigibles in Cuers and Pierrefeu-du-Var: http://perso.wanadoo.fr/m.coterot/

Lighter than air

As you leave the village Pierrefeu-du-Var, a big surprise is in store: a monument in the form of a wing, 14 m high … This is the "Dixmude" monument.*

During the First World War, which inaugurated aerial warfare, dirigible balloons demonstrated their efficacy for bombardments, naval or terrestrial reconnaissance, and escorting ship convoys. The German forces built the most outstanding examples under the generic name "Zeppelins" after the aristocratic designer of this type of aerostat. The basic principle was to stretch an envelope filled with hydrogen over a rigid structure made from a light alloy

The history of these Zeppelins, the first of which took flight in 1900, included the first aerial bombardment of Paris in 1916, the first commercial crossing of the Atlantic in 1928, and the Hindenberg fire which took 35 lives in New York in 1937, a tragedy that marked the end of the dirigible saga due to their basic structural defect, the fact that they were inflated with an inflammable gas.

During the 1920s, in the course of war reparations, Germany furnished France with two of its enormous dirigibles, including one that would be rebaptized Dixmude. 266 m long and 28 m high, containing 70,000 m3 of hydrogen gas, the dirigible was transported to the base at Cuers-Pierrefeu, where the construction of immense new hangars for these flying objects had just been completed.

On 21 December 1923, the dirigible, no doubt hit by lightning, caught fire and exploded while in flight off the shore of Sicily. Only the body of its captain, Lieutenant Commander Du Plessis, was recovered from the sea that swallowed the other 49 victims. It was then decided to erect this monument in Corsican granite that now lends an original touch to the village of Pierrefeu-du-Var.

An association, Friends of the Dixmude, perpetuates the memory of this tragedy. You can contact the former president, Monsieur Tissier, always ready to tell this dramatic story.

The French Navy still makes use of the aerodrome near Pierrefeu-du-Var and preserves, carefully packed away in a wooden box, a strikingly realistic model of the Dixmude, 3 m long. It might be a good idea to take it out one day and put it on display …

*The name of Dixmude was given to this dirigible to honour the memory of the Belgian resistance to German occupation. Dixmude is a town in Belgium where a bloody battle took place. The Belgians put up a heroic fight there against German assaults in November 1914.

EXTRAORDINARY EX-VOTOS

13

• Sanctuaire Notre-Dame-des-Anges
Frères Franciscains de l'Immaculée, 83790 Pignans
T• el: 04 94 59 00 69 • E-mail: ffindanges@immacolata.com
• The sanctuary is open daily, with daily Mass at 7.00 and on Sunday at 10.30 and 17.00

A caiman dedicated to the Virgin Mary

10 km from Pignans, the Notre-Dame-des-Anges chapel that sits on a peak in the Massif des Maures is worth a visit for its extraordinary collection of ex-votos, although unfortunately a number of them have been stolen.

One of them, hanging from the chapel ceiling, is an actual stuffed caiman, said to be a victim of Jules Gérard's rifle (see page 118). But the most moving of these ex-votos is probably the photo that features on the cover of the small booklet by Henry Levert (sold by the monks for €10) and representing the execution of four men by a firing squad of eleven soldiers, with Toulon harbour in the background. It's a pity that someone stole another photo showing a hunter of Pignans whose gun had exploded and found himself surrounded by flames, "while the Infant Jesus, in the arms of his mother, peed on the gun". (Source: Guide de la Provence mystérieuse, Éditions Tchou).

Legend has it that Nymphe, the sister of St Maximin and servant of Mary Magdalene, lived here long before the existing chapel was built in the 19th century. She is said to have sculpted the statue of the Virgin that stands there today. It was lost but then found again, hidden away in the bushes. The parishioners of Pignans put it inside their church for safekeeping, but the statue returned of its own accord to the bushes. It was then decided that a pilgrimage should be made each year on the first Sunday of July to Notre-Dame-des-Anges. Since 2001, monks from the order of the Frères Franciscains de l'Immaculée live in keeping with their vows inside the sanctuary. On the narrow road that climbs to the summit there is a sign nailed to a tree that seems appropriate: la beauté de ces lieux fait oublier les peines de la route [the beauty of this place makes one forget the difficulties along the way].

UNUSUAL STREET NAMES

In Pignans, when you pass through the door that leads inside the second set of medieval walls by way of the passage de l'Église, you find yourself confronted with a metaphysical choice: on the right you have rue de l'Église [Church] and on the left, rue de l'Enfer [Hell]. But as it happens, this enfer is derived from the old Provençal word, infèrs, meaning residues of olive oil, because there was once an olive press in this street [at No. 10]. You'll notice that one of the two pretty ceramic panels, illustrating the road to Paradise on the right and the road to Hell on the left, has been broken, no doubt deliberately. Guess which?

THE FOUNTAIN OF MARIUS

Rue Fontvieille, 83910 Pourrières

The pyramid of the "putrid fields"

It was here on the plain surrounding Pourrières, a Var commune below the Sainte-Victoire mountain, that the Roman general Caius Marius stopped the advance of a barbarian horde of Teutones, Ambrones and Cimbri, in 102 BC. There was once a monument celebrating his triumph along the route of the present-day RN7, but it was eroded over time and "replaced", in a manner of speaking, by the present fountain of Pourrières, which is also pyramid-shaped and was built using stones from the previous monument.

The fighting that took place here was incredibly violent. After two days of repeated assaults and an enveloping attack on the Teutone rear, the Romans are reported to have killed 200,000 enemy soldiers and taken 90,000 prisoners. The Ambrone women almost changed the course of the battle by taking up arms in the place of their men, accusing them of cowardice. The historian La Pise (17th century) recounts that the Teutone women drew up their skirts and presented their "privates", saying, "If you are afraid, enter these places from which you came forth, that they may serve as a refuge for you!" It was in any case the shortest and most bloody battle ever to take place on French soil.

It was said that the River Coenus ran red with blood and that the bodies on the battlefield were left unburied. This would explain the origin of the name of Pourrières, derived from campi putridi [putrid fields] ... But some people claim that it stems far more prosaically from champs de poireaux [fields of leeks], which are abundant in Pourrières. Then again, legend has it that the peasants used the bones of dead warriors to build fences and attach their grapevines.

SIGHTS NEARBY

THE MEMORY OF HUMILIS

Maison de Germain Nouveau, 5, rue Germain Nouveau, 83910 Pourrières

SCULPTURE OF GERMAIN NOUVEAU

Place du Château, 83910 Pourrières

Around the year 1900, one particular beggar could sometimes be seen standing in front of Saint-Sauveur cathedral, in the exact spot where today the Cézanne plaque may be found (see page 19). It's said that Cézanne himself used to give alms to this man. He was Humilis, also known as Germain Nouveau, a poet born in Pourrières in 1851. A friend of Verlaine and Rimbaud, he was the founder of the cercle zutique (a group of French sceptics, so-called because they said, "Zut!" to everything). From the place du Château, behind the church, there is a magnificent view of Sainte-Victoire mountain. There is also a sculpted face of the poet, made by Gaston Secondi in 1967.

THE STATUE OF JULES GÉRARD

- Place des Écoles (near schools and the boulodrome)
- Birthplace of Jules Gérard (the present-day town hall)

7, place de la Mairie, 83790 Pignans

Jules Gérard, lion killer

On 14 June 1817, there was born in Pignans, a wine-growing village in central Var, a certain Jules Gérard. Having lost both his parents early on, the young man demonstrated his desire to live by developing his physical capacities. He practised hunting because Pignans, surrounded by woods (including the pines that lend the village their name) was rich in game. Fencing and chausson (ancestor of French boxing) gave him a taste for combat. When he was 23, he joined up with the corps of Spahis (North African troops serving in the French Army) and was sent to Algeria.

Jules Gérard would devote himself to exterminating the lions that were decimating flocks in the region of Kabylia and sometimes even attacked men.

With the tacit approval of his superiors, he improved on existing techniques for hunting lions. He established procedures to optimize tracking and approaching the wild beasts and helped perfect the weapons that were available at the time. In the mid-19th century, hunting rifles were still relatively primitive.

He shot his first lion in Kabylia in July 1844, at night and using a double-barrelled gun (of which one barrel didn't work), with a single bullet. The beast was over a metre long and weighed 200 kg. From being just another roumi (as foreigners were called, in reference to the previous Roman occupation), Jules Gérard came to be a respected figure among the native people, then, as his list of kills grew longer, he received the nickname of Katel Sioud: master of lions.

News of the exploits of the "lion killer" crossed the Mediterranean and became a topic of conversation around dinner tables in Paris. In 1853, Jules Gérard was presented to Emperor Napoleon III. Alphonse Daudet read works by Jules Gérard and was inspired by them to write Tartarin de Tarascon in 1872. But the ridiculous, swaggering character in this book had little in common with the real Jules Gérard.

After killing his 25th lion, Jules Gérard devoted himself to exploration and drowned in the River Jong during an expedition in Sierra Leone. He was 46 years old.

In the place des Écoles at Pignans, you can see the bronze fountain by sculptor Olivier Decamps, inaugurated in 1964 to commemorate the centenary of Jules Gérard's death. And near the door of the town hall, which has a medallion with a lion's head and two stone lions on either side, there is a plaque that recalls that this was the birthplace of Jules *Gérard: Officier des Spahis, chasseur de fauves et écrivain cynégétique dit le tueur de lions* [Spahi officer, hunter of wild beasts and writer on the art of hunting, known as the lion killer].

LAC DU GRAND LAOUTIEN

- On the D64 between Gareoult and La Roquebrussanne
- Parking

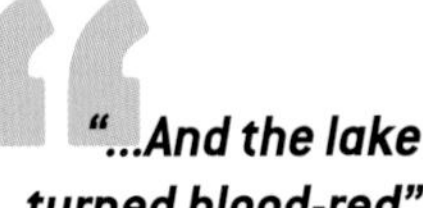

"...And the lake turned blood-red"

An improbable, unexpected, breathtaking and somewhat disturbing spot, the Lac du Grand Laoutien (Provençal for "basin") lies at the bottom of a veritable crater that inevitably brings to mind a volcano or even the impact of a meteorite.

The lake is 130 m across and 43 m deep, with sheer cliffs rising 30 m in places above the water's surface. The water is green and conceals its shadowy secrets. A strange sensation, looking down into this natural curiosity, and a feeling of contentment on leaving it without having fallen in …

In the past, the inhabitants of the two nearest villages, Gareoult and La Roquebrussanne, were convinced that the lake was a dormant volcano. Each year, on the second Sunday in May, the priest of La Roquebrussanne would have to go down to the shore to bless the waters. If he ever refused, it was said that the volcano would awaken within the year. The phenomenon that took place in 1775 did not reassure anyone as to the mysterious nature of the lake. That year, simultaneously with the earthquake that destroyed the city of Lisbon, the lake turned blood-red.

Another curiosity, the animal species living within this lake are very rare and not found in other French lakes, but only in Nordic countries. It's as if they have survived the warming of the local climate, evolving in an underground environment connected to some yet-to-be-explored network. Of the 13 species of hydracarian present, three are normally only found in northern Europe, two in tropical Africa, and one in Morocco and the Banyuls area. Lastly, we should mention the Limnogeria lougiseta, for which this lake is the only known habitat in the world.

As for the volcano, experts think that the Grand Laoutien was once an underground cavity whose roof, overloaded with the weight of trees and rocks, suddenly collapsed.

Two aerial views of the site:
http://www.carto.net/verdon/ste_baume/laloube/laoucien_aerien.htm

```
                S V L A S A S A L V S
                  L A S A T A S A L
                    S A T R T A S
                      T R E R T
                      R E C E R
C R V X               E C I C E A N G E L I C A
                      C I H I C
M                     I H I H I                 M
V I                   H I M I H               C V
I G V                 I M X M I             M E C
G V F E R I H I M X V X D O     M I N I M E
V F E R I H I M X V R V X D     O M I N I M
F E R I H I M X V R C R V X     D O M I N I
V F E R I H I M X V R V X D     O M I N I M
G V F E R I H I M X V X D O     M I N I M E
I G V                 S E X E S             M E C
V I                   T S E S T               C V
M                     Q T S T Q                 M
                      V Q T Q V
S. T H O M A E        A V Q. V A de A Q V I N O
                      M A V A M
                      S M A M S
                      E S M S E
                      M E S E M
                      P M E M P
                      E P M P E
                    A R E P E R A
                  O D A R E R A D O
                O R O D A R A D O R O
<- - - - - - -  1 5 , 8 c m . - - - - - ->
                295 caractères
```

THE PALINDROME OF NOTRE-DAME-D'INSPIRATION

Notre-Dame-d'Inspiration
• Chemin de la Chapelle, 83136 la Roquebrussanne
Access from the village of La Roquebrussanne: take the path to the chapel that runs west from the centre of the village. Leave your car in the parking space next to the oratory at the foot of the path. The climb takes a good quarter of an hour by this route, at first paved with pebbles (and good intentions), then becomes a dirt track.

The bell of the Notre-Dame-d'Inspiration chapel is unusual in that it has a curious palindrome inscribed on its sides. Brought from Rome in 1730, it was cast by a certain Casini, "caster of the reverend works of St Peter in the Vatican". The palindrome, in the shape of a cross, is composed of 295 characters which were decrypted by Abbé Menin, a former priest, as follows: "The cross is for me certain salvation. It is the cross that I worship always. Angelic cross. The cross of the Lord with me. The cross is for me a refuge, Saint Thomas Aquinas." But that's only the tip of the iceberg. The essential part of the palindrome is obscure, to say the least.

"The 295 characters of the palindrome inscribed upon the bell still preserve their secret

The palindrome is displayed on the visible portion of the bell, but given the height of the belfry, you'll need binoculars or a good telephoto lens to see it. And to actually read it, you'd better bring a ladder …

The Notre-Dame-d'Inspiration chapel is at the top of a hill overlooking the village of La Roquebrussanne, which also features the ruins of a chateau and a beautiful amphitheatre built by a former priest using stones from this chateau. It is almost regrettable that this amphitheatre, capable of seating over a thousand people, has not been put to use by some festival or other, given its splendid location.

PALINDROMES

A palindrome is a sentence that can be read in both directions, starting from the right or the left. There are palindromes of letters, syllables, or whole words. Here are some famous examples of palindromes in French: *Tu l'as trop écrasé, César, ce Port-Salut, Un roc cornu, Cerise d'été, je te désire.* (to be read in a circle, with the "C" in the middle), *Non à ce canon !, Karine égarée rage en Irak, Oh, cela te perd répéta l'écho …*
The longest palindrome in French literature is that of Georges Pérec: "Le Grand Palindrome" (1969), included in La Littérature potentielle, Collection Idées, Gallimard, 1973.

OFFICE DE TOURISME DE LA ROQUEBRUSSANNE
15, avenue Georges-Clemenceau, 83136 La Roquebrussanne
• Tel: 04 94 86 82 11 • www.la-roquebrussanne.fr

THE RENAISSANCE WINDOW OF ROUGIERS 

• Grand'Rue, 83170 Rougiers
7 km south of Saint-Maximin-la-Sainte-Baume

"*The sculpted window bears witness to the village's past wealth*

You don't just stumble on Rougiers. Far from the main roads, this village with its thousand inhabitants seems rather sleepy. You stroll along the main street admiring the pretty building façades with their handsome doors, when suddenly a wall of colour draws your eye. This double Renaissance window with mullions bears witness to the village's rich past and is so striking that it's hard to tear yourself away. The window seems to be supported by a stone cornice that stretches between two cupids on either side, with the word passo inscribed beneath one, and lasso beneath the other, which can be roughly translated from the Latin as: "Everything passes, and one grows weary of everything." But you could never tire of this window …

SIGHTS NEARBY

A WALK TO THE CASTRUM 

It would be a shame to leave Rougiers without visiting the castrum (Roman chateau) and the Saint-Jean chapel. The walk follows a loop that leaves the old part of Rougiers by a narrow little road that leads in the direction of La Sainte-Baume. At the top of the ridge, follow the arrows that direct you to the site of the chateau. The girth of its towers (and what remains of the ramparts) speaks for itself. Restoration work is now in progress. At the far end of the plateau, you'll find the chapel and an extraordinary view of the entire region. You go back down by the path below this chapel that crosses "old-old" Rougiers, the village that existed before the present-day Rougiers, just beneath the chateau walls.

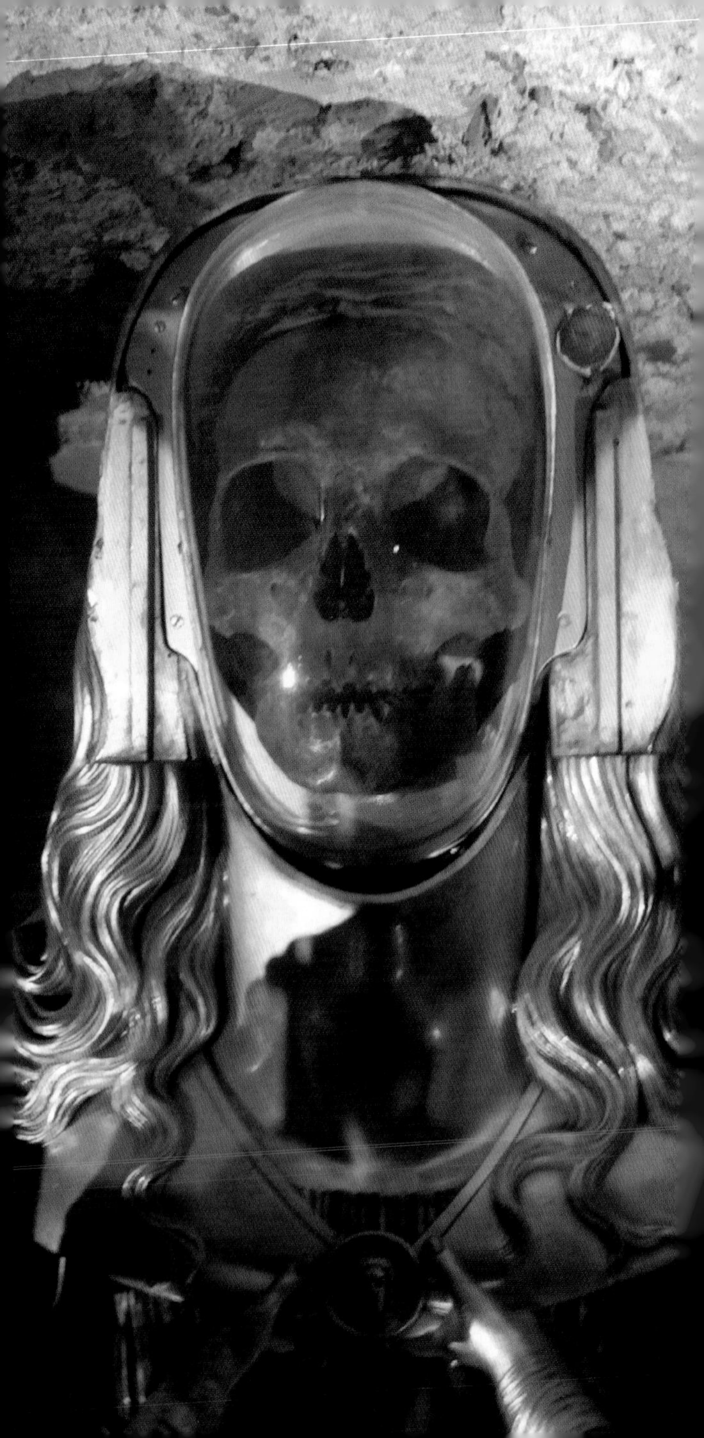

THE TOMB OF MARY MAGDALENE

22

• Basilique
Place de l'Hôtel de Ville, 83470 Saint-Maximin-la-Sainte-Baume

Relics, sarcophagi, tombs, and holy flasks: when Catholicism mixes with the fantastic

After landing at Les Saintes-Maries-de-la-Mer, Mary Magdalene is supposed to have sought refuge in the grotto of La Sainte-Baume where she was fed by the angels. You can see her tomb in the Basilica of Saint-Maximin-la-Sainte-Baume, described in all the guidebooks and considered to be the third most important tomb of Christianity (after that of Christ in Jerusalem and St Peter's tomb in Rome). The saint's skull, encrusted with gold, is most impressive. Inside a vial, protected behind glass and a metal grill, you also glimpse a scrap of skin found intact on the forehead of the saint when her sarcophagus was discovered in 1279. This piece of skin is from the exact spot where Jesus laid his finger, after his resurrection, saying to Mary Magdalene, Noli me tangere: "Do not touch me ..."

What is less well known is the fact that this scrap of skin remained in its place, attached to the saint's forehead, until 1780. The approach of the Revolution and fear of anti-religious looting may well explain its removal…

Curiously, the French Revolution also led to the loss of another very important relic that once could also be viewed in the Basilica: the Sainte Ampoule, a glass flask containing pebbles and earth from Golgotha, imbibed with Christ's blood. They were brought from Palestine by the saints when they landed at Les Saintes-Maries-de-la-Mer. Each year, on Good Friday, this black earth turned red as the blood it contained liquefied. Practically all the kings of France, from François I to Louis XIV, and including Louis XI, Louis XIII and Charles VII, came to witness this miracle. On these occasions, a one-way itinerary was organized within the basilica: in order to cope with the flow of pilgrims from all over the world, they entered by one door, followed the path indicated by arrows, and were then pushed out the exit.

The Sainte Ampoule was stolen during the night of 6–7 October 1904. In his flight, it seems that the thief dropped it, because shards of glass were found on the ground. Nevertheless, a renowned diviner declared several years ago that he was certain that the Sainte Ampoule had never left the town of Saint-Maximin and was hidden in a house somewhere near the Basilica …

A flask of a similar type, containing the blood of St Januarius, also exists in Naples. The blood still continues to liquefy three times each year.

LEGEND OF "LES SAINTES"

Shortly after the Passion of Christ, his immediate entourage, persecuted by those who had secured his crucifixion, had no choice but to go into exile. According to legend, it was aboard a small fishing boat without oars or sail that the three Marys (Mary Magdalene; Mary Jacobe, sister of the Holy Virgin; Mary Salome, mother of the apostles James and John) came to Les Saintes-Maries-de-la-Mer. Their boat is said to have been propelled by the finger of God from the shores of Palestine to Provence. They were accompanied by Martha, who would spread the Gospel along the banks of the Rhône and would also vanquish "La Tarasque", a monster that was terrorizing the inhabitants of the region, thus becoming the patron saint of Tarascon. Lazarus who was resuscitated by Christ, Maximin who was one of the 72 disciples, Joseph of Arimathea who brought with him the Holy Grail (see below), and Sara, the servant of the three Marys, also made this journey with them. Some people maintain that it was Sara who greeted the others on the beach. Sara is honoured every 24 May by the famous Gypsy pilgrimage to Les Saintes-Maries-de-la-Mer, where Mary Salome and Mary Jacobe also settled.

Father Morel, a former priest in Les Saintes commune, rejected the thesis of the boat without oars or sail, and recalled the fact that at that time a regular shipping route linked the coast of Palestine with Greece, Rome and Provence. But, as we mentioned earlier, the legend concerning "Les Saintes" was reinforced by the discovery of the bodies of the two Marys beneath the crypt of the village church and by the sarcophagus of "Marie de Magdala" found at Saint-Maximin-la-Sainte-Baume. The famous Marseille tarot deck is also said to be connected with this legend (see Marseille insolite et secret, published in the same series as this guide): according to Philippe Camoin, the heir of a master card manufacturer of Marseille in the 17th century, Mary Magdalene and Lazarus were keepers of esoteric knowledge to be handed down, both having witnessed the resurrection of Christ (it is interesting to note that it was Joseph of Arimathea, who accompanied them to Provence, who brought Christ down from the Cross and placed Him in his tomb). The Marseille tarot would thus be the vehicle of this secret message. Deeply encoded, it is believed to contain a revelation concerning the mystery of eternal life.

It was at the beginning of the 1980s that Michael Baigent, Richard Leigh and Henry Lincoln published their book, Holy Blood, Holy Grail (Century UK), calling into question the established legend with a thesis that demolished religious certainties. According to this version, Jesus did not in fact die on the Cross but instead married Mary Magdalene and had children with her. Thus, the Holy Grail that Joseph of Arimathea brought from Palestine was not a cup which had contained the blood of Christ, but the progeny of Jesus himself, the Sang Real ("royal blood", because Jesus claimed to be King of the Jews) which ran in the veins of his descendants. This would also tend to explain the role of the Templars, who are said to have been charged with keeping this explosive secret.

THE "LITTLE" SAINT-PILON

The summit of the hill above the grotto of La Sainte-Baume is named Saint-Pilon (994 m). Once there was a sculpture representing Mary Magdalene being borne by angels. Today, a sculpture depicting this same scene is to be found on the RN560, also known as the "Marseille road" as it enters Saint-Maximin, at the crossing with the sliproad leading to the motorway. It's said that this was the very spot where Mary Magdalene was set down by the angels, so that St Maximin could take care of her, give her Holy Communion, and prepare her tomb. Some people believe that the Saint-Pilon sculpture and this statue are one and the same. But who could have transported it from one site to the other? That remains a complete mystery ...

OFFICE MUNICIPAL DU TOURISME DE SAINT-MAXIMIN-LA-SAINTE-BAUME
Hôtel de ville, 83470 Saint-Maximin-la-Sainte-Baume • Tel: 04 94 59 84 59
• Fax: 04 94 59 82 92 • e-mail : office.tourisme.stmaximin@wanadoo.fr

SIGHTS NEARBY

CLOISTER OF THE COUVENT ROYAL 23

The Couvent Royal (Royal Monastery) of Saint-Maximin and its splendid cloister is today a hotel and restaurant. During the day, you can freely visit both the cloister and the adjacent halls, including the monks' great refectory. In the evening, however, only the restaurant diners are able to enjoy these cloistered halls ...

LE CORBUSIER'S UNDERGROUND BASILICA 

RD80, 83640 le Plan-d'Aups

Upon the plateau surrounding Plan d'Aups, between the hospice and the village, one can see the remains of the aborted project for an underground basilica of Sainte-Baume. The original concept, elaborated by Edouard Trouin among others, was an architectural plan with an initiatory purpose, presenting a coherent layout for pilgrims on their way to the sanctuary dedicated to the sinner saint in the grotto of La Sainte-Baume ('baume' is the Provençal word for grotto). Shops, hotels, and parking space would also be provided below the surface. Aware of the ambiguous nature of this scheme, the town council halted excavation and in the end decided to convert the buildings already erected above ground into a multipurpose space for cultural and sporting activities.

L'HÔTELLERIE DE LA SAINTE-BAUME 

83640 le Plan d'Aups • Tel: 04 42 04 54 84

Maintained by Benedictine sisters, La Saint-Baume hospice today welcomes pilgrims, couples preparing for marriage, and ordinary guests. The atmosphere is a little austere, but the prices are unbeatable: €7 for a bed in the dormitory, and from €18.50 for a private room with single bed.

VALBELLE PARK AND CHATEAU

• Montée du Château, 83170 Tourves
Tourves is 7 km south-east of Saint-Maximin-la-Sainte-Baume.
To visit this site, park at the end of boulevard Gambetta (which starts at the cooperative wine cellars), near the public bathhouse. The entry to the chateau is signposted.

Swept away by the Revolution

Pillaged and to a large extent destroyed during the Revolution, Tourve's chateau today lies in ruin. The Provençal people clearly had had enough of the local nobility that flaunted its illegitimate superiority over them with its arrogant monuments: the Valbelle family, who became the holders of the marquisate of Tourves, owed their noble title to marriage, their own family tree going back to an apothecary in Marseille, himself descended from a shoemaker from Beausset (Var).

Other than the chateau itself, the site boasts an astonishing obelisk, 20 m high, as well as a copy of the pyramid of Sextus in Rome, a sly reference to nearby Aquae Sextiae (the Roman name for Aix-en-Provence).

President of the Parlement de Provence, Count de Valbelle was an important figure in his day, dividing his time between his Aix townhouse and frequent visits to Marseille and Paris. For 20 years he was the lover of "La Clairon", a famous tragic actress who introduced him to Voltaire, d'Alembert, Diderot and Rousseau. No doubt at least one of these philosophers stayed in Tourves, where the count spent six or seven months per year, in a home that he wished to make into a small Provençal version of Versailles.

Facing the obelisk, the grand balcon [colonnade] is a very large monument that the revolutionaries did not succeed in destroying thanks to the strength of its construction. The 10 Doric-style monolithic columns, each 5.5 m in height, were made of marble from the nearby Mazaugues quarry.

Lastly, on the opposite side of the chateau from the obelisk, you can make your way to the pyramid, although it's difficult to find among the encroaching brambles. From the outside, it now looks like a large but rather shapeless block. The local inhabitants removed much of the stone cladding that provided its Egyptian pyramidal style. Inside, there is a niche where once a white marble mummy was set on a black pedestal.

ST PROBACE – THE RAIN-MAKER SAINT

Upon the heights overlooking Tourves, the Saint-Probace chapel shelters the rain-making saint. Whenever drought becomes a worry, the local people go to seek him in his hermitage and keep him hostage in the church until the rain comes. But Tourves being located on the flat lowlands, sometimes St Probace overdoes it. In that case, the water rises and you start to appreciate the height of some of the village pavements.

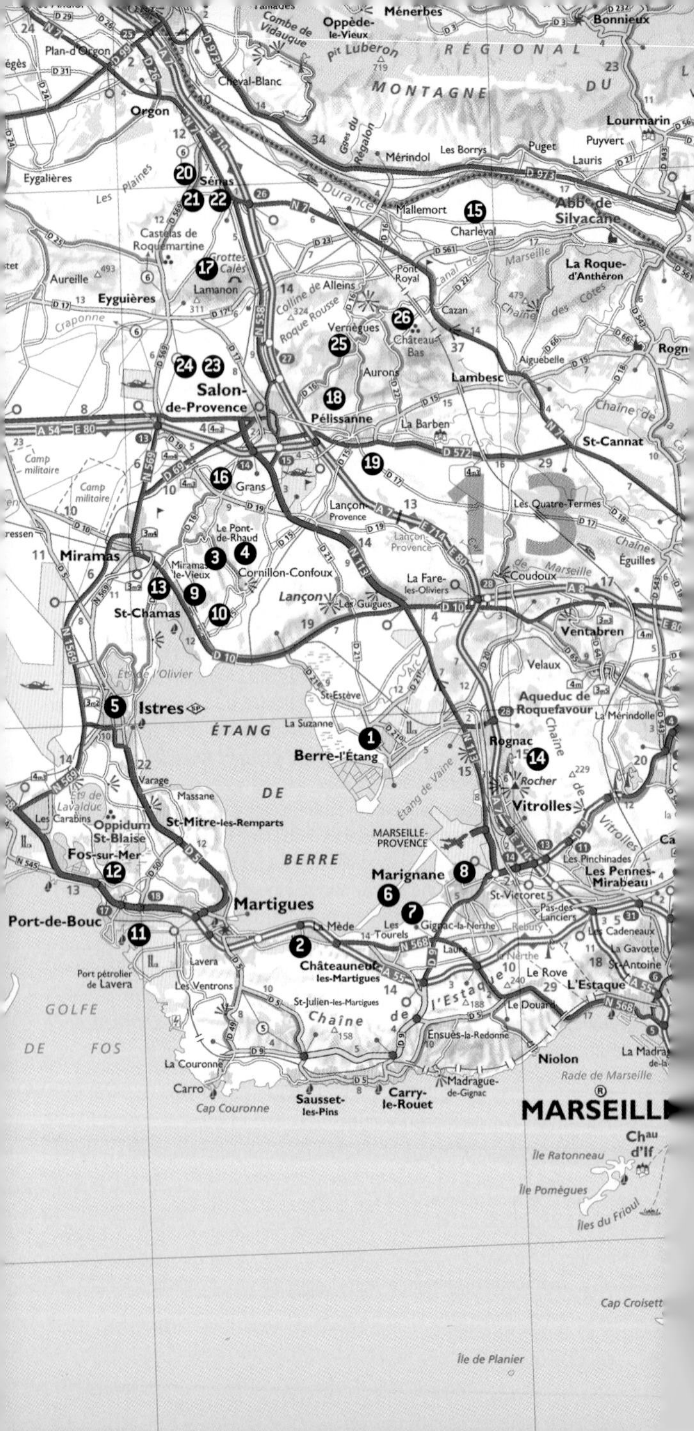

Ménerbes
Oppède-le-Vieux
Bonnieux
MONTAGNE DU LUBERON
Orgon
Cheval-Blanc
Plan-d'Orgon
Lourmarin
Puyvert
Lauris
Mérindol
Puget
Sénas
Eygalières
Mallemort
Charleval
Abb. de Silvacane
La Roque-d'Anthéron
Durance
Castelas de Roquemartine
Aureille
Eyguières
Lamanon
Colline de Alleins
Vernègues
Château-Bas
Cazan
Pont Royal
Chaîne des Côtes
Rognes
Lambesc
Aurons
Salon-de-Provence
Pélissanne
La Barben
St-Cannat
Grans
Lançon-Provence
Les Quatre-Termes
Éguilles
Miramas
Le Pont-de-Rhaud
Miramas-le-Vieux
Cornillon-Confoux
La Fare-les-Oliviers
Coudoux
St-Chamas
Lançon
Les Guigues
Ventabren
Velaux
Istres
Aqueduc de Roquefavour
La Mérindolle
La Suzanne
St-Estève
Berre-l'Étang
Rognac
ÉTANG DE BERRE
Rocher
Vitrolles
Étang de Vaïne
Varage
Massane
Oppidum St-Blaise
St-Mitre-les-Remparts
Les Carabins
Fos-sur-Mer
MARSEILLE-PROVENCE
Marignane
Les Pinchinades
Les Pennes-Mirabeau
St-Victoret
Martigues
Port-de-Bouc
La Mède
Les Tourels
Gignac-la-Nerthe
Pas-des-Lanciers
Les Cadeneaux
La Gavotte
Châteauneuf-les-Martigues
Le Rove
L'Estaque
St-Antoine
Port pétrolier de Lavera
Lavera
Les Ventrons
St-Julien-les-Martigues
Chaîne de l'Estaque
Le Douard
Ensuès-la-Redonne
GOLFE DE FOS
Niolon
La Couronne
Carro
Cap Couronne
Sausset-les-Pins
Carry-le-Rouet
Madrague-de-Gignac
Rade de Marseille
MARSEILLE
Île Ratonneau
Île Pomègues
Îles du Frioul
Chau d'If
Cap Croisette
Île de Planier
13

AROUND L'ÉTANG DE BERRE AND SALON-DE-PROVENCE

PISCINE CLAUDE JOUVE

• Avenue du 8 mai 1945, 13130 Berre-l'Étang
Open Monday to Friday 9.30–12.30 and 17.00–19.00, Saturday 14.00–18.00, Sunday 9.30–12.30
Admission: €2.80, children 14 and under €2

A swimming pool in a former aerodrome

If Berre-l'Étang is famous above all for its Shell petrochemical complex, the biggest industrial site in Europe (covering almost 800 hectares), which you can visit by booking at the tourist office in Berre, the most surprising place in this town is the municipal swimming pool.

The size of the building makes you gasp. Rightly so, because this swimming pool was installed in one of two immense hangars at the former naval aerodrome in Berre, which from 1919 to 1942 was one of the most important in France. It was built following a decision taken in 1918 to transfer the training school for seaplane pilots to Berre from Hourtin in Gironde.

Among the reasons for this transfer was the proximity of both the military aeronautics school in Istres and the étang [lagoon] whose waters were less choppy than the sea, but still salty … The latter detail was important, because takeoffs for the under-powered seaplanes back in those early days were easier on relatively dense salt water, compared to the fresh variety …

At the time the aerodrome was also home to fighter squadrons, training units, bombers and torpedo planes. But the war put an end to debates over the relative merits of normal aircraft, amphibious planes and seaplanes. Now only Canadairs use the lagoon, but over on the opposite side at Marignane.

OFFICE DE TOURISME DE BERRE-L'ÉTANG
Avenue Roger-Salengro, 13130 Berre-l'Étang • Tel: 04 42 85 01 70
• Fax: 04 42 85 07 15 • e-mail : tourisme.berre@free.fr

HENRI FABRE, SAILOR OF THE SKY ❷

• Avenue Henri Fabre
La Mède, 13220 Châteauneuf-les-Martigues
From Marignane or Marseille, follow the signs for Martigues on the A55 motorway, then take the exit for La Mède. Drive towards the refinery on the RN568 and turn right in the direction of La Pradine. You'll see the monument as you drive along the avenue Henri Fabre towards L'Étang de Berre.

"The world's first seaplane flight

It was on 28 March 1910, in La Mède, a neighbourhood of Châteauneuf-les-Martigues, at the spot where the monument stands, that Henri Fabre succeeded in taking off from L'Étang de Berre, flying 500 m, then splashing down again, aboard a flying machine with a novel design. He had conceived and built this machine himself, and gave it the affectionate nickname "Duck". It was the world's first seaplane. During the First World War, he set up a company employing 200 people to mass-produce military seaplanes.

Born on 29 November 1882 in Marseille, Henri Fabre passed away on 29 June 1984, in his 102nd year. While in retirement, he invented a little folding boat, made from four plywood boards and a waterproof canvas bottom, with a small mast and sail. He transported his invention around on the roof of his car and was thus able to go sailing whenever he pleased. He called this last invention the bateau-claque [click-clack boat].

Henri Fabre's "Duck" is on display at the Musée de l'Air et de l'Espace of Le Bourget, in the northern suburbs of Paris. A replica of the same plane was previously installed on the roof of the international terminal of the Marseille-Provence airport. But due to recent building work, it was dismantled and removed to an out-of-the-way hangar, from which nobody seems to know when it will re-emerge!

A video cassette about Henri Fabre has been released by the Institut National de l'Audiovisuel: Henri Fabre, marin du ciel [Henri Fabre, sailor of the sky] - VHS - Length: 52 min - Publishers: INA MÉDITERRANÉE / France 3 SUD

OFFICE DE TOURISME DE CHÂTEAUNEUF-LA-MÈDE
3, rue Léon-Blum, 13220 Châteauneuf-les-Martigues • Tel: 04 42 76 89 37
• Fax: 04 42 79 80 25 • e-mail : infos@chateauneuflesmartigues-tourisme.com
• www.chateauneuflesmartigues-tourisme.com

THE BEE WALL OF CORNILLON-CONFOUX ❸

• Quartier de Camp-Long, 13250 Cornillon-Confoux
• From the village take the D70 in the direction of Lançon-de-Provence and Salon-de-Provence. The road descends from the village, lined with Roman milestones, then levels out. About 1.5 km from the village, turn left onto the small, paved road. A sign indicates an equestrian club while a wooden arrow points the way to the mur d'abeilles [wall of bees]. You can see it on the right from the road. To the left is a detached house with a dovecote.

For most people, the phrase "wall of bees" doesn't ring any bells. Although you may not expect much, this place is in fact very impressive. Remarkably restored, l'apier, as it's called here, is the second largest bee-wall in France. Built entirely of drystone, it is 60 m long and contains 56 niches or cells to house the individual beehives.

> ***"Along the 60-metre wall, 56 niches protected the beehives from inclement weather***

Made from the bark of cork oaks or rye straw, these hives were thus protected from bad weather and animal predators. This technique, which appears to have been used by the Romans, was still in use at the end of the 19th century. The positioning of these walls was not left to chance: the south-south-east orientation lets the bees stay in the sun while sheltering them from the mistral.

The biggest bee-wall in France is to be found at the site of La Baume, in Montfrin (Gard), with 75 niches hewn in the rock.

GETTING THERE ON FOOT

The Bouches-du-Rhône tourist committee has published a brochure in its Topo Randonnée [Hiking Routes] series which sets out a walk in the hills around Cornillon-Confoux. The entire route, taking about two and a half hours, takes you to the bee-wall by way of some magnificent scenery and wide panoramas. You'll come across bories [drystone shelters], ruins, sections of Roman roads, and the majestic Château de Confoux, which is private property and is not open to visitors.

COMITÉ DÉPARTEMENTAL DU TOURISME DES BOUCHES-DU-RHÔNE 13, rue Roux-de-Brignoles, 13006 Marseille • Tel: 04 91 13 84 13 • e-mail : cdt13@visitprovence.com • www.visitprovence.com	OFFICE DE TOURISME DE CORNILLON-CONFOUX Place de l'Église, 13250 Cornillon-Confoux • Tel: 04 90 50 43 17 • Fax: 04 90 50 47 60 • e-mail : ot.cornillonconfoux@free.fr

THE VIRGIN OF CORNILLON-CONFOUX

• Place de l'Église, 13250 Cornillon-Confoux

A very pregnant Virgin Mary crushes the serpent with her feet

The little known village of Cornillon-Confoux possesses a very strange statue of the Holy Virgin: installed in a niche outside the church, it represents a Virgin who is manifestly several months pregnant. As they say in Provence, enceinte jusqu'aux yeux [pregnant up to the eyes] …

Erected in 1865, the statue is one of the rare representations of the parturient Mother of Christ, and this despite the 16th-century decree by the Council of Trent banning "unusual images in Catholic churches". There are only 11 other examples of representations of the parturient Mother of Christ in France: in the cathedral of Reims (Marne), in Brioude (Haute-Loire), Plomeur (Finistère), Laroque-des-Albères, Prades and Perpignan (both in Pyrénées-Orientales), Chissey-sur-Loué (Jura), Oulchy-le-Château (Aisne), Arcachon (Gironde), Belpech and Cucugnan (both in Aude).

One other peculiar feature about this statue, originally placed inside the church, is that it portrays the Virgin as she appeared to Catherine Labouré, at the convent of Les Filles de la Charité, 140 rue du Bac, Paris, in 1830.

During this vision, Mary was seen by Catherine just as the statue in Cornillon depicts her: pregnant, with 12 stars above her head (since vanished from the statue), and crushing a serpent with her foot (a detail that often goes unnoticed). This Parisian miracle also led to the creation of a "Miraculous Medal" and has been regarded as representing two passages from the Bible: Genesis (3: 15), where the woman crushes the serpent; and Revelation (12: 1–2), which says: *"And there appeared a great wonder in heaven; a woman clothed with the sun, and the moon under her feet, and upon her head a crown of twelve stars; And she being with child cried, travailing in birth, and pained to be delivered."*

TO FIND OUT MORE

http://www.chapellenotredamedelamedaillemiraculeuse.com
Representations of the pregnant Virgin in statues and on medals:
Chapelle Notre-Dame de la Médaille Miraculeuse
140, rue du Bac, 75007 Paris

OFFICE DE TOURISME DE CORNILLON-CONFOUX
Place de l'église, 13250 Cornillon-Confoux • Tel:04 90 50 43 17
• Fax: 04 90 50 47 60 • e-mail : ot.cornillonconfoux@free.fr

THE CHURCH OF LA SAINTE-FAMILLE ❺

• 24, boulevard Victor Hugo, 13800 Istres • Tel: 04 42 55 00 72
• http://paroisseistres.free.fr

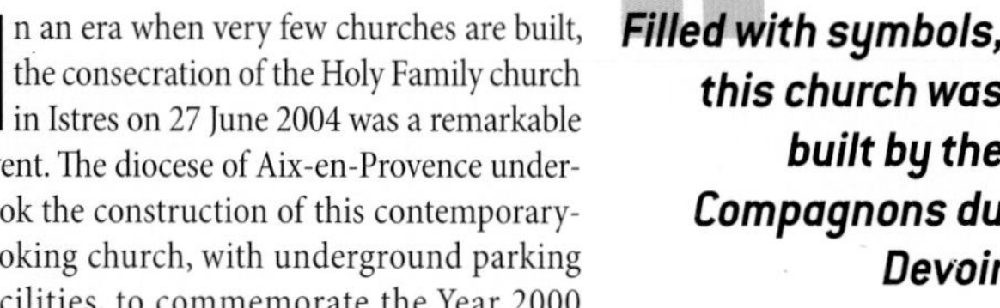

Filled with symbols, this church was built by the Compagnons du Devoir

In an era when very few churches are built, the consecration of the Holy Family church in Istres on 27 June 2004 was a remarkable event. The diocese of Aix-en-Provence undertook the construction of this contemporary-looking church, with underground parking facilities, to commemorate the Year 2000 Jubilee. The architect was François Gautier and the building work was carried out by the Compagnons du Devoir.

If the church makes an impact when viewed from the outside, it is within that surprise is heaped upon surprise. Composed on 820 hexagonal stones, each weighing exactly 1 tonne, from the Ménerbes quarry, the nave is most impressive. The stones are bevelled to eliminate sharp angles, creating empty lozenges at their joints, which allows sound to be trapped within the dome. At the top of the nave, 19 m high, an oculus lets in natural light.

The church is full of symbols, starting with its east-west orientation, pointing towards the Near East from whence Christ came. The altar is made from ivory-coloured stone with blue and red veins from Tavel, left rough at its base, cut and smoothed in the middle section, and sanded and polished at the top. Masterpiece of expert mason Enrique Barbossa, "Bordeaux's soul of patience", the baptistery is octagonal in form, 8 being the number symbolizing baptism because it evokes the day of Christ's resurrection.

Suspended by 12 cables attached to 12 stones (symbolizing the 12 apostles), the chandelier is 10 m in diameter and also houses the sound system, smoke detectors and fire alarm, so that no wires run across the dome. One strange detail shouldn't be overlooked: behind the baptistery are plaques citing the church's generous donors. You wonder who this "Zeze" could be, who signs his name with a boat and two fish (one of which is a shark) …

OFFICE DE TOURISME D'ISTRES
30, allée Jean-Jaurès, 13800 Istres • Tel: 04 42 55 51 15 • Fax: 04 42 56 59 50
• e-mail : ot.istres@visitprovence.com

LA PLAGE DU JAÏ 6

Shore of L'Étang de Berre between Marignane and La Mède.
Access from the town centre of Marignane: follow the signs posted in a somewhat anarchic manner. Access from La Mède, which forms part of the commune of Châteauneuf-les-Martigues, follow the signs, here again posted in a haphazard fashion ... Please note that the two access roads don't meet up, unless your vehicle has good tyres and a very resistant suspension ...

Villas, huts, and "castles"

It was a time that people under 40 will never know... A time when people would willingly go for a swim in L'Étang de Berre. A time when beach bars and restaurants (but that's perhaps too fine a word ...) had names like "Twist-Bar", served little fried fish caught in the lagoon itself, and played songs by Alain Barrière and Gilbert Bécaud from jukeboxes resting unsteadily upon the sand ... Today, the Plage de Jaï suffers from the freshwater dumped into the lagoon by the nearby EDF power plant at Saint-Chamas.

All along this tongue of land surrounded by water, called the "Jaï dune cordon", you pass by beach huts and other precarious shelters, luxurious villas, camping sites, prefab chateaux, barbed wire and breeze-block walls. In short, this is a popular beach that packs in the crowds during the summer, and where "class mixing" is no idle expression.

The Plage du Jaï is in fact a double cul-de-sac. Whether you come from Marignane or from La Mède, in theory you should be able to get from one to the other, but the state of the unpaved road will soon force you to give up trying. Films are also often shot here, because the area still exudes an atmosphere difficult to reproduce in the studio.

SIGHTS NEARBY

L'ETANG DE BOLMON 7

"Behind" the Plage du Jaï, two other aquatic universes meet: L'Étang de Bolmon, which makes the Jaï strip a "dune cordon", and even closer to the mainland, the Rove canal which, coming from Marseille and having crossed the Estaque massif, reaches Marignane and runs alongside the lagoon, protected by dikes, to Martigues (see Marseille insolite et secret, in the same collection as this guide).
The fauna and flora of l'étang de Bolmon reserves its share of surprise.

THE WINGLESS LARK

Nombre d'Or roundabout on avenue du 8 mai 1945 in Marignane.
A French Alouette [Lark] helicopter in stationary flight above one of Marignane's roundabouts reminds visitors that the town is Europe's "copter capital", thanks to the presence of the Eurocopter factory (a subsidiary of the EADS aeronautics consortium). It's the largest European manufacturer and the world's largest exporter of helicopters, with 8,000 aircraft flying in 132 countries.

PARK OF THE FORMER GUNPOWDER FACTORY 9

• RD10, 13140 Miramas
• The park is open Wednesday 14.00–17.00 (18.00 April–October), and the first and third Sunday of each month, 10.00–17.00 (18.00 April–October).

It is accessible from the RD10, between Miramas-le-Vieux and Saint-Chamas, by the gate on the right. Alternatively take the path that leaves Miramas-le-Vieux or, lastly, the entry in the port of Saint-Chamas. Paradoxically, the majestic main entrance to the gunpowder factory in Saint-Chamas cannot be used by visitors.

Blast zone...

The park surrounding the former powder factory is a great place for taking walks, with its fauna, flora and loaded (!) history, after three hundred years of manufacturing gunpowder and other explosives. Prior to its creation, gunpowder was produced in the Huveaune valley, but the interference with the flow of the river sometimes prevented the peasants from irrigating their crops. The site of Saint-Chamas, where the waters of the Canal de Craponne joined the River Touloubre, was chosen instead and a new powder factory was built there in 1690.

It was only in 1974 that this factory closed its doors for the last time. Since then, the grounds have been decontaminated and "de-mined" by the French Army. Today, you can visit a large part of these 135 hectares and discover the industrial buildings, fallow land, canals, marshes and a large variety of fauna, the park being made up of several different habitats such as dry hills, humid forest (rare in Provence), and marshland. Observation posts are available, from where you can see some astonishing terrestrial wildlife as well as birds found throughout the Camargue (pink flamingos, herons, egrets, teals). Local birds of prey soar above the park.

At the entrance to the park, a building contains reminders of some of the major dates in the factory's long history, but does not offer the anecdotes that only former workers could tell you. For example, the manufacturing buildings all have very lightweight roofs and were surrounded by trees, so that in case of an explosion the blast would be directed upwards. Workers in direct contact with gunpowder were only allowed to work for 40 minutes at a time, after which they had to go out and breathe fresh air because of the toxic atmosphere inside. The buildings were often surrounded by vegetable gardens tended by workers during their "respiratory breaks".

The powder factory regulations were, of course, very strict due to the ever-present fear that a mistake in handling substances would lead to disaster. It was absolutely forbidden to smoke on the premises, and workers had to leave any matches or cigarettes in the changing rooms. But all this failed to prevent an explosion on 16 November 1936 that killed 53 people, while injuring another 200. The blast was felt throughout Provence and windows along the Canebière in Marseille were shattered. To foil possible searches, inveterate smokers would stock up at the bar-tabac opposite the factory entrance, which sold single cigarettes, easier to hide ...

THE CLOCK OF SAINT-CHAMAS

10

• Office de Tourisme de Saint-Chamas
Montée des Pénitents (Be warned that it's a real climb from the base of the bridge, so steep in fact that you may be too breathless to even say hello on reaching this tourist office.)
13250 Saint-Chamas • Tel: 04 90 50 90 54 • Fax: 04 90 50 90 10
E-mail: tourisme-saintchamas@tele2.fr • http://www.saintchamas.fr.st

The town's "Ghoul" takes its last victim

Divided into two by a cliff that is today breached by a passage surmounted by a bridge, an aqueduct and the municipal clock, Saint-Chamas is a highly unusual village.

Tourists have a tendency to pass it by, merely stopping to admire the Flavian bridge at the entrance to the town, a magnificent remnant of the times of the Roman emperor Augustus. With a single span and twin triumphal arches crowned by lions, the bridge is truly magnificent, both timeless and extraordinary, left in this place thanks to some mysterious preserving spirit.

Even the people of Provence think they know all about Saint-Chamas without having actually been there. Before the advent of the TGV, the PLM (Paris, Lyon, Mediterranean) spur line serving Arles, passed by Saint-Chamas and you could see the cliff from the train.

The village was originally built above this cliff (called the "Baou"), using the soft, blue cobalt-bearing rock, and subsequently spread to the edge of L'Étang de Berre following the departure (or settlement) of barbarian hordes. Divided by the cliff, it thus has two sections: the port, known as the "Pertuis" neighbourhood, and the inland neighbourhood around the town hall, called Le Delà [Beyond]. Some means, therefore, had to be found of linking the two.

A naive but superb ex-voto facing the entrance to the local museum explains better than a long description how the inhabitants of the two neighbourhoods of the village once communicated. La Goule [Ghoul] was a cold, damp dark tunnel dug into the rock. However on 18 December 1863 this tunnel collapsed, causing the death of Joseph Trovero and his team of horses, as a plaque on the cliff walls reminds us. It was then decided to abandon the Ghoul by opening a breach in the Baou, but then the two sides of the gap had to be joined at the top. This impressive bridge, the Aqueduc du Plan, is 62 m long and 23 m high. It cuts the village in half and also bears the weight of the municipal clock.

From the tourist office, you can climb a few steps to visit the local museum and then, carrying on, you come to the edge of the breathtaking gap that can be crossed by walking on either side of the water that still runs along the middle of the aqueduct. If you suffer from vertigo, you might want to give this crossing a miss ... But on the far side of the bridge lies the Moulières hill where some curious heads, sculpted in the rock, seem to await youth's evening antics ...

MUSÉE MORALES 11

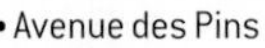

• Avenue des Pins
13110 Port-de-Bouc

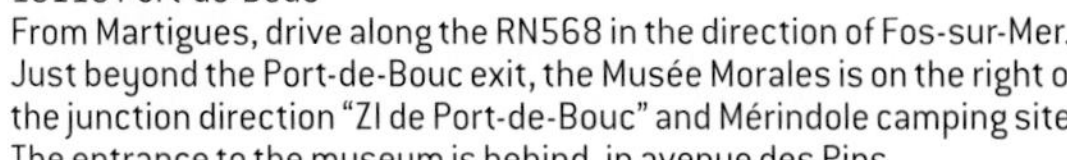

From Martigues, drive along the RN568 in the direction of Fos-sur-Mer. Just beyond the Port-de-Bouc exit, the Musée Morales is on the right of the junction direction "ZI de Port-de-Bouc" and Mérindole camping site. The entrance to the museum is behind, in avenue des Pins.

He welded, twisted, and tortured tons of scrap metal

Anyone who drives around L'Étang de Berre will know of the Musée Morales, even if they haven't visited it: traffic lights placed just in front of the museum force drivers to halt and contemplate for a moment the bizarre metal forms that make up this collection.

Charles Morales is what you might call a "roadside genius". It is here, alongside the RN568, in the commune of Port-de-Bouc that he assembled, welded, sculpted, twisted and tortured tonnes of scrap metal to create a rusty bestiary of his many different fantasies …

There are more than 700 pieces exhibited here across an area of 5,000 m2, enough to give any child nightmares and make them ask questions that will disturb their parents. At the entrance, Morales clearly warns visitors that he's nobody's fool: Ô toi qui entres ici et qui t'appliqueras à comprendre ce que tu verras du commencement à la fin tu me diras si tant de mer*es ont été créées afin de tromper ou bien pour l'amour de l'art [O you who enter here and will try to understand what you see from beginning to end, tell me if so much sh** has been created in order to deceive or for the love of art] (Morales 79).

But the (iron) curtain is about to fall on this fascinating project, because the museum is closed "for building work" and the phone no longer answers at this number. It appears that Charles Morales has passed on to weld in a better world. You can, however, still get a fairly exhaustive glimpse of the work on display in his now posthumous museum from the outside.

SIGHTS NEARBY

THE SOLLAC STEEL PLANT AT FOS-SUR-MER 12

A visit to a steel-making plant is always spectacular: the sight of the molten metal, particularly during the milling process, is very impressive. Luckily for the people of Provence, the Sollac plant at Fos-sur-Mer is one of the rare places where a visit can be booked. Over and above the indispensable tour of the facilities, the 3-hour tour gives an insight into the world of steel and the stages in its manufacture. Once you've seen the size and range of tools needed for the process, you'll look at your car door, beer can or teaspoon with a new eye. The tour also includes a presentation by the Arcelor group (which owns part of the site), one of the world leaders in steel manufacture comprising the former Usinor, Arbed of Luxembourg and Aceralia of Spain. Reservations: Sollac Méditerranée (groupe Arcelor), site de Fos, 13776 Fos-sur-Mer. Communication service: 04 42 47 25 01.
www.arcelor.com and www.sollacmediterranee/.com

TROGLODYTE DWELLING FOR RENT

13

• Chez Monsieur and Madame Ravel
22, quartier des Pénitents, 13250 Saint-Chamas
12, chemin des Costes 13127 Vitrolles
• Tel: 04 42 89 58 83 / 06 32 25 91 04
• E-mail: sylvette.ravel@wanadoo.fr or richard.ravel@wanadoo.fr
Brief description: 60 m2 surface area. Sleeps four, but ideal for a couple. Fireplace, terrace with panoramic view of the village, fishing port and lagoon
Weekly rent: €240–€480, depending on season

"**Between two worlds...**"

Hewn into the cliff at Saint-Chalmas, a troglodyte dwelling, complete with all mod cons, offers the chance of a truly astonishing stay by the shores of L'Étang de Berre.

When you read the brochure about holiday lets in Saint-Chamas, you may not realize the extraordinary location of some of the furnished accommodation on offer, with respect to the village's internal layout. So the troglodyte home of Monsieur and Madame Ravel, 60 m2 for four persons, at first sight may only stand out because of the use of that strange word, "troglodyte". In fact, this particular let is quite an extraordinary place.

First of all, the house is traversier [transversal]: the entrance is in the sloping neighbourhood of Le Delà, the inland part of Saint-Chamas, and at the other end you find yourself on a terrace overlooking the port neighbourhood of Le Pertuis, with a panoramic view of L'Étang de Berre. This double orientation really gives you a sense that it's attached to two completely different worlds.

The configuration of the house, dug into the brown limestone rock of the cliff, with a cavernous ceiling, and the fabulous view from the northern entrance through to the southward-looking terrace, is simply amazing.

Many of those who have stayed here in the past have become regulars. This not only means that it is difficult to reserve a holiday stay, but also that acquiring your own "hole-in-the-wall" at Saint-Chamas is likely to be very expensive. But we should also explain that these cliff dwellings are not merely separated by walls, but metres of limestone, so there's no need to worry about soundproofing. Ideal for honeymoons …

THE ROCK OF VITROLLES

From the A7 motorway take the Vitrolles-Village exit. Follow the signs for "Le Rocher" et "Village". At the cemetery, behind the rock, park your car and follow the sign "Théâtre de verdure" or take the tarred road reserved for residents' vehicles that circles the rock.

Despite the dizzying ascent, the fantastic view from the top is worth the effort

Vitrolles is a very large commune adjoining the A7 motorway and has one of the biggest commercial zones in the region. The contrast between the new town and the old village is striking. The imposing, craggy rock, topped by a tower and a chapel, can be seen from a great distance.

The site is spectacular, and was presumably impregnable. It is reminiscent of those Tuscan landscapes known as paesine, dotted with eroded marble. You can only visit the rock on foot. First you cross the théâtre de verdure [open-air theatre], named after Jean Giono, which each summer hosts "Les Nuits du Rocher" with a programme of classical and jazz concerts, theatre and dance. Then you pass in front of the old cemetery before beginning a very steep climb (75 steps). The chain anchored in the rock to provide handholds is useful, especially on the way back down. From the top of the Roucas (Provençal for "rock"), the panorama is fantastic. You can see right across L'Étang du Berre and the view stretches to the Mediterranean, to the hills surrounding Marseille and to Sainte-Victoire mountain, but also includes the plumes from the oil refineries and the runways at Marseille-Provence airport. The statue of the Holy Virgin on the roof of the Notre-Dame-de-Vie chapel (over 1,000 years old) is commonly invoked as the "Madonna of aviators", protecting foolhardy flyers. A Saracen tower dating back to the 11th century completes the tour of the rock.

After this feast of visual delights, especially at sunrise or sunset, a walk through the old village of Vitrolles banishes any misgivings aroused by the new town that has grown up next to it. Without false affectations, souvenir shops, or the usual arts and crafts, the village today remains in a condition such that Pagnol could film one of his Provençal stories here. Whoever had the idea of putting up plaques next to the handsome doors of the village houses, saying who lived there and the professions they exercised, should also be congratulated. Let's just say that there have been an awful lot of public notaries in Vitrolles ... You can also see the ramparts over the portalet, formerly the main gate to the village, and inside the church admire an altar attributed to Pierre Puget, the celebrated architect from Marseille.

OFFICE DE TOURISME DE VITROLLES
Place de Provence, 13127 Vitrolles
• Tel: 04 42 10 40 00 • Fax: 04 42 10 59 81
• e-mail : office-tourisme@vitrolles.com • www.vitrolles.com/office-tourisme

THE VILLAGE OF CHARLEVAL 

> ***A village with a reputation for rectitude…***

No need to search for the unexpected at Charleval, everything is unexpected. First of all the ground plan, incompatible with the self-contained, recalcitrant and shady (especially in summer …) character of its occupants. A town laid out in straight lines, its streets impeccably parallel, its rows of houses – even though everybody has tried to personalize their home you'd think you were in the USA or a Sim City computer game.

Charleval was designed in 1741 by César de Cadenet, who decided to establish a new village, probably with the intention of attracting labourers to increase his income from farming. By a charter of 6 November 1741, de Cadenet assigned a plot of land to the families on a long lease which stipulated that it was up to them to build in a specific place and to a defined style and size. Hence the square village.

But the curiosity value of Charleval also comes from the many details that keep up a Disney-like atmosphere. The 19th-century Gothic Renaissance chateau, superbly kitsch, where you expect to see Micky, Donald and friends coming out, the central square with a doll's house town hall and a statue of the lord of the manor on his pedestal, gazing at the sky and seeming to excuse himself for having exercised his rights in this land of hills and valleys …

Cartesians fond of rectitude shouldn't miss the walk along the alley lined with ancient plane trees, which runs straight as a die alongside the Canal de Craponne.

OFFICE DE TOURISME DE CHARLEVAL-EN-PROVENCE
2, place André-Leblanc, 13350 Charleval
• Tel/Fax: 04 42 28 45 30 • e-mail : office-tourisme-charleval@wanadoo.fr

THE MARY-ROSE FOUNTAIN

16

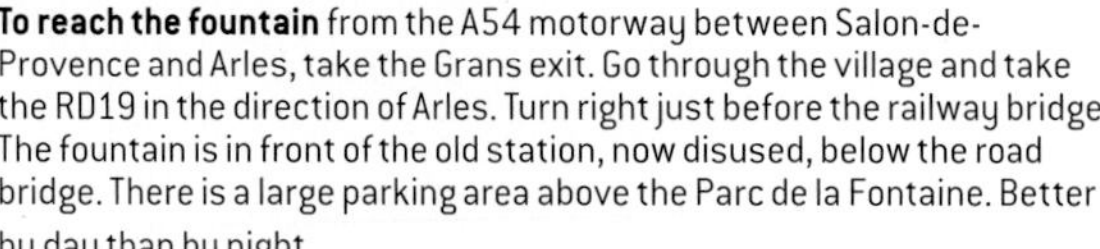

• Parc de la Fontaine, 13450 Grans
To reach the fountain from the A54 motorway between Salon-de-Provence and Arles, take the Grans exit. Go through the village and take the RD19 in the direction of Arles. Turn right just before the railway bridge. The fountain is in front of the old station, now disused, below the road bridge. There is a large parking area above the Parc de la Fontaine. Better by day than by night ...

Auguste Saurel was born at Cavaillon in 1892 and went to live at Eyguières in the Alpilles. When he was 18 he got involving in building a glider in which he had an accident, injuring his shoulder and ear.

Marie-Rose Carias was born on 26 January 1896 at Mazan and her parents settled in Eyguières where they kept the Café de Commerce. Like everybody else she knew about Auguste's accident.

Some time later Auguste went to Grans, where he attracted the attention of Marie-Rose who was also visiting the town. They had each come for different reasons, to walk to the Canebière fountain a little distance from the village. Without a word ever being spoken between them, there grew a love nourished by a few distant glimpses and by the poems of Auguste, who had found his muse. Alas, before this love could become anything other than platonic, at the age of 15 Marie-Rose was struck down by a fatal illness.

Auguste went off to war, became a teacher, lived in Lyon, Clamart and Cassis and dedicated his poet's life to the girl he called Mary-Rose. The "y" got round the problem of the silent "e" in Marie, which didn't fit in with his rhyming schemes. In 1912, he met Monsieur Bedarrides, the mayor of Grans, and told him the story of the meeting with Marie-Rose. Moved by this, after the war in 1919 the mayor renamed the Grans fountain "Fontaine Mary-Rose". A plaque was mounted beside it:

[To a soul / A fountain simply adorned
With the name of Mary Rose, / And crowned by the muses,
Where I have from the beginning / Gathered for you the flowers of glory
Virgin, such is the monument / That I dedicate to your memory]
Auguste Saurel

Another plaque was erected in March 1977 on Saurel's death.

Marie-Rose Carias is buried in Eyguières cemetery (gate No. 3, second row of graves, on the right). Look out for the ornamental yews in this cemetery, which are cut in a particular way, like neatly spaced hayricks. On the tomb of the Carias family there is a single name, that of Saurel. Today the grave is still regularly covered with flowers, nobody knows by whom.

SYNDICAT D'INITIATIVE DE GRANS
Boulevard Victor-Jauffret, 13450 Grans • Tel: 04 90 55 88 92 • Fax: 04 90 55 86 27

THE GIANT OF LAMANON

• Allée du Château, 13113 Lamanon
From the tourist office or the church square, head towards the chateau. After a short distance go down the wide avenue opposite the chateau. The plane tree stands on private property but you can see it very well from the road. It has been listed and the landowners are obliged to preserve it. The field is private property and access is prohibited.

The oldest plane tree in Provence

The Lamanon plane tree, some 300 years old, stands 20 m high, has a circumference of 7.5 m, and its crown covers 1,500 m2 from top to bottom. Although it takes seven people joining hands to encircle its trunk, it isn't the largest example in the world. The Hippocrates Plane, on the island of Kos in the Greek Dodecanese, is over 2,000 years old and has a circumference of 14 m. Otherwise there is a plane at Barjols in Provence which is not so old but whose exposed roots give a total circumference of 12 m (see page 103). The plane tree is ubiquitous in Provençal towns and villages, the breadth and depth of its shade much appreciated. It is found in courtyards, squares, in front of bastides and along the roadside, where it has proved to be dangerous to the point that a number of associations have been formed to demand that the trees should be cut down …

THE PLANE TREE IN PROVENCE

This tree is a relatively recent introduction to Provence. At the beginning of the 19th century, elm, lime, chestnut and hackberry shared the green spaces, elm being the favourite. The plane was chosen by municipal authorities for the deep shade of its canopy and because it is less susceptible to insects. The origin of the word "plane", via the Greek platanos, is platus meaning broad. The common or London plane, with its maple-like leaves, is the type most frequently found in France. It is a hybrid between the American and the Oriental planes, developed in England in the 17th century. In Greek mythology the plane is a symbol of regeneration, as its bark renews itself in flakes, rather like the scales of a snake. The Trojan horse was built from plane wood.

However the Provençal planes are sick and, since the Second World War, they have gradually been decimated by the canker brought over by the American liberators in 1944. It's said that wooden ammunition boxes stored at Borely Park in Marseille harboured the deadly fungus. The disease is spread mainly when pruning tools have been in contact with an affected tree. Elaborate precautions are now taken when these trees need cutting.

ORPI

THE PELICAN FOUNTAIN AT PÉLISSANNE

• Rue Wilson, 13330 Pélissanne

> ***Once every year, rosé wine miraculous flows from the Pelican Fountain***

The story of the Pelican Fountain is interesting: not every day is water turned into wine.

Listed as a historic monument in 1942 (so some classification of monuments went on during the war …), the fountain consists of a tall, smooth column topped by a partly Ionic, partly Corinthian capital. On top is a pelican in its nest nourishing, as is its wont, its offspring with its flesh.

The pelican is the creature shown on the town's coat of arms. In Roman Catholicism it symbolizes the sacrifice of Christ shedding his blood to save mankind. Also from the symbolic point of view the bird with its outstretched wings evokes aviation, an unmistakable reminder of the proximity of the Salon-de-Provence air base, flight school and preferred training ground of the Patrouille de France, the international aerobatic team from the French air force. Finally, it shouldn't be forgotten that "Pelican" is unfortunately often associated with forest fires, being the nickname of the Bombardier Canadair and other amphibious firefighting aircraft.

Walking around the fountain you come across four marble plaques, one at each corner of the monument, giving its history since it was erected in the 18th century. Designed in 1769 by Jean-Baptiste Louche, master-mason at Pélissanne and Bernus, master-sculptor at Salon-de-Provence, the fountain was *"completed during the reigns of Louis XV, MDCCLXX (1770) and Napoleon I MDCCCIX (1809)"*. Following "improvements", it was completely restored under the Third Republic (1870–1940).

The most surprising thing is that this fountain, whose water is unfit for drinking, is transformed once a year into a fountain of wine, the logical and sustaining outcome of the pelican symbol and a natural prolongation of the wine festival. So you should come to Pélissanne on the third Sunday of October during the great craft fair, to drink the fresh rosé miraculously flowing (but for one day only) from the aptly named "cannons" of the Pelican Fountain.

OFFICE DE TOURISME DU MASSIF DES COSTES
Parc Roux-de-Brignoles, 13330 Pélissanne • Tel.: 04 90 55 15 55
• Fax: 04 90 55 01 86 • e-mail: ot.massif.des.costes@wanadoo.fr
• www.ot-massifdescostes.com

REMAINS OF ROMAN ROADS IN PROVENCE 

• Visits to the Via Aurelia
Bruno Tassan • Tel: 04 90 56 68 93 • Member of the Association pour les Journées de l'Antiquité (AJA) – Département des Sciences de l'Antiquité, Maison Méditerranéenne des Sciences de l'Homme (MMSH, Aix-en-Provence) • http://www.via-aurelia.net
• Leave the village of Pélissanne heading for the Salon-de-Provence air base via the RD68. Take the motorway, which crosses the Canal EDF (state-owned energy utility). At the end of the road, after "Béton de France" turn left onto the RD68E, which rejoins the canal. The former Roman road starts there in the direction of "Gigery". The milestone is on the left after about 1 km. The arrow-straight track becomes paved again when it meets the RD17
• Web site of joint project sponsored by 17 European regions giving information about the Roman roads in the Mediterranean and their preservation: http://www.viaeromanae.org

A letter posted in Arles took a week to reach Rome

Provence, which took its name from the first Roman provincia beyond the Alps, has always been an attractive destination and since Antiquity the site of routes that would become, under the Roman Empire, rapid and well-maintained carriageways.

The Via Aurelia, the Gaulish part of which was built by Augustus at the end of the 1st century BC and the beginning of the 1st century AD, was the principal axis linking Rome with Provence. Running alongside the Mediterranean in its southern section, the Via Aurelia left the coast behind in Provence and reached Arles inland. The Via Domitia, on the other hand, arrived in the north of Provence after crossing the Alps. Today you can still see certain sections and milestones as well as artworks on this ancient route, providing you can find it among the old tracks, motorways and high-speed railway lines.

Bruno Tassan offers guided walks around Salon-de-Provence, where the Via Aurelia passes, during which he sets the history of the route in context. For some 4 km you can see for yourself the principles by which the Romans built their roads.

Primarily intended for military use, these roadways were traced out along existing routes while favouring straight lines and as short distances as possible. Bends are rare on low-lying ground, thanks to superb mapping. Before construction started, a geometric survey was carried out to find the best layout, avoiding zones liable to flooding or over-steep escarpments.

In the countryside, the surface was of packed gravel and rocky patches were levelled. In urban areas, the road was paved or a mosaic of pebbles was laid. The road was around 5 m wide with a stone to mark every mile, either every 1,000 paces, which corresponds to 1,481 m, as opposed to the nautical mile (1,852 m) or the statute mile (1,609 m). The milestones bore the name of the emperor who had ordered the building or remaking of the road, together with the distance from the last stage.

It's difficult to imagine today the achievements made possible by these Roman roads: urgent mail was dispatched at the rate of 150 km a day, the carrier changing horse at each staging post. So a letter from Arles took less than a week to reach Rome – not until the end of the 19th century would such an efficient postal service be seen again. Despite the 20 centuries since the building of these roads, the barbarian invasions and the lack of maintenance in the Middle Ages, you can still travel along sections of them today and appreciate the exceptional quality of Gallo-Roman workmanship.

OTHER REMAINS OF ROMAN ROADS TO SEE IN PROVENCE

PONT FLAVIEN

Entering the town of Saint-Chamas, a spectacular ensemble comes into view: as well as a bridge built by a local notable known as Flavien, there is a very unspoiled section of Roman road with deep ruts worn in the stone by chariot wheels (see page 143).

LA VIA DOMITIA

Alpes du Sud tourist offices have a leaflet on "La Via Domitia" listing the main points of interest that can still be seen along the road linking Italy and Spain. To give just one example, Pont Julien near Apt, crossing the River Calavon and built in 3 BC, is a remarkable construction of three arches with a system of hollows in the pillars to clear heavy floodwaters.

MUSÉE DE L'ART SINGULIER DE RAYMOND REYNAUD 20

• Quartier la Peyronnette, 13650 Sénas, Tel.: 04 90 57 23 18
• Admission free

If you'd like to visit the museum you're strongly advised to book. Call in at Sénas tourist office where the genial and efficient Karine and Sophie will arrange things for you and explain how to get there, complete with plan. As Raymond Reynaud is over 80, it's best to respect his kindness.

"You'll either love it or hate it"

As Sophie in the Tourist Office said, "you'll be bowled over" and "you'll either love it or hate it". We were, and we loved it.

The Musée de l'Art Singulier de Raymond Reynaud is a strange private museum created by a real visionary, sincere, affable and modest. Mr Reynaud welcomes visitors to his house which, apart from a few external signs of a unconventional mason, seems normal sized.

During the visit, however, you get the impression of having toured an immense museum, there is so much exhibition space and such astonishing works.

Although in his early days he painted canvases in black and white on the theme of the seven deadly sins, which seemed to him to be timely in these days of the consumer society, he later added "acoustic" colours – green, red. Finally he tackled polychrome, breaking down the barriers of the plastic arts in producing whatever his flights of fancy brought into his head. Apart from the paintings, his sculptures are just as captivating. Made from burnt wood (not flotsam, too aesthetic for his taste), they are not very cheerful but they are spectacular.

Notable among the canvases are the immense Don Quixote et Sancho Panza, Jean de Florette and Tartarin as well as Pagnol's Marius, whom he compares with Ulysses in his earthly love for Fanny.* If through these popular and emblematic characters he sought to communicate with everyone, everyone does not have access to art. The paradox of this creator is that his desire to be universal hasn't met with popular recognition. There are indeed many visitors to his museum, but most of them are Japanese or American. How many people from Sénas have seen his work? One is never a prophet in one's own land.

The visit is free and you'll leave with postcards offered by the artist. You can however make a contribution and thank the Reynauds in buying a beautifully produced book, Raymond Reynaud, un singulier de l'art, text by Alain Paire, published by Images en Manœuvre at €20.

*French writer and film-maker Marcel Pagnol's "Marseille trilogy" of films – Marius (1929), Fanny (1931), and César (1936) – deal with the lives of a Marseille fishmonger, Fanny, and her lover Marius who goes off to sea.

THE BELLTOWER OF THE ÉGLISE DE SÉNAS 21

• Avenue André Aune, 13650 Sénas

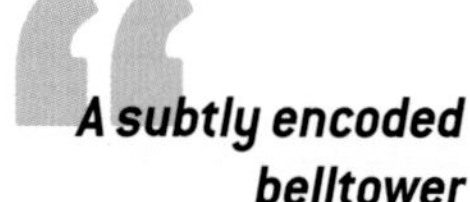

Saint-Amand in Sénas is an ancient chapel dating from the 12th century, modified and enlarged over the centuries. The belltower, built between 1555 and 1559, is in the form of an octagonal spire embellished with rostres (stone spurs), which gives it an unexpected hedgehog-like aspect. There are 56 of these rostres, seven on each of the eight spines.

Among the suggested interpretations the most probable is that of the hierarchy of human experience. At the bottom, the basest aspects of the human soul, animality, passion and hedonism illustrated by beaks, claws, spikes and, in the next row up, phallic symbols. Higher up the rostres are rougher and less figurative, with a greater sense of serenity. Finally, at the top below the cross, two rows of spikes evoke the crown of thorns of Christ's Passion. The cross at the apex of the spire is surmounted by a cock recalling St Peter's three denials.

The impression is of being in the presence of the work of comrades who liked to leave personal messages for their successors. The phalluses sometimes found on buildings are indeed rarely commissioned pieces, especially when a church is involved. Gargoyles urinating (or worse) on the faithful were also added to some buildings ... an ironical gesture towards the sacred and impunity for so-called mortal sins.

This belltower has opened the way for generations of local jokers' wordplay on the number of "noses" (nas in Provençal) per spine – seven – and the name of the village of Sénas, which can be rendered as sé nas or sept nez (seven noses). In fact the name of the village comes from séno mago: an ancient Gaulish settlement.

SIGHTS NEARBY

THE GATE OF THE CHURCH RELIQUARY 22

The small gate that protects the reliquary of Sénas church was made by a certain Poussel, a local craftsman who had two professions, locksmith and innkeeper. His house had two doors, each representing one of his activities. At the east door you entered the bar under the sign of Bacchus and at the west door you went to see the locksmith after opening it with a golden key. Hence the name of the street behind the town hall, which is still known as rue de la Clé d'Or.

THE TOMB OF NOSTRADAMUS

• Église Collégiale Saint-Laurent
Square Saint-Laurent, 13300 Salon-de-Provence
Just in front of the tourist office, where cours Gimon leads into cours Victor Hugo, take rue Maréchal Joffre, which goes straight on whereas cours Victor Hugo turns left.
• Open Monday to Friday, 13.30–17.00 and during Mass, although you're advised not to look around the church then.

"The desecrator bore the name of Wretched, he was hanged shortly thereafter

Although he was born at Saint-Rémy-de-Provence, most traces of Nostradamus can be found at Salon-de-Provence, where he lived from 1547 to 1566. His house is a major tourist attraction and there are two statues of him in the town. For those in the know, no visit to Salon is complete without taking in the tomb of the "Sage". It is to be found in the collegiate church of Saint-Laurent in the side wall of the third chapel on the left.

This is the second tomb of Nostradamus: originally he was buried upright in the Église des Cordeliers (in the rue des Cordeliers, where almost nothing of the church remains today), with pen, paper, ink and a candle so that he could continue to make his predictions. Curiously, he had requested in his will to be buried in the Collégiale Saint-Laurent but had changed his mind. In 1791, Cordeliers church was sacked by the soldiers of the National Guard from Vaucluse. It's said that the desecrator who broke open the coffin with an axe found "a copper plaque with the date of the violation of the sepulchre and a curse on the sacrilegious" on the ribs of the skeleton. The desecrator in question, who bore the fateful name of "Malheureux" [Wretched], was hung shortly thereafter for other wrongs he had committed.* Behind the wall of the chapel therefore remains what could be saved from the sacking of Cordeliers church. The original epitaph has been destroyed, but you can read a reconstitution of the text made in 1813:

"Here lie the bones of Michel Nostradamus, alone among all mortals worthy of recording, with a pen almost divine, the great events which, in future, will come to pass in the universe, under the influence of the stars. He lived 62 years, 6 months, 17 days. Posterity will not begrudge him his rest. Anne Ponsard de Salon hopes for eternal bliss for her husband."

*Guide de la Provence mystérieuse, Éditions Tchou.

SIGHTS NEARBY

THE BOURG-NEUF TOWER

24

Between the tourist office and the Collégiale Saint-Laurent, you pass the gate of Bourg-Neuf – one of the gates leading onto the ramparts of Salon. If the light is favourable, you can clearly see wavy marks in the stone on the inner wall to the left. These were made by the edges of the shackles and dangling chains worn by the condemned (disgraced thieves or usurers attached outside the walls) as they scraped the surface.

THE OLD VILLAGE OF VERNÈGUES

The village was erased from the map by an earthquake at precisely 7.14 pm

At 7.14 pm on 11 June 1909, an earthquake of magnitude 5.3 on the Richter scale shook the Salon-de-Provence region and devastated a number of villages, including Lambesc, Rognes, Saint-Cannat, Pélissanne and Vernègues. The shock was felt throughout Provence; 46 people were killed and thousands of homes destroyed, of which 1,500 at Aix-en-Provence.

A study led by the Ministry of the Environment in 1982 simulated the impact of a quake equivalent to that of 1909 which would have happened in the same place but with the current population and ground plan – there would have been between 400 and 1,000 fatalities. A quake of such amplitude happens on average once a century in France.

In contrast to the villages of the plain, which were rebuilt on the same site, Vernègues did not rise again. The inhabitants created a new village below the old one. So when you visit old Vernègues you see nothing but the ruins of houses, the church and the chateau. The vaulted cellars of the houses are the only bits left of the former village. On the plateau, where mobile phone operators have taken the opportunity to install their antennae, you'll find one of the most spectacular panoramas of Provence.

CHÂTEAU BAS

26

• Cazan, 13116 Vernègues, Tel: 04 90 59 13 16, Fax: 04 90 59 44 35
• E-mail: contact@chateaubas.com • http://www.chateaubas.com/
• North-east of Salon-de-Provence.

Access via the RN7, direction Sud Nord, at the exit for the hamlet of Cazan follow the sign for "Château Bas" on the left. Park in front of the chateau and tour the property on foot: the temple is at the end of the garden. On the way back there's no harm in trying the chateau wine.

Temple of excess, wedding photos forbidden...

Just behind Château Bas, a splendid historic property with a renowned vineyard, there is a Roman temple dating from the 1st century BC with a 16th-century chapel attached to it. The site is of exceptional beauty despite the railway viaduct of the TGV Méditerranée line, 40 m high and almost 1 km long, which passes overhead about 300 m from the temple, ignoring the historic monument buffer zone.

Château Bas is above all a 16th-century construction on the site of an ancient little town, of which the temple is the only visible remains today.

Going around the chateau, you plunge back 21 centuries in time with this ancient temple in the Corinthian style, of which a large part of the base built in huge blocks of local stone endures, as well as a fine Corinthian column, which marks the site with its vertical momentum.

Christianity also benefited from this place, reusing it from the 11th century: in 1054 the two archbishops of Arles and Apt consecrated a church dedicated to both Saint-Pierre and Saint-Césaire.

Sit down on the grass among the oaks and poplars, and close your eyes, imagining that men and women came here to worship Diana, the huntress goddess. Even if the name "Temple of Diana" is ancient, and now totally obsolete in the light of recent discoveries, it's still not known to what cult the temple belonged.

A notice at the start of the track, placed there by the owners of the chateau, forbids wedding photographs in front of the temple "compte tenu des débordements constatés" [considering the excesses that have been noted]. Proof that the romanticism of the site brings out spontaneous impulses, which is the least that a temple still dedicated to Diana in the local collective imagination could do …

The passage of the high-speed train so close to this magical place has caused great prejudice to the chateau owners and to lovers of the site. The affair is now before the courts …

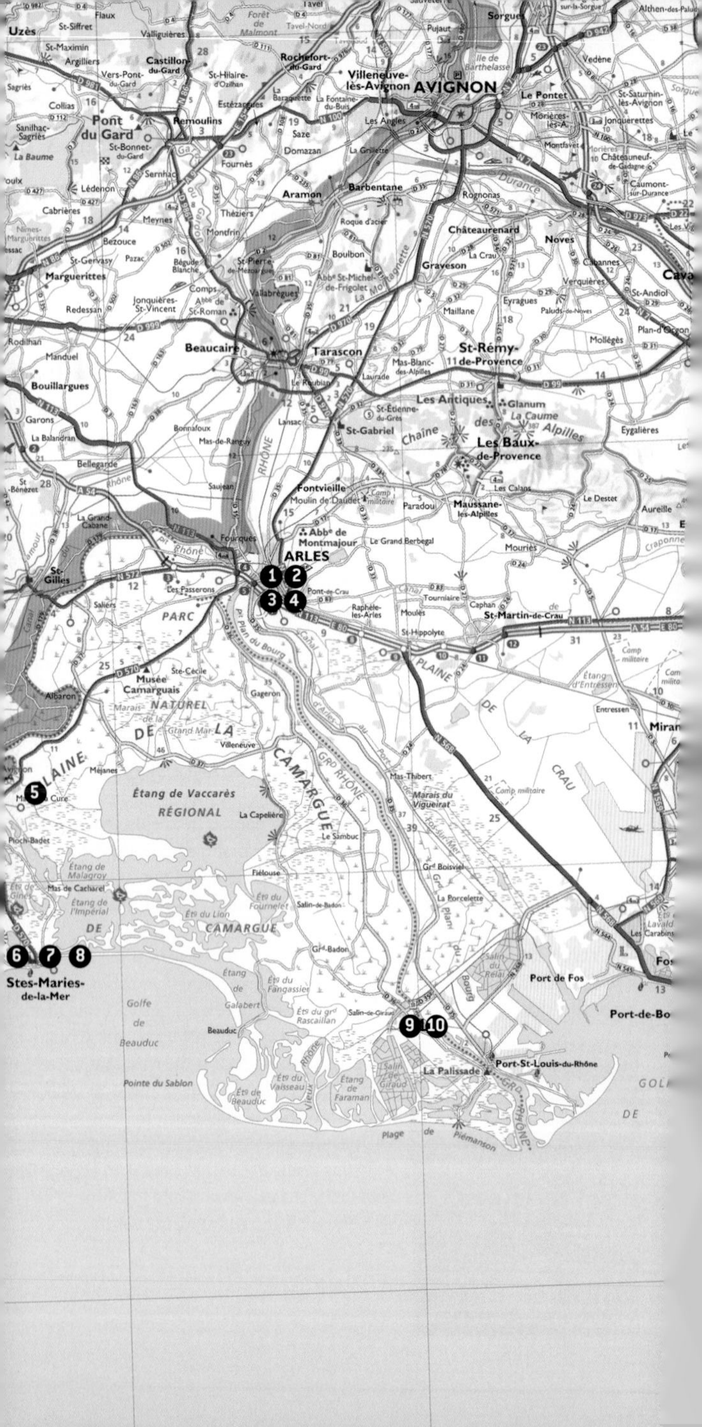

Uzès
St-Siffret
Flaux
Valliguières
Tavel
Forêt de Malmont
Sorgues
Althen-des-Paluds
St-Maximin
Argilliers
Castillon-du-Gard
Rochefort-du-Gard
Pujaut
Vedène
Vers-Pont-du-Gard
St-Hilaire-d'Ozilhan
Villeneuve-lès-Avignon
AVIGNON
Île de Barthelasse
Sagriès
Le Pontet
St-Saturnin-lès-Avignon
Collias
Estézargues
La Baraquette
La Fontaine-du-Buis
Pont du Gard
Remoulins
Les Angles
Morières-lès-A.
Jonquerettes
Sanilhac-Sagriès
St-Bonnet-du-Gard
Saze
Domazan
La Grillette
Montfavet
Châteauneuf-de-Gadagne
La Baume
Fournès
Durance
Caumont-sur-Durance
Sernhac
Lédenon
Aramon
Barbentane
Rognonas
Cabrières
Meynes
Théziers
Roque d'acier
Châteaurenard
Nîmes-Marguerittes
Bezouce
Montfrin
Noves
Boulbon
La Crau
Cabannes
St-Gervasy
Pazac
Bègude Blanche
St-Pierre-de-Mézoargues
Graveson
Marguerittes
Abbe St-Michel-de-Frigolet
La Montagnette
Verquières
Vallabrègues
Comps
Eyragues
St-Andiol
Redessan
Jonquières-St-Vincent
Abbe de St-Roman
Maillane
Paluds-de-Noves
Plan-d'Orgon
Rodilhan
Mollégès
Beaucaire
Tarascon
St-Rémy-de-Provence
Manduel
Mas-Blanc-des-Alpilles
Laurade
Le Roubian
Bouillargues
Les Antiques
Glanum
La Caume
Eygalières
St-Étienne-du-Grès
Chaîne des Alpilles
Garons
Bonnafoux
Lansac
St-Gabriel
La Balandran
Mas-de-Ranguy
Les Baux-de-Provence
Bellegarde
RHÔNE
St-Bénezet
Saujean
Fontvieille
Camp militaire
Les Calans
Moulin de Daudet
Paradou
Maussane-les-Alpilles
Le Destet
Aureille
La Grand-Cabane
Abbe de Montmajour
Le Grand Berbegal
Fourques
Mouriès
ARLES
Petit Rhône
St-Gilles
Pont-de-Crau
Tourniaire
Caphan
Les Passerons
Raphèle-lès-Arles
Moulès
St-Martin-de-Crau
Saliers
PARC
Pt Plan du Bourg
St-Hippolyte
PLAINE DE LA CRAU
Ste-Cécile
Étang d'Entressen
Musée Camarguais
Gageron
Entressen
Albaron
NATUREL
Marais de la Grand Mar
DE LA
Villeneuve
CAMARGUE
Canal d'Arles au Port de Bouc
Miramas
PLAINE
Méjanes
Mas-Thibert
Marais du Vigueirat
Étang de Vaccarès
RÉGIONAL
La Capelière
GRD RHÔNE
Pioch-Badet
Le Sambuc
Étang de Malagroy
Gd Boisviel
Fiélouse
Mas de Cacharel
Étang de l'Impérial
DE
Étg du Fournelet
La Porcelette
Étg du Lion
CAMARGUE
Salin-de-Badon
Les Carabins
Gd Badon
Salin du Relai
Port de Fos
Stes-Maries-de-la-Mer
Étang de Galabert
Étg du Fangassier
Golfe de Beauduc
Étg du grd Rascaillan
Salin-de-Giraud
Port-de-Bouc
Beauduc
La Palissade
Port-St-Louis-du-Rhône
Pointe du Sablon
Étg de Beauduc
Étg du Vaisseau
Vieux Rhône
Salin de Giraud
Étang de Faraman
GOLFE DE
Plage de Piémanson
1
2
3
4
5
6
7
8
9
10

CAMARGUE

TWO SHOPS FOR GARDIANS

1

• Camille , 5, boulevard Clémenceau, 13200 Arles • Tel: 04 90 96 04 94
22, rue Jean Granaud, 13200 Arles • Tel: 04 90 96 20 87

Clothing fit for the herdsman, not for the herd

There are two shops in Arles that will enable you to dress like a proper gardian [herdsman] and roam the Camargue, whether on foot, on horseback, or by car.

By the way, we won't add here to that useless debate: in French, should we say en Arles or à Arles? Say what you like, but if you want to buy clothing you should know where to find the real thing. First off, there's Camille at 5 boulevard Clemenceau, which prolongs boulevard des Lices, the town's principal axis. Although this establishment was founded in 1932, the display window dates from the 1960s and tends to catch the eye. And yet this is in fact a temple of traditional Carmargue clothing and in no way a boutique for tourists.

Start with the shirts in bright colours – reds, yellows, blues, blacks with Indian patterns. From €39 to €84. Next the tie, which goes around the collar and falls to the chest, a cordelière [cord tie] rather than an ordinary cravate, for about €11. As for the jacket, you'll need to choose between a corduroy herder's jacket, which might be worn by the head of a family, a landowner, or someone used to giving orders in the mas [house] or at the counter. Or else choose the gentle herdsperson's version, in smooth black velvet with a bright red lining for between €239 and €305.

The pants are beige, brown or white "moleskin", starting at €60. For women, there are jupes-culottes, for around €98. The zippers are metal and placed at the front, so that they won't be exposed to the buffeting of the saddle when the horse gallops. Lastly, the hat in black felt costs €56. In all, the whole outfit does not come cheap (between €400 and €500), but if you simply must have it …

Rue Jean Granaud is opposite Camille and to the left of the theatre starting from boulevard Clemenceau. Here they make boots to measure (and only to measure): Camargue boots, western boots, motorcycle boots … €250 per pair. That seems expensive, but they will last forever and resist all the nasty surprises the Camargue can spring on you: wire, water, mud and stones. The workshop is in the store.

THE ARLES BRIDGE SHEEP PASSAGE 

Access: at the end of boulevard Clemenceau, near the Rhône and on the side of the bridge over the river, a ramp leads down to the underground passage.

> ***Going where the grass is greener***

Under the motorway bridge spanning the Rhône, a tunnel lets sheep cross the river, protected from traffic, in the course of their seasonal migration.

When the Arles bypass on the RN113 linking Salon to Nîmes was built, a new bridge over the Rhône was needed. The engineer Paul Geniet took into account the seasonal movement of sheep and included within this structure, inaugurated in 1969, a wide lane underneath the main deck of the bridge that lets the stock make a dry, safe crossing.

In those days, each spring thousands of sheep left the plains of lower Provence on their annual migration to the green pastures, cooler temperatures and wide open spaces of the Alps. For about three weeks the shepherds, on foot of course, accompanied, guided and watched over these enormous flocks that had to be fed, watered and led to their destination. And even where trains could replace travel by road, the sheep had to be taken to those trains, and these departed from Arles, on the left bank of the Rhône, the opposite side of the river from the pastures in the Camargue. So if they reached Arles safely, at least, the sheep could make the rest of the trip by rail.

But crossing the Rhône with thousands of animals, in the midst of traffic, was no small matter. And hence this very ingenious solution of creating a sheep passage incorporated into the body of the Rhône bridge.

This passage still exists, but it seems to have become a magnet for graffiti artists ...

OFFICE DE TOURISME D'ARLES
Boulevard des Lices, BP 21, 13633 Arles Cedex • Tel: 04 90 18 41 20
• Fax: 04 90 18 41 29 • e-mail : ot.arles.courrier@wanadoo.fr
• www.tourisme.ville-arles.fr

READ ALL ABOUT IT

Transhumance 1951 – Photographer Marcel Coen and writer Maurice Moyal accompanied migratory shepherds and a flock of 2,000 merino sheep from Arles on their slow journey to the Alps.
Order from: Maison de la Transhumance, Hôtel de Ville, 13310 Saint-Martin-de-Crau, France
Price: €35 + €4 carriage

LA CHAPELLE DE LA GENOUILLADE

❸

• On the RN113 between Arles and Pont de Crau

From boulevard des Lices in Arles, head in the direction of Pont de Crau and Marseille. At the end of a straight stretch, the street/road turns right above the former SNCF rail train workshops. The chapel is 100 m further on the right. You can walk there from the centre of town in less than 10 minutes. Otherwise, park in rue Frédéric Chevillon which starts on the left, opposite the chapel.

One can still see upon the altar the mark left by Christ's knee

When Mary Magdalene and the other saints landed in Provence at Les Saintes-Maries-de-la-Mer, they were accompanied by St Trophime. He brought with him the severed head of his cousin, St Étienne [Stephen], which became a treasured relic. Trophime wanted to evangelize Arles and became the town's first bishop. His first act was to reserve part of the Roman cemetery of Alyscamps for Christian tombs. He summoned to this ceremony seven other bishops from among the first disciples of Christ. They included St Maximin of Aix, St Saturnin of Toulouse and St Serge of Narbonne. According to legend, it was then that Jesus himself appeared to bestow his blessing on the cemetery by bowing a knee, whose print remained as a mark on the stone. This stone later became the altar in the Chapelle de la Genouillade [Kneeling Chapel], created in this place to commemorate the event. After falling into ruin, it was rebuilt in the 16th century.

In the past, people concluded their walk or visit to Alyscamps with a stop at this chapel. But when it became a question of whether Arles or its rival Aix would be served by the Paris-Marseille railway line, the inhabitants of Arles sent a petition with 4,700 signatures to Lamartine, chairman of the parliamentary commission studying the railway bill. The poet deputy took the side of Arles in this debate and declared from the tribune: "If the amendment triumphs, if you assault the Rhône, the sea, and nature, make no mistake as to the fate of unhappy Arles. Inscribe on the map of France: ruins and debris." In 1848, Arles won its train, its station, and the dismemberment of Alyscamps. The Chapelle de la Genouillade then found itself cut off on the other side of the railway and was forgotten. Indeed, when you ask where La Genouillade is, most people in Arles simply point you in the general direction of the neighbourhood that bears its name ...

LA CHAPELLE DE LA CHARITÉ

• Hôtel Jules César, Boulevard des Lices, BP 116, 13631 Arles Cedex
Tel: 04 90 52 52 52 • Fax: 04 90 52 52 53
• Rooms from €158

In this moving chapel, Manitas de Plata recorded his first album

The Hotel Jules César is ideally situated on the main avenue of Arles at the entrance to the old part of town. It's a four-star hotel installed in a former Carmelite convent with its Chapelle de la Charité, whose façade rises above boulevard des Lices. As it belongs to the hotel, this chapel can only be visited by appointment and when members of the hotel staff are available to open it.

The chapel, very beautiful and very moving, just happens to be the place where Manitas de Plata, the Gypsy musician also known as Ricardo Baliardo, recorded his first album. Although at that time he was only known to a small circle of fans, Manitas was being hounded by an American producer to make a record. But in those days, nobody could have convinced him to take a plane and fly to the US. Instead he proposed that the producer come to Arles and record at his place. That's what they did, but a Gypsy caravan proved a little too cramped to set up a sound studio. So they finally made the recording in this chapel.

Since then, everyone knows about the musical career of the man whose pseudonym means "little hands of silver". A free and generous Gypsy, Manitas de Plata has lived his life on his own terms, totally incompatible with what today is considered politically correct.

FLOATING COFFINS

In ancient times, many people wished to be buried in Alyscamps. They expressed as their last wish that their body should be placed in a barrel along with the contribution necessary to buy burial rights and launched upon the Rhône. Some sly folk in Beaucaire intercepted one of these floating coffins and removed the money. The barrel then kept returning to the point along the bank where this theft took place. That attracted the attention of the authorities, who arrested the thieves.

DOMAINE DU CHÂTEAU D'AVIGNON 5

- RD570, 13460 Les Saintes-Maries-de-la-Mer
- Tel: 04 90 97 58 58 ou 58 60 • Fax: 04 90 97 58 78
- Open from 1 April to 31 October, 10.00–18.00, except Tuesday
- Admission: €3, reduced rate €1.50, free for under-18s
- E-mail: chateau.davignon@lapote.net

A thoroughly modern folly

Contrary to what the name suggests, this chateau is nowhere near Avignon, but a dozen kilometres from Les Saintes-Maries-de-la-Mer. It owes its name to the Avignon family, who converted this property into a highly productive agricultural estate thanks to irrigation works carried out using water from the Petit Rhône river. It belongs today to the Conseil Général des Bouches-du-Rhône and is open to the public, in its original state.

In 1893, Louis Prat-Noilly, a producer and trader of wines and liqueurs from Marseille, bought this 3,000 hectare estate and decided to refurbish the chateau as a hunting lodge (although it's really much, much more!). This wealthy man, curious about the latest technical innovations of his day, turned this residence into a veritable catalogue of every possible modern luxury and comfort that could be integrated into a dwelling at the end of the 19th century.

Outside the chateau, an outbuilding housed the heating system, with an English boiler that produced hot water for both the bathrooms and central heating. The heating technician lived on the premises, and in the east wing of the building there was a garage and a petrol pump.

The living quarters were spread out over three levels. The second floor was reserved for the staff: the three members attached to the chateau who lived there all year round, plus all the others who followed Louis Prat-Noilly wherever he went. Note that he also had a townhouse in Marseille, a seaside property at Montredon and another estate near Vauvert (Gard), as well as a large apartment in Paris.

In the big laundry room there's an icebox, and in the pantry a water-heated chafing dish, a distant ancestor of the microwave oven. Also in the pantry is a board, like those once found in hotels, that relayed calls from the bedrooms requesting an evening tisane or a late-night liqueur.

Running water on every floor, which was an immense step forward in most 20th-century homes, was already in use at the chateau. Water was in fact a key element in the operations of the estate, for the irrigation system that extended as far as the Vaccarès pond by means of dense network of roubines,* but also for the desalinization of these lands, because in the Camargue planting has always suffered from the high concentrations of salt in the soil. The storage and pressurization of water were made possible thanks to the water tower, built in a neo-medieval style, which can be seen in the park. Drinking water was filtered by the Pasteur procedure.

*Roubine: (local term), canal dug or adapted for water drainage.

HERDSMAN'S HUT TO LET

• Patrick Biermann
13, avenue Riquette Aubanel, 13460 Les Saintes-Maries-de-la-Mer
• Tel: 04 90 49 67 67 et 06 20 78 25 35 • E-mail: pbie@wanadoo.fr
• http://www.maisondegardian.com • Rates: €700 to €1,180 for a week, according to season and number of persons . There are other cabanes de gardian [herdsman's huts] to let in the commune, so enquire at the local tourist office.

Home on the Provençal range

There are only a few authentic herdsman's huts available as seasonal lets. The location of this one, in front of the Plage des Saintes-Maries, and its authenticity, will soon make you a real Santois (inhabitant of Les Saintes-Maries).

A symbol of the traditional Camargues habitat, the herdsman hut is shaped like an inverted ship, the rounded side (the apse) facing towards the prevailing wind (mistral) and bearing an inclined cross; the main façade is gabled, and all of it is whitewashed with lime, windowless, beneath a steep reed roof. Originally, this precarious lodging was intended for herdsmen who moved with their herds as they grazed. Easy to build, consisting mainly of reeds tied in bundles that are called manons, these huts provided shelter from the rain and the wind. But in the Camargue, the wind is often extremely violent, which is why a cord ties the apse to a stake planted in the ground to hold down the structure. It is the apse, with its high vault, that served as a stable for the gardians, the famous mounted herdsmen of the Camargue. Today, these huts have become more like chaumières [cottages], some of them fairly luxurious. Windows have been opened up in walls, the space beneath the apse has been converted into a vast living room, or upstairs bedrooms have been added.

The cabane belonging to the Biermann family is ideally situated in the village of Les Saintes-Maries-de-la-Mer: Only a 3-minute walk from the centre, it sits on a tongue of land looking out at the beach to the south and L'Étang des Launes to the north. This neighbourhood, known as the "Pont du Mort", was reserved in the 1950s solely for these cabanes de gardian in order to preserve the village's traditional appearance, at a time when new buildings were springing up everywhere.

OFFICE DE TOURISME DES SAINTES-MARIES-DE-LA-MER
5, avenue Van-Gogh, BP 73, 13732 Les Saintes-Maries-de-la-Mer Cedex
• Tel: 04 90 97 82 55 • Fax: 04 90 97 71 15
• E-mail : info@saintesmaries.com • www.saintesmaries.com

It was Alphonse Daudet who best described how it feels being inside a cabane de gardian, in the evening, when the door has been closed: [How good it is when the wind / Knocks at the door with its horns / To be all alone in the hut / All alone like a house in Crau / And to see by the little hole / There, far away in the glassworts / The marshes of Giraud gleaming / And hear nothing but the wind / Knocking at the doors with its horns / Then from time to time the bells / Of the horses of La Tour de Brau.]

LA CROIX GARDIANE

• Avenue Riquette Aubanel, 13460 Les Saintes-Maries-de-la-Mer
From the tourist office, follow the seashore along avenue Van Gogh which then becomes avenue Théodore Aubanel and finally avenue Riquette Aubanel (in Provence, "Riquette" is a diminutive of the feminine first name Frédérique). When the avenue leaves the shore, take the path on the right of the big gate with the "Camarguais" sign. The path is protected from vehicle by four large boulders.

A "logo" invented by the Marquis de Baroncelli

Here's a tough question that may make locals hesitate for an instant: "Where is the original Croix Gardiane?" In principle, they should be able to answer in under 10 seconds, otherwise it might be a tourist you're asking ... Sometimes called the Croix de Camargue, it is everywhere, even on the roundabout of the Arles road at the entrance to the village of Les Saintes-Maries-de-la-Mer.

Folco de Baroncelli was born in 1869 to a noble Tuscan family that had emigrated to Provence in the 14th century. The young man's first contacts with the Gard manades,* then with Spanish bullfighting, and finally with the félibrige movement (founded by Frédéric Mistral and others), aroused in him a veritable passion for Provence, and more particularly for the Carmargue, and led him to invent this famous cross.

In 1895, he settled in Les Saintes-Maries-de-la-Mer and created the Manado Santenco herd. From then on, he actively sought to restore the full nobility of local customs in the Rhône delta. He codified the rules to Camargue-style bullfighting (in which the bulls are not put to death) and also instilled pride in the occupation of herdsman by founding Nacion Gardiano. It was no accident that he became friendly with members of the Sioux tribe who came to Europe as part of Buffalo Bill's circus. Indeed, he often compared the fate of Native Americans with that of the Gypsies, and even claimed to perceive a physical resemblance. It was this view of things that impelled him to make the Gypsies' procession a regular ceremony, which would take place each year on 24 May. Since his death, two days later, the Marquis is also honoured every 26 May by herdsmen, Gypsies and the Saintois, as the people of Les Saintes are known.

It is logical that the Marquis wanted to create a symbol to unite the Provençal people of the Camargue, "people of the earth, people of the sea, united by the heart". This symbol was the Croix Gardiane, whose forms signify faith with the cross, hope with the anchor, and charity with the heart. It was named Gardiane because the three points prolonging the arms of the Cross evoke the herdsman's trident. Created at the request of the Marquis by painter Hermann Paul, its first public representation was the one you can still see today on the Pont du Mort, although not indicated as such by any sign, and was executed in 1930 by Gédéon Blatière, a wrought-iron craftsman from the village of Le Cailar (Gard), where there has since been a boulevard Baroncelli. Three years later, he designed the nickel-plated trident that surmounts the flagpole of the Confrérie des Gardians [Herdsmen's Brotherhood].

*Manade: herd of bulls raised in the Camargue

SIGHTS NEARBY

MUSÉE BARONCELLI 

Musée Baroncelli - Rue Victor Hugo, 13460 Les Saintes-Maries-de-la-Mer • Tel: 04 90 97 87 60 • Days and opening hours are quite variable

Everything you've always wanted to know about the "Marquès" (Provençal for "Marquis"). We can't to go into further detail here about the incredible and extraordinary life of Folco de Baroncelli, but those of you who are curious can find out more about the character of this defender of the oppressed, tireless innovator, and lover of his region, of animals, of men and of … women. 2 km down the road towards Aigues-Mortes, at the point where his mas, Le Simbeu [The Symbol] once stood (since destroyed), you can see his grave, on the left between the new Le Simbeu mas and the landing stage of the Tiki III boat.

ROURE AND AMOUR

In 1904, Folco de Baroncelli glimpsed a young woman who would come to haunt his poems thereafter. He finally managed to meet her in Arles in 1908. Jeanne de Flandresy was 34, the widow of a Scottish count and the daughter of an archaeologist with whom she had written several books on the history of Provence. The passionate affair between them would only be interrupted by the death of the Marquis. Out of her love for him, she bought back the Palais du Roure, the Baroncelli family home in Avignon, which she transformed into a magnificent museum devoted to the culture of Provence and the Camargue, and which is visited today: Palais du Roure, Hôtel de Baroncelli-Javon, 3, rue Collège du Roure, 84000 Avignon, Tel: 04 90 80 80 88.

OFFICE DE TOURISME DES SAINTES-MARIES-DE-LA-MER
5, avenue Van-Gogh, BP 73, 13732 Les Saintes-Maries-de-la-Mer Cedex
• Tel: 04 90 97 82 55 • Fax: 04 90 97 71 15
• E-mail : info@saintesmaries.com • www.saintesmaries.com

THE FÉLIBRIGE MOVEMENT

Le Félibrige is an association whose purpose is to restore legitimacy to the Provençal language and maintain its traditions. It was founded on 21 May 1854 at Châteauneuf-de-Gadagne (Vaucluse), under the patronage of St Estelle, by seven young poets: Frédéric Mistral, Joseph Roumanille, Théodore Aubanel, Jean Brunet, Paul Giéra, Anselme Mathieu and Alphonse Tavan. The origins of the word félibre are threefold:

— Félibre comes from the Latin felibris meaning infant. Poets, through the ages, have been called "infants of the Muses".

— Félibre is also derived from the Greek felibos, or "friend of the beautiful".

— Lastly, félibre comes from the Provençal words fe and libre, that is, "free by faith".

NAVIS IN PELAGO
16
33

L'ÉGLISE ORTHODOXE DES SALINS

• The Orthodox Church of Salin-de-Giraud can only be visited by appointment.
Contact: Monsieur Démosthène Maillis: 04 42 86 83 31 - Madame Hélène Herrera: 04 42 86 82 78
• Mass is said there every other Sunday at 10.00 (on alternate Sundays, the Orthodox pope says Mass on the other side of the Rhône at Port-Saint-Louis-du-Rhône).

"Greek immigrant workers built their church in a former military shelter

In Salin-de-Giraud, a town created specifically for extracting salt, workers of all origins have lived together, including a particularly large Greek community that gathers today around an unlikely Orthodox church built in a former military shelter.

Salin-de-Giraud is a small town with a population of a little over 2,000 inhabitants, which depends administratively on the commune of Arles (40 km away) and is known above all for its production of sea salt.

Here the unusual is ever-present. Unusual and superb: the views of the Camargue from which the mounds of white salt emerge. Unusual and surprising: the town is divided into two entities, each of which revolves around a separate industrial giant: Solvay on one side and Salins du Midi (which replaced Pechiney) on the other. Also unusual is the housing, composed for the most part of dwellings built on the lines of the corons [mining villages] of northern France. Lastly, we can't talk about Les Salins (as the locals refer to their town) without mentioning the fact that it is almost completely cut off from the world after the last departure of the Barcarin ferry across the Rhône, in the evening.

To extract the salt over the years, workers have had to be found who will accept this difficult and exhausting labour. And so it has come to pass that Russian, Italian, Spanish, Armenian and Greek immigrants have all been recruited to work at Salin-de-Giraud, which in some respects has become their second country. The largest community represented is that of the Greeks, with some hundred families still living there. Many of them came to Les Salins from the island of Kalymnos in the Dodacanese archipelago close to the Turkish coast, just after the First World War, when it became obvious that they could no longer support themselves as sponge fishermen.

Soon, these Greek immigrants were integrated into the life of this original industrial town on the very doorstep of the Camargue. But as in the case of any immigrant community, they faced the problem of maintaining their ties with the mother country through the use of their language, the preservation of traditions and customs, and the practise of their religion. The majority of them being Orthodox Christians, they have managed to remain on good terms with the French Catholic authorities, but they had to wait a long time before they were able to gather together in a church they could call their own.

In 1939, faced with the imminent prospect of war, the French state decided to install a military powder factory at Salin-de-Giraud. Built by the Batignolles construction company to house workers, the shacks at this site were soon abandoned after the defeat in 1940, and this neighbourhood of Les Salins took on the name of Batignolles. After the war, the Greeks, now organized in the Communauté Orthodoxe Franco-Héllenique de Salin-de-Giraud, obtained one of these shacks for the purpose of converting it into a church. It was consecrated in 1952. From an architectural point of view, it could be said that this Orthodox church is unique in the world. And if the military look of its dome may seem surprising from the outside, inside it does prove well suited to religious uses. For many years now, the faithful have worked on a voluntary basis to improve the church and make it a place to remember their faraway island, with language classes, dance classes, and on the wall of the adjoining premises a map of Greece just like the ones found in Greek primary schools, so that the third-generation children don't forget the mother country.

SIGHTS NEARBY

SALT TRAIN

Tel: 04 42 86 71 80 • http://www.salins.com

This little salt train is the only means of going inside the private industrial property of Les Salins. Although miniature trains always seem to have a somewhat negative image, the one in Salin-de-Giraud actually recapitulates an unusual bit of heritage. In past summers a little train used to take workers to the beach, which was some distance from the town. The locomotive was supplied in turn by the two companies, Solvay and Pechiney. The workers at Les Salins du Midi still benefit today from exclusive access to an immense private beach. Rumours to the effect that you only need go to the corner bar to obtain the access card from one of the beneficiaries no longer have any basis in fact.

BARCARIN FERRY

http://www.camargue.com.fr/bacs/

How do you get to Salin-de Giraud, 6 km as the pink flamingo flies from Port-Saint-Louis-du-Rhône, given that there is no bridge over the Grand Rhône before Arles, 40 km away? Men have often defied the river, but not to the point of building a bridge on the unstable banks of this vast flowing mass of water. Therefore the only way to cross is by means of the Barcarin ferry, at a cost of 4.50 for a light vehicle such as a car. The ferry ride is in itself an unusual experience, one that young children will particularly enjoy. And when Barcarin 3 or Barcarin 4 "rev their engines" to get clear of the quay, you don't feel cheated as to their power (about 1,000 horsepower). The two Barcarin ferries pass by one another, and in a few seconds you find yourself on the other bank, almost regretting that the crossing was so short.

OFFICE DE TOURISME D'ARLES BP 21, 13633 Arles Cedex • Tel: 04 90 18 41 21 • Fax: 04 90 93 17 17 • E-mail : ot-arles@visitprovence.com • www.tourisme.ville-arles.fr	ACCUEIL DE SALIN-DE-GIRAUD Place des Gardians, 13129 Salin-de-Giraud From Easter to the end of October: Information at 04 42 86 89 77

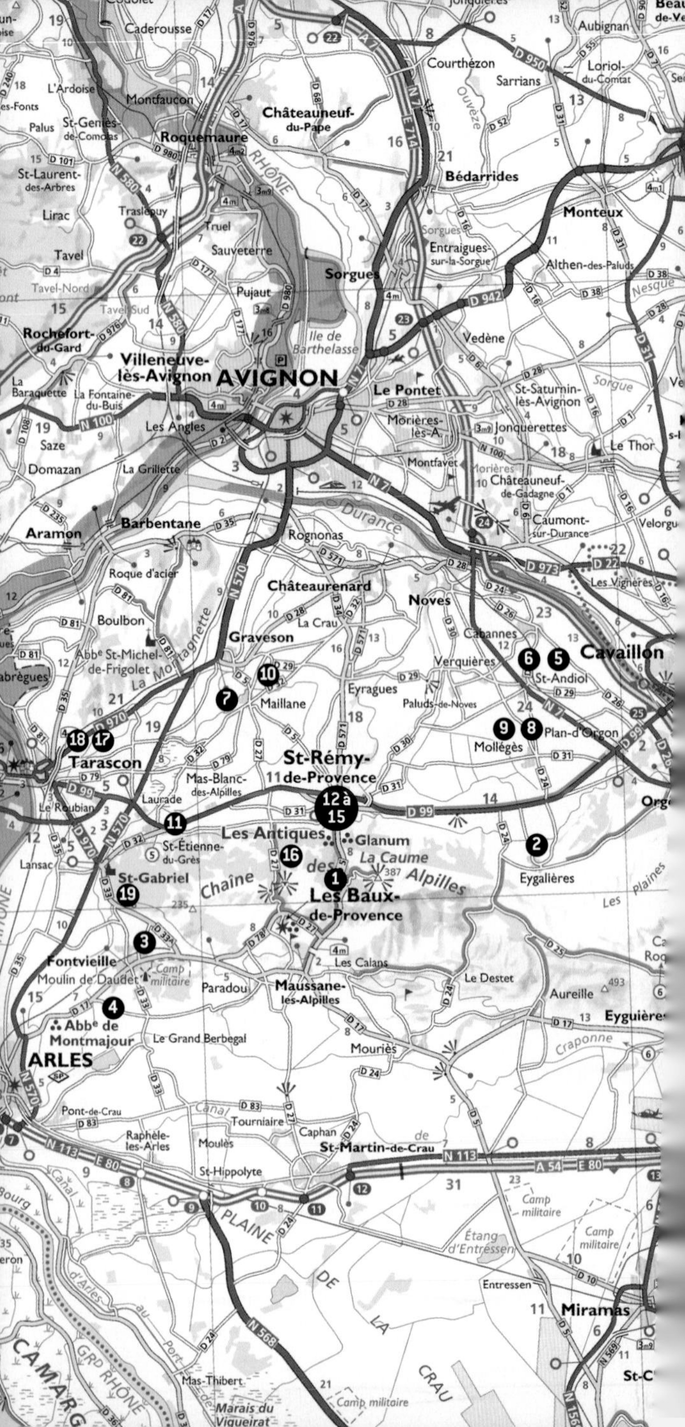

Caderousse
Courthézon
Aubignan
Loriol-du-Comtat
Sarrians
L'Ardoise
Montfaucon
Châteauneuf-du-Pape
St-Geniès-de-Comolas
Palus
Roquemaure
St-Laurent-des-Arbres
Bédarrides
Lirac
Traslepuy
Truel
Sauveterre
Monteux
Tavel
Entraigues-sur-la-Sorgue
Althen-des-Paluds
Sorgues
Pujaut
Tavel-Nord
Tavel Sud
Rochefort-du-Gard
Ile de Barthelasse
Vedène
Villeneuve-lès-Avignon
AVIGNON
Le Pontet
La Baraquette
La Fontaine-du-Buis
St-Saturnin-lès-Avignon
Les Angles
Morières-lès-A.
Jonquerettes
Saze
Le Thor
Domazan
La Grillette
Montfavet
Châteauneuf-de-Gadagne
Durance
Aramon
Barbentane
Rognonas
Caumont-sur-Durance
Velorgues
Roque d'acier
Châteaurenard
Les Vignères
Noves
Boulbon
La Crau
Graveson
Cabannes
Cavaillon
Abbe St-Michel-de-Frigolet
La Montagnette
Verquières
St-Andiol
Maillane
Eyragues
Paluds-de-Noves
Mollégès
Plan-d'Orgon
Tarascon
St-Rémy-de-Provence
Mas-Blanc-des-Alpilles
Laurade
Le Roubian
Les Antiques
Glanum
La Caume
St-Étienne-du-Grès
Lansac
St-Gabriel
Chaîne des Alpilles
Les Baux-de-Provence
Eygalières
Les Plaines
Fontvieille
Moulin de Daudet
Camp militaire
Paradou
Les Calans
Maussane-les-Alpilles
Le Destet
Aureille
Eyguières
Abbe de Montmajour
Le Grand Berbegal
Mouriès
Crapone
ARLES
Pont-de-Crau
Canal
Tourniaire
Caphan
Raphèle-les-Arles
Moulès
St-Martin-de-Crau
St-Hippolyte
PLAINE DE LA CRAU
Étang d'Entressen
Entressen
Miramas
CAMARGUE
GRD RHÔNE
Mas-Thibert
Marais du Vigueirat
Camp militaire
RHÔNE

ALPILLES

LES "TRÉMAÏÉ"

It's preferable to visit this site on foot after finding a parking space at Les Baux-de-Provence (not always easy, especially during the tourist season). From the esplanade Charles-de-Gaulle at the exit to the village near the car park, take the road on the right in the direction of the motorway. At the first bend, you'll see a dirt track on the right with a small sign indicating "Trémaïé". Follow this track until you reach the Chapelle des Saintes-Maries, the stele is just above. To reach the stele of the "Gaïé", continue along the track until you come across a wooden sign indicating the little path on the right, 250 m from the "Trémaïé".

The three Marys of Les Baux-de-Provence

The site of the "Trémaïé" lies in the small valley of Entreconques, directly below the cliffs of the village of Les Baux and consists of a stele carved in the rock representing three figures in Roman costume. Tradition has it that this is a portrait of the three Marys who landed at Les Saintes-Maries-de-la-Mer: Mary Magdalene, Mary Jacobe and Mary Salome. The name of the chapel below, Les Saintes-Maries, seems to support this hypothesis.

Some people favour another interpretation, according to which the three figures are instead the Roman general Marius, his wife Julia and his official "pythoness" (soothsayer), Martha. This Martha, not to be confused with the St Martha who arrived with the three Marys and later vanquished "La Tarasque" (a local monster), is said to have played an important part in the famous victory of Marius against the Teutones at the foot of Sainte-Victoire mountain. Born in the region and of Salyen (Celto-Ligurian) origin, Martha made herself indispensable to Marius due to her talents for sorcery, but above all, her physical attractions ... The least glorious, but most plausible explanation presents the three figures as the "photo" of a wealthy family of Les Baux who posed before the chisel of the portrait artist. A little further along the path, the other stele depicting the "Gaïé" completes the mysteries of this site, all the more so because the rock has eroded and makes it difficult to decipher the two figures in togas. The scene appears to represent an altar where a sacrifice is being celebrated: you can see a channel allowing blood to pour into bowls offered to the ancient divinities. Some illegible inscriptions may have revealed more, but the local people have always believed that it included the same Marius mentioned above and the name "Gaïé" is derived from his first name, "Caïus".

As for the experts, they claim that it is a funeral monument commissioned by a certain Montanus, to honour the memory of his parents.

AU HASARD BALTHAZAR

The lords of Les Baux were the masters of Provence for several centuries. "A race of eagles who were never vassals", as Frédéric Mistral wrote, they claimed to be descended from one of the three Magi, Balthazar, hence their motto, Au hasard Balthazar [Into peril, Balthazar]. And also their emblem, a star with 16 rays, symbolizing the star that pointed the three Magi in the direction of the grotto in Bethlehem.

THE ALCHEMIST'S GARDEN

❷

- Mas de la Brune, 13810 Eygalières • Tel: 04 90 90 67 67
- Fax: 04 90 95 99 21 • E-mail: contact@jardin-alchimiste.com
- http://www.jardin-alchimiste.com
- Admission: €5
- Guided tours for groups of eight or more, by appointment.

Open daily from 1 May to 3 October, 10.00–19.00

"Down the garden path to the Philosopher's Stone

Le Mas de la Brune, a rare vestige of Renaissance architecture in Provence, has become a bijou hotel of refined luxury. In the 1990s, having found out that the original builder of this house was in all likelihood a savant with similar pursuits to those of Nostradamus and Paracelsus, the present owners, Alain and Marie de Larouzière, created an astonishing "Alchemist's Garden", with the help of two landscape gardeners, Éric Ossart and Arnaud Maurières.

The garden visit is in three stages: the Chemin de Berechit, the Jardin Magique and the Jardin de l'Alchimiste, the latter also having three components: L'Oeuvre au Noir, L'Oeuvre au Blanc and L'Oeuvre au Rouge …

You first pass through a labyrinth of plants whose form, visible only from a bird's-eye view, spells Berechit, the first Hebrew word in the Bible, signifying origin or commencement (Genesis).

Then you enter the Jardin Magique, which presents the magical powers ascribed to plants by medieval popular belief. In contrast to these old prejudices, alchemy was the opposite of magic and sorcery.

Next you come to the Jardin de l'Alchimiste, organized according to the three great works in the alchemists' quest, ultimately leading to the Philosopher's Stone.

Your initiation starts with L'Oeuvre au Noir, which corresponds with the first age of life. Under the sign of Saturn, you follow a long tunnel of plants lined with basalt slabs stamped with the symbol for lead, ophiopogons (tubers) and aeoniums (cacti), to discover the slate basin, whose stagnant waters confirm that the dominant colour here is indeed black …

L'Oeuvre au Blanc reflects the period of intellectual and emotional development. The ruling celestial body in this section is the moon and the featured metal is unstable mercury. A progression through white "Fées des Neiges" roses, "Gauras" and "Miscantus" evokes the brief bedazzlement of the rational and reasonable. Finally, L'Oeuvre au Rouge represents the climax of the alchemical quest. This Red Garden is placed under the sign of the sun and of sulphur. Between the pomegranate trees, Bellegarde roses form 33 alignments around the double triangular basin in which 33 goldfish (in French, poissons rouges …) swim, the number 33 being that of universality.

As you leave the garden, you'll notice the handsome façade of the Mas de la Brune and its watchtower which protects the statue of a mermaid playing a lute. Beneath is a rather dire warning: Mortel vivant, pense et croy, que ta fin sera enfer ou paradis sans fin [Living mortal, think and believe, that your end will be eternal heaven or hell].

L'AUTEL DE LA COQUILLE

Carrière Romaine, RD17, 13900 Fontvieille

To visit l'Autel de la Coquille, leave the village of Fontvieille by the RD17 in the direction of Saint-Rémy and Les Baux-de-Provence. After 3 km, turn left onto the road leading to Les Baux-de-Provence. You'll pass the Carrières de Provence [quarries] on your right, then, 500 m further on, you should see a dirt track that goes off to the right between two stone walls. The start of this track has a great many "no entry", "one way" and "private property" signs. To park opposite, it's best to go further on and turn around, because traffic on this road is quite busy and fast-moving. Pedestrians on the dirt track are tolerated by the nearby owners. Finally, you should note that there is no sign indicating that this is the way to L'Autel de la Coquille ... but you'll find what you're looking for 200 m down the track on the right. Above all, don't forget that this track is private.

Birth of venus or trace of St James?

L'Autel de la Coquille is a sculpture in the form of a scallop shell, on the wall of the former stone quarry of Fontvieille, next to the quarry in use today.

Although the sculpture is not very big, it does arouse some emotion. First because you'll need to search awhile to find it, and then because of the symbolism it embodies.

It was the Romans, always great users of stone, who sculpted this altar and motif into the rock. It represented the pearly altar from which Venus arose at her birth, just as Botticelli painted her several centuries later. Originally, there was a votive dedication engraved on the altar, accompanied on the left by the image of a bull being led to sacrifice. The monument is said to have been dedicated to a local divinity associated with water.

Later, when pilgrims on their way to Santiago de Compostela took this route, they halted here for a moment of prayer before what they believed to be a Christian oratory. It was indicated as part of the pilgrimage route and presented as an emblem of St James, another of the many instances where Christianity cleverly integrated traces of previous pagan faiths.

Finally, the people of Provence have a third interpretation, according to which the pecten [scallop shell] represents fertility linked with the worship of water spirits.

OFFICE DE TOURISME DE FONTVIEILLE
Rue Marcel-Honorat, 13900 Fontvieille • Tel: 04 90 54 67 49
• Fax: 04 90 54 69 82 • e-mail : ot.fontvieille@visitprovence.com
• www.fontvieille-provence.com

THE HYPOGEA OF MONT DES CORDES 

- Restaurant le Parc des Cordes
Route d'Arles, RD17, 13990 Fontvieille
- Tel: 04 90 54 67 85 – 06 18 03 17 23
- Musée de l'Arles et de la Provence Antiques
Presqu'île du Cirque Romain, BP 205, 13635 Arles Cedex
- Tel: 04 90 18 88 88 • Fax: 04 90 18 88 93• E-mail: info.mapa@cg13.fr
- http://www.arles-antique.cg13.fr

Secret sacred tombs

A hypogeum is an excavation dug by man, usually for a tomb. The expression allée couverte (a series of dolmens arranged to form a covered walkway) is often employed, because although the tomb is a corridor dug in the rock, the ceiling is constituted by megalithic stone slabs. The most spectacular collection of hypogea in Provence are those found near Fontvieille. One of them, L'Hypogée du Castelet, is on public land and very easy to visit because it lies at the side of the RD17 as you leave Fontvieille in the direction of Arles. It is small and not very prepossessing, but nevertheless moving.

You can visit two more hypogea on private property by having lunch or dinner at the Parc des Cordes, where the Hypogées de Bounias and de la Source await you. The restaurant in the countryside serves (outside on the terrace when weather permits) traditional local cuisine using fresh produce from the market (at Arles) and meat grilled on a wood fire. Access to other hypogea in the area is restricted due to the lack of security systems.

There are several hypotheses as to the date of their excavation and the identity of the people buried in them. In 1835, Prosper Mérimée claimed that they were the work of a prehistoric civilization. These covered walkways might be several thousand years old (5000 BC), and if more recent objects were recovered within them, it would be because the hypogea were later re-used by other peoples. In 1866, a son of the Bounias family who was ferreting for rabbits* on the Plateau du Castelet, stumbled across another tomb, which relaunched speculation concerning their age. The Musée de l'Arles et de la Provence Antiques presents in its first room a model of L'Hypogée des Fées discovered on Mont des Cordes, as well as a display case with objects found in the course of archaeological digs in the Fontvieille hypogea.

*Ferreting [chasse au furet]: The ferret is a carnivorous mustelid mammal (Mustela putorius furo), an albino or semi-albino variety of the polecat originating from North Africa, raised and trained for hunting. The hunter sends it into rabbit burrows to drive out the occupants.

ACCESS
To reach the hypogées (hypogea, or underground chambers) leave the village of Fontvieille by the RD17 in the direction of Arles. Once you see L'Abbaye de Montmajour, watch for a small brown sign on the right that reads "L'Hypogée du Castelet". There is a car park just beyond it. The two other accessible hypogea are on the property of the Parc des Cordes restaurant. This is close by L'Hypogée du Castelet, but on the opposite side of the road, on the left driving towards Arles. Enquire at the restaurant about visiting them.

SAINT-VINCENT CHURCH

• Place de l'Abbé Fernand Singerlé, 13670 Saint-Andiol

The church, was fortified against attacks by mercenaries

The village of Saint-Andiol is on the RN7, near Cavaillon. Its name is that of one of the saints who evangelized Provence and was martyred by the Roman emperor Septimius Severus. It would be shame not to make a short stop there to admire the church, a rare example of a fortified church and a faithful copy (only smaller in size) of the one in Les Saintes-Maries-de-la-Mer.

It was around the 10th century that the monks of the powerful abbey of Saint-Victor in Marseille came to drain the marshes here, and then erected the church in the 12th century.

It was fortified in the 14th century to protect it from attacks by mercenaries who, left unemployed by the peace treaty of Bretigny in 1360, devastated and pillaged everything in their passage. Hence this surprising architecture, including crenellations, machicolations and a covered way, lying on top of a Roman sanctuary. Inside, the Gothic tabernacle (ciborium) alone, dating from the 15th century, 4 m high and in the form of a tower, is enough to justify a visit.

TO VISIT, ENQUIRE AT THE OFFICE DE TOURISME DE SAINT-ANDIOL
Lotissement Lou Mistraù - avenue Alphonse-Daudet, 13670 Saint-Andiol
• Tel: 04 90 95 48 95 • Fax: 04 32 61 08 79
• e-mail : saint-andiol-tourisme@wanadoo.fr • www.saint-andiol.fr

SIGHTS NEARBY

HOME OF JEAN MOULIN 6

Along the RN7 as it runs through Saint-Andiol, the family home of the Resistance hero Jean Moulin bears a discreet commemorative plaque. Although born in Béziers, Moulin was baptized in the village church and took refuge here following his first arrest by the Nazis in 1940. In fact, the Jean Moulin route, called "Chemin de la Liberté", starts off from Saint-Andiol. It then passes through Eygalières, where you find the Bergerie [sheepfold] de la Lèque, a shelter used by Moulin when he parachuted into France on 1 January 1942, and ends at the Jean Moulin memorial on the RN538 as it enters Salon-de-Provence from the north.

MUSÉE FRÉDÉRIC MISTRAL

11, rue Lamartine, 13910 Maillane
• Tel: 04 90 95 74 06 (Syndicat d'Initiative)
Open April to September, 9.30–11.30 and 14.00–18.30; October to March, 10.00–11.30 and 14.00–16.30. Closed Mondays and public holidays

Frédéric Mistral, friend of Buffalo Bill?

In the office of the museum-home of Frédéric Mistral, a cushion on one of the armchairs may attract your attention. Made from beige leather and roughly sewn, it bears the portrait of a face. This "cushion of life" belonged to the Native American chief, Silver Eagle, who passed through Les Alpilles during the Buffalo Bill circus tour of France at the start of the 20th century.

How did this cushion end up here? Nobody seems to know. According to Native American custom, such cushions are passed down to the owner's descendants. What we do know, on the other hand, is that when the "Wild West Show" of William F. Cody, alias Buffalo Bill, came to Nîmes and Marseille, the Marquis Folco de Baroncelli became enamoured with the persecuted native peoples of North America and twisted the history of civilizations in order to make them cousins of the Gypsies. Note that during its second French tour of 1905–06 (the first took place in 1890), the circus left behind one of the Native American troupe members, Charging Elk, due to illness. Penniless, he dragged himself around the city of Marseille, from alleyways to hospitals, unable to speak a word of French, until his lonely death in a foreign land. His sad story is told poignantly in a novel by James Welch, The Heartsong of Charging Elk.

As for the cushion, we won't say more than we know, which is practically nothing. There's another pleasant tale to be told, even if it's not necessarily entirely true: when Buffalo Bill visited Maillane, it seems that he "forgot" his dog, or according to other sources, gave it to Mistral. The latter, who did not want to be encumbered with an animal, domesticated or otherwise, was vexed. But when he went to pay his respects at the family tomb in the village cemetery, the mutt preceded him and promptly lay down on the marble slab of his ancestors … Touched by this, he adopted him under the name of Moun chin (my dog).

FRÉDÉRIC MISTRAL (1830–1914)

Born at Maillane in Les Alpilles, Frédéric Mistral is considered to be Provence's greatest poet. He published his first major poem, Mireille, in 1859. Dubbed the "new Homer" by Lamartine, he devoted himself to the cause of the Provençal tongue, regarded at the time as a lowly patois, and along with six other poets he founded the Félibrige literary movement (see page 182).
He received the Nobel Prize in 1904.

THE GUEST ROOMS OF L'AMPHITHÉÂTRE 8

• Avenue du Comtât, 13940 Mollégès • Tel: 04 90 95 42 45
• Rooms from €47–€52, breakfast included.

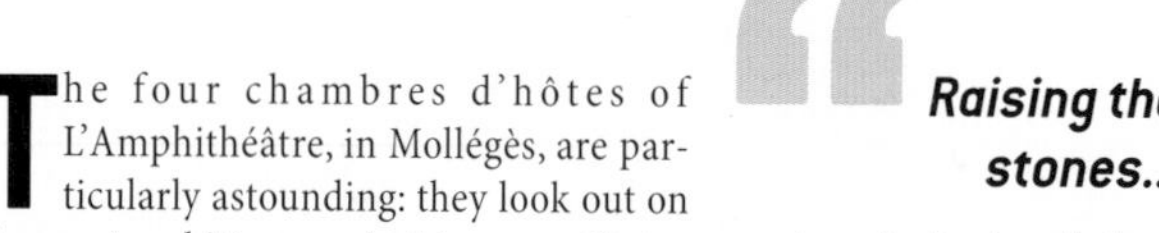

Raising the stones...

The four chambres d'hôtes of L'Amphithéâtre, in Mollégès, are particularly astounding: they look out on the most ambitious project to reconstitute an ancient site in the whole of Provence.

Jean Vargas, a retired museum guard, kept watch over the exhibits at the Louvre and the archaeological site of Glanum until his visual acuity fell to 1% in each eye. Practically blind, he has continued to sculpt "by touch" and through the eyes of his wife, Marie. He has produced 583 pieces in all, including his masterpiece, a copy he made of the "Paysan Cavare", a statue representing a peasant from the Cavaillon found in the vicinity and now on display at the Louvre.

In addition to his sculptures, the astonishing Jean Vargas is an original character: he decided to embark on nothing less than the reconstruction of a theatre, amphitheatre and arena from ancient times. As he must fit all this on the same site, he is quite simply inventing a Latinized version of an all-purpose sports stadium. His planning timetable is also very tight. In 2005, he inaugurated the bas-relief of a Roman bullfight known as the jeu crétois [Cretan game]. In 2006, he intends to build the bull pen, and in 2007, a Gaulish tavern. Each inauguration is scheduled for the first Sunday of June and is the occasion for drinking, a concert and general partying.

If you've the slightest desire to learn more about sculpture, there's no better way than to rent a room or two at L'Amphithéâtre.

THE DRAUGHT HORSE OF MOLLÉGÈS 9

• Place du Lavoir, 13940 Mollégès
The website of Micheline and Jacques Bersia, which presents the village:
• http://perso.wanadoo.fr/papijaque/
The "horse" monument is signposted

"In the rock, sculpted, I, here, bear witness"

It was at the end of the 1980s that Claude Parraud and several other inhabitants of Mollégès (the "s" at the end is pronounced) decided that they should give a more visible identity to their village, which until then had never been described, or even mentioned, in the main tourist guidebooks.

On reflection, it occurred to them that the draught horse, who was in a sense the "king" of the village fête of St Eloi, deserved to be remembered for posterity, especially since horses were no longer used much for pulling loads, the motorized power of the tractor having replaced horse and bag of oats.

On 7 May 1989, the monument, which is now a source of village pride, was inaugurated. The horse was carved from a single block of stone from the Oppède quarry by Camille Soccorsi, a Tarascon sculptor who is well known for the two bulls that have made the reputation of Beaucaire (a rival town to Tarascon in the Gard département): Clairon and Goya.

The lines inscribed on the statue's pedestal were borrowed from the work of the Provençal poet, Charles Galtier:
[We cannot guess what tomorrow will bring / And so that in future we can still be sure / Of the happiness that binds man and horse, / In the rock, sculpted, I, here, bear witness.]

SIGHTS NEARBY

BOURRELLERIE FATTORE 

Rue de la Poste, 13690 Graveson • Tel: 04 90 95 72 55

In the village of Graveson, an unlikely boutique perpetuates a tradition that has become rare in these times.

Born in Graveson, Louis Fattore became a bourrelier-harnacheur [harness-maker]. If in the rest of France the term is usually bourrelier-sellier, in Provence they prefer the word harnacheur. The main thing is not to get his profession mixed up with that of a bourrelier-matelassier [saddler] if you want him to have a chat with you.

His workshop is to be found in rue de la Poste right in the centre of the village. Above the shop window the legend reads: ancienne maison Coeur fondée en 1870 [former Coeur house founded in 1870].

Louis Fattore makes, to measure and by hand, everything you need to equip a team of horses, either horses pulling carriages or draught horses, now only used during occasions such as the feast of St Eloi.

THE PILGRIMAGE TO NOTRE-DAME-DU-CHÂTEAU 

Avenue Notre-Dame-du-Château, 13103 Saint-Étienne-du-Grès
Saint-Étienne-du-Grès is a small village with a little over 2,000 inhabitants, 7 km to the east of Tarascon. To reach the Notre-Dame-du-Château chapel, leave the village to the west, and at the fork in front of the town hall, be sure not to take the RD99 towards Saint-Rémy, but the little unclassified road to the right. A sign indicates that this road is narrow and some handsome dwellings can be glimpsed behind gates and beneath shady trees. About 3 km further on, you can park on the left side of the road, opposite the entrance to the Château Dalmeran, a wine-growing domaine that produces an AOC (appellation d'origine contrôlée) Baux-de-Provence. The route is signposted, to the right of the road, and you should expect a good quarter hour's climb up to the chapel.

An Alpine Virgin in Les Alpilles

The Notre-Dame-du-Château chapel of Saint-Étienne-du-Grès is the centre of the extraordinary veneration surrounding the "Belle Briançonne".

In 1346, the inhabitants of Briançon (Hautes-Alpes), decided to ask the patron saint of Tarascon, St Martha, to intercede in their favour by driving from their territory the terrible threat of the Black Death, or plague. Famous for having vanquished the dragon/monster/crocodile, justly named "La Tarasque", St Martha seemed powerful enough to meet this challenge. The outcome of her intervention proved successful and, the plague having relinquished its grip, the people of Briançon sent a delegation to Tarascon to thank the saint in person. To show their fervour, they took with them a wooden statue of the Virgin from one of their chapels.

Once their mission was accomplished, they returned home and put the statue of the Virgin back in her place. But when the neighbouring Vaudois later invaded their territory, the hermit Imbert, who guarded the statue, took the initiative of placing her in safety at Tarascon, where she had already stayed briefly. This explains her presence today in the Notre-Dame-du-Château chapel in Saint-Étienne-du-Grès.

Each year, the pilgrimage to Notre-Dame-du-Château takes place on the first day of Rogations (the Sunday before Ascension). In fact the date has become somewhat confused in modern times, but the principle remains the same: the statue is transported from Notre-Dame-du-Château chapel to Tarascon where she is placed in a niche at the porte Saint-Jean, long enough for the bearers to rest for a few hours before taking her to the Collégiale Sainte-Marthe church. She stays there for 40 days and her costume is changed daily.

Even if the celebration originates from a legend that no one can verify, the walk to Notre-Dame-du-Château is very pleasant. Along the way, you cross a stream by an ancient bridge, and on the left of the path there are steps cut into the rock leading to a troglodyte dwelling. From the chapel you have a very fine view of La Montagnette (the mount on which stands the abbey of Saint-Michel-de-Frigolet), of Tarascon, and of the whole area of Les Alpilles.

HÔTEL LES ATELIERS DE L'IMAGE

• 36, boulevard Victor Hugo, 13210 Saint-Rémy-de-Provence
• Tel: 04 90 92 06 14 • Fax: 04 90 92 56 54
• E-mail: info@hotelphoto.com • http://www.hotelphoto.com
• Price of rooms: from €155–€380.
Hut €240–€600, depending on the season

A hotel room in 4-star treehut

Les Ateliers de l'Image is a superb and particularly original hotel: installed in a former cinema on the boulevard Victor Hugo that encircles Saint-Rémy's ancient ramparts, it also boasts a magnificent room in a hut.

This hut is the extension of a 45m2 suite equipped with a Bang & Olufsen hi-fi system, linked by way of a impressive drawbridge. Once this is raised, the hut is completely isolated from the outside world. Ideal for a honeymoon, or even a farewell weekend ...

SIGHTS NEARBY

HÔTEL GOUNOD VILLE VERTE ⓭

Place de la République, 13210 Saint-Rémy-de-Provence
• Tel: 04 90 92 06 14 • Fax: 04 90 92 56 54
• E-mail: contact@hotel-gounod.com • http://www.hotel-gounod.com/
Suite No. 24 (Gounod Room) €165–€215, depending on the season.
Other rooms from €80.

Frédéric Mistral's masterpiece, Mireille, was first published in 1859. Although Mireille is now a common first name in Provence (and elsewhere in France), it was in fact invented by Mistral. It's difficult to imagine just how big an impact this poem had at the time.

Charles Gounod became interested in the work and started to prepare a lyrical version in 1863. He came to Maillane to pay a visit to Mistral and then stayed in Saint-Rémy-de-Provence, at the Hôtel Ville Verte, in order to imbibe the atmosphere of Provence for a couple of months (from March to May 1863). He took up residence in room No. 24 (now a suite), whose windows overlooked the Collégiale Saint-Martin church. A plaque in memory of the composer's stay here is affixed to the hotel façade. Founded in 1660, the establishment is today a hotel with quiet charm, with rooms named after arias from the opera Mireille.

LES “TOURS DE FORCE”

• Roundabout at the end of avenue Frédéric Mistral
Leave Saint-Rémy in the direction of Maillane by avenue Frédéric Mistral (Maillane is the birthplace of the Provençal poet). The flour mill is on the right just before the first roundabout, and the first of the three “Tours de Force” faces this same roundabout.

Towers of Power

A medieval keep? An Eiffel Tower in concrete? Located on the edge of an ordinary roundabout, the Saint-Jean tower surprises the passing motorist with its rusty wheel, which seems to be immobilized, on the top.

It is in fact one of three towers whose purpose was to transmit the power of the turbines from one mill to another.

Between 1868 and 1887, the Mistral Frères company, owner of four wheat-flour mills along the Réal canal, embarked on a programme to modernize and mechanize its equipment. The company installed turbines in its Saint-Bernard and Saint-Jean mills to replace the traditional paddle-wheels, with the idea of coupling the turbines in these two mills. Therefore three towers were built to support a cable transmitting power from one mill to the other. The 15 horse-power thus transferred boosted the power of the Saint-Jean mill to 36 horse-power.

The idea was sound, but as was often the case failed to consider the bigger picture. The Camargue turned out to be very poor ground for growing wheat, notably because of the high concentrations of salt in the fields. The Mistral brothers soon faced financial ruin and the mills, not profitable enough, were finally closed down in 1910.

PARKING IN SAINT-RÉMY

As anyone who has approached Saint-Rémy during the tourist season already knows, the whole area surrounding the old town centre (partly pedestrianized) is invaded by traffic and parking is expensive (€1 per hour). But there is a very economical way to park your car in Saint-Rémy: you just need to procure a parking disk from the municipal police. The police station is very easy to find, it’s right next door to the tourist office building. For the price of 1, you simply attach the disk behind your windscreen, while respecting the parking duration. But watch out, while you’re inside the police station getting your disk, your car will be in the tourist office’s paying car park ...

OFFICE DE TOURISME DE SAINT-RÉMY-DE-PROVENCE
Place Jean-Jaurès, 13210 Saint-Rémy-de-Provence • Tel: 04 90 92 05 22
• Fax: 04 90 92 38 52 • www.saintremy-de-provence.com

MAS DE LA PYRAMIDE

• Chemin des Carrières, 13210 Saint-Rémy-de-Provence
• Tel: 04 90 92 00 81
• Admission: €4, Meal: €20
Open daily, 9.00–12.00 and 14.00–17.00 (19.00 in summer)
The Mas de la Pyramide is signposted from the RD5 which links Saint-Rémy to Les Baux-de-Provence. As you leave Saint-Rémy, turn left opposite Les Antiques and go around the Saint-Paul de Mausole monastery.

"The family that lives in a Roman quarry

You don't just visit the Mas de la Pyramide, you go to see Lolo Mauron, the owner of the place. It's a truly magical spot, situated in a steep-sided valley around the remains of a Roman quarry that was mined during four centuries and whose stones served to build Glanum (see box below). The troglodyte mas [house] at this site has been preserved in its original state by Lolo Mauron.

Today you'll discover in this surprising habitation all the ingenious arrangements that allowed people to live here comfortably in Roman times: "central heating", running water, and hollows in the stone for attaching slaves …

The Mauron family has lived here for generations since first arriving from Marseille in 1609. They raised up to 150 sheep that were kept in an underground sheepfold where the family also grew champignons de Paris for 10 years.

Visiting this place is very moving because, beyond its absolute strangeness, you find yourself witness to a family saga on display in the ancestral portrait gallery. On the house façade, you'll see an iron plaque from La Confiance, an insurance company that affixed this plaque when the contract was signed only to remove it again if the client failed to keep up premiums. Hence the shotgun pellets that have turned it into a sieve, a way of discouraging over-keen insurance agents …

Other than a tour of the place, Lolo Mauron also offers meals at the farm for €20. It is by far the best address in Saint-Rémy.

The symbol of the quarry, to which the mas owes its name of "Pyramide", is a stone column that emerges in an incongruous manner from the grass in the middle of the valley, reaching a height of 20 m. The column testifies to the depth of the quarry, left there to measure how far the men had dug into the rock. It probably also served as the observation post of the Roman sentinels at the quarry, making sure the slave labourers kept busy.

GLANUM

Glanum was a very important ancient site, but until 1921 the only known parts of it were the two famous Roman monuments still standing in Saint-Rémy-de-Provence: the mausoleum and the municipal arch, which are together referred to as "Les Antiques". The archaeological digs undertaken in the first half of the 20th century, however, uncovered a vast city. Temples, houses, the forum and the baths make up a unique ensemble of remains dating from the Roman occupation.

LES "VERDINES" DU MAS DES FIGUES 

• Mas des Figues
Vieux chemin d'Arles, 13210 Saint-Rémy-de-Provence
• Information and reservations, Monday to Friday, 9.00–19.00
• Tel: 04 75 41 55 96 / 06 08 42 77 76 • Fax: 04 75 40 81 30
• E-mail: info@provencehotel.fr
• http://figues.hotels-en-provence.com
€75–€135 per night in caravan, according to season
Leave Saint-Rémy-de-Provence in the direction of Arles and Tarascon. After the Intermarché petrol station, drive for 3 km until you see a sign indicating "Les Baux". Turn left onto the RD27 and drive 1.5 km. At the second crossroads, turn right onto the old Arles road and drive 500 m further to reach the Mas des Figues.

Sleep in a Gypsy caravan

These are historic horse-drawn Gypsy caravans, just like the ones that "travellers" used in the past during their peregrinations. They come from Romania, are made from painted wood and are known as verdines in French because of their largely green colour. Inside two adjoining caravans, you'll find such mod cons as air conditioning and a mini-bar, although no phone or TV … it's your choice.

Each caravan has a name, one Sara and the other Salome, an allusion to Mary Salome who was the mother of the apostles James and John. As for Sara, she is also a saint venerated by Gypsies who is the object of their famous pilgrimage each year on 24 May to Les Saintes-Maries-de-la-Mer.

After having had their fill of the thrills of modern living and the "joys" of consumer society, Philippe and Anne-Marie Michelot decided on a change of pace. The Mas des Figues represents their new existential choice, which they share with their guests. It's a return to basics and the term "farm inn" is not a cliché in this case, it really is a farm, without "celebrities", but with animals, vegetables and a natural rhythm of life. They have just received the official stamp of approval as a Ferme Auberge from the Chamber of Agriculture of Bouches-du-Rhône.

OTHER CARAVANS TO LET IN PROVENCE

LES ROULOTTES DU MAS DOU PASTRE (SEE OPPOSITE)
Hôtel le Mas dou Pastre, Quartier Saint-Sixte, 13810 Eygalières
Tel: 04 90 95 92 61 • Fax: 04 90 90 61 75
• E-mail: contact@masdupastre.com • http://www.masdupastre.com
Caravan rates: small caravan: €70 per night , La Romantique: €105 per night, La Manouche: €105 per night
Leave Eygalières in the direction of Orgon, the Mas dou Pastre is less than 1 km on the left, opposite the Chapelle Saint-Sixte on the right.
The Hôtel le Mas dou Pastre is a charming place surrounded by olive trees, cypresses and lavender, in one of those much sought-after landscapes of Les Alpilles. In addition to the classic hospitality of its hotel, this mas also makes available three old caravans with all mod cons.

GUEST ROOMS AT THE HÔTEL DE MOLIÉRES 17

Y. and Y. Jumeau, 7, rue du Progrès, 13150 Tarascon
• Tel/Fax: 04 90 43 52 52 • E-mail: y.jumeau@wanadoo.fr
• http://www.chambres-tarascon.com
• Antiques stay (three days and two nights): €215 per person in a double room

"Luxury accommodation and an introduction to the antiques trade

In Tarascon, a couple who run an antiques business propose to enliven your stay in their guest rooms in a very beautiful private townhouse dating from the 17th and 18th centuries, by an introduction to the antiques trade.

This stay is by no means intended to give you "training" in this profession in just three days. It simply provides an overview with commentary on furniture in the principal styles, from the 17th to the 19th centuries, both in Tarascon itself and at L'Isle-sur-la-Sorgue, 30 km away, France's antiques capital after Paris.

In addition to antiques, several other related topics are proposed by Monsieur and Madame Jumeau: the art of decorative painting (imitation marble, ornamentation, false mouldings and patinas), the art of gilding with gold leaf, and lastly, the restoration of gilded wood.

You have to have visited the Hôtel de Molières to understand what staying in this place really means. The private dwelling of the Clerc de Molières family who founded the first Mont de Piété (a French charitable institution) and the Tarascon hospital, this building was conscientiously restored several years ago and today is revealed in all its splendour. It boasts a superb staircase, an inner courtyard full of charm, an outer courtyard laid out as a medieval garden, a library, authentic decorative woodwork and painted ceilings. The rooms are spacious and can be combined to sleep large families. But when it comes to the bathrooms, there's an abrupt change of century: the plumbing was designed by Philippe Starck.

SIGHTS NEARBY

THE COLLÉGIALE SAINTE-MARTHE CHURCH 18

Situated just opposite the Hôtel de Molières, the Collégiale Sainte-Marthe church was first erected in the 10th century and then rebuilt in the 12th century once the body of the saint was discovered. Unfortunately, the sarcophagus today lies empty. Martha, who came to Provence from Palestine in the boat without oars or sails that carried the other saints (Mary Magdalene, Mary Jacobe, Mary Salome, etc.), would go on to convert the inhabitants of the region to Christianity. She was called upon to drive out a monstrous animal that was terrorizing the neighbourhood: "La Tarasque". Martha first paralysed it with holy water, then forced the beast to look upon the cross, and immobilized it with her belt. The people of the town that would later become Tarascon finished the job.

SAINT-GABRIEL CHAPEL AND TOWER

• 5 km south of Tarascon on the RD32
The leaning house serves as a landmark. There is a car park in front of the chapel. Access to the tower is restricted in summer. Enquire at the tourist office in Tarascon.

Boatmen, bags, and embossed stones

Near Tarascon, an 11th-century chapel is worth a visit, not to mention the hidden curiosity at this sight, a monumental tower built with very large embossed stones.

La Chapelle Saint-Gabriel stands on the site of the ancient town of Ernaginum, along the Via Aurelia at the point where it entered marshlands. It was there were goods were transferred onto wooden rafts, supported by inflated goatskin bags and guided by utriculaires (from the Latin uter, meaning "bag"), boatmen specializing in the art of navigating shallow, marshy waters.

But the draining of the marshes led to the disappearance of this town, leaving only two traces of its existence.

The chapel, built in the 12th century in Romanesque style, possesses a superb façade oriented towards the setting sun. Two scenes are represented on the tympanum: "Daniel and the Lions" and "Adam and Eve", who have just succumbed to sin.

By lining yourself up with the chapel apse, you'll find the narrow path that climbs for several minutes. A great surprise waits at the end: the tower, some 10 m wide and 20 m high, is truly impressive. It dates perhaps from the same period as the chapel (late 12th century), but curiously is not indicated by any sign nor mentioned in any guidebook.

Henri-Paul Eydoux (in his work, Monuments méconnus, *Provence*, Éditions Perrin) quotes Prosper Mérimée who visited Saint-Gabriel and included the following description in his *Notes d'un voyage dans le Midi de la France* in 1835: *"At the top of the hill behind the church, there rises a tall, square tower, built with large embossed stones. Two other square towers of smaller girth, today almost completely in ruins, were placed on either side of the main tower and about 50 feet in front of it. The crenellations of the main tower have been destroyed or perhaps never existed."*

The most spectacular feature of this tower is the great care with which the stone-cutters created the embossed surfaces of these stones and aligned them. As Henri-Paul Eydoux remarks, the joints are so fine that no plant or weed, so frequently found in ruins, has grown between the stones.

When you leave Saint-Gabriel, don't forget to take a picture of the leaning house at the crossroads, which was once a restaurant.

OFFICE DE TOURISME DE TARASCON
59, rue des Halles, 13150 Tarascon • Tel: 04 90 91 03 52 • Fax: 04 90 91 22 96
• e-mail : tourisme@tarascon.org • www.tarascon.org

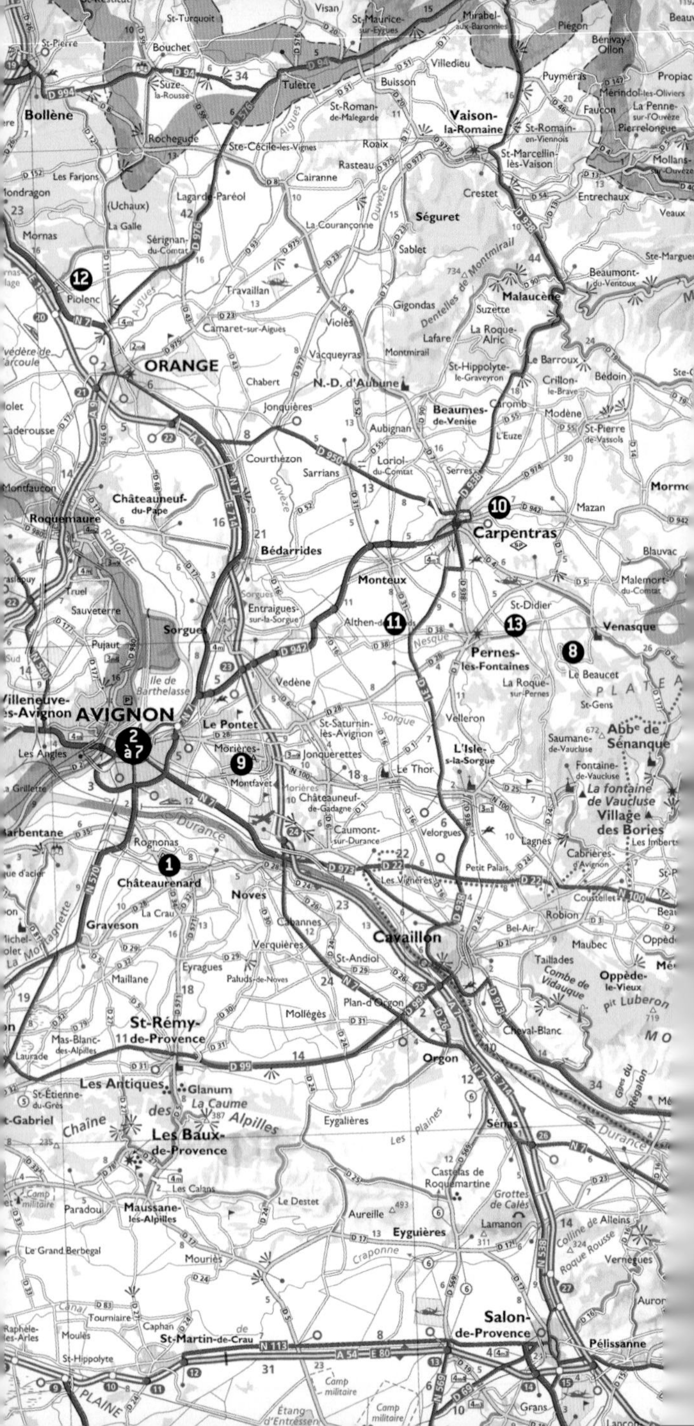

Bollène
Orange
Vaison-la-Romaine
Séguret
Gigondas
Malaucène
Carpentras
Châteauneuf-du-Pape
Bédarrides
Monteux
Pernes-les-Fontaines
Venasque
Avignon
Villeneuve-lès-Avignon
Le Pontet
L'Isle-sur-la-Sorgue
Abbe de Sénanque
La fontaine de Vaucluse
Village des Bories
Châteaurenard
Noves
Cavaillon
St-Rémy-de-Provence
Les Antiques
Glanum
Les Baux-de-Provence
Chaîne des Alpilles
Maussane-les-Alpilles
Eyguières
Salon-de-Provence
Orgon
Sorgues
Pélissanne
St-Martin-de-Crau

AVIGNON REGION AND COMTAT-VENAISSIN

MARCHÉ D'INTÉRÊT NATIONAL DE CHÂTEAURENARD 

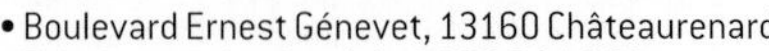

• Boulevard Ernest Génevet, 13160 Châteaurenard
• Telephone to book a visit: 04 90 94 14 90
• Open 6.30–7.30 from Monday to Saturday

> "*Europe's biggest open trading market for fruit and vegetables*"

Your first thought might be that a visit to the Châteaurenard "Market of National Interest" (MIN) isn't really a traditional tourist activity: the market is held early in the morning between 6.30 and 7.30. No good arriving at 7.45 then, there won't be a thing left to see. On the other hand, by ringing for details and turning up well before 6.30, you can take part in this immutable and amazing ceremony that helps shift a lettuce from a peasant's truck onto your plate.

Watch out though, this is a wholesale market not a farmers' market. You can't buy anything, but there's no harm in taking a basket along: sometimes produce falls to the ground …

In the small hours, vehicles loaded with fruit and vegetables arrive to take up their places in what looks like the parking space of a supermarket. These are the peasant farmers who come here to sell their produce. Behind the barriers the buyers, wholesale dealers and distributors chat while waiting for opening time. At 6.30 precisely, a wartime siren opens the trading. Then everything happens at once. It all goes very quickly and there is every likelihood that you won't see much: these are private deals in which the price is negotiated individually with no limits other than the law of supply and demand. The most impressive thing about it is the closing of a deal: no paper or banknotes are exchanged, only glances, head movements and incomprehensible gestures seal the contracts, everyone subscribes to the idea that your word is your bond …

As for the buyers, they have to rush down the alleys to be the first to unearth a bargain, or a magnificent load of early produce which already has a buyer.

At the close of the market you sometimes see a few trucks taking their load away again. When the market is closed and people get talking, you can learn so much more about the crisis in farming than at any number of election meetings …

300,000 tons of fruit and vegetables pass through MIN each year. You'll need to be very careful as there is a constant flow of cars, trucks and huge lorries in a zone where the highway code is sometimes put aside as soon as the market starts.

OFFICE DE TOURISME DE CHÂTEAURENARD
11, cours Carnot, BP 129, 13838 Châteaurenard • Tel: 04 90 24 25 50
• Fax: 04 90 24 25 52 • e-mail : ot@chateaurenard.com • www.chateaurenard.com

SAINT-VÉRAN CEMETERY

2

• Avenue Stuart Mill
Between route de Lyon and avenue de la Folie, 84000 Avignon
• Tel: 04 90 80 79 95• Open from 1 November to 31 March 8.30–18.00 and from 1 April to 31 October 8.30–19.00
• R.M. Fleurs Mathieu, avenue du Cimetière, 84000 Avignon
• Tel: 04 90 86 55 70

To save her father's life, she drank the blood of a beheaded man

The superb Saint-Véran d'Avignon cemetery is remarkable for its variety of shady and luxuriant greenery.

Apart from the beauty of the place, you'll come across some original characters who merit a posthumous visit …

From the main entrance, go down on the left to the end of the first row, where you'll find the grave of Marie-Maurille Virot de Sombreuil (1774–1823), known as Mademoiselle de Sombreuil, who saved her father from the guillotine in September 1792. As the death sentence was about to be carried out, she climbed on the scaffold, called the crowd to witness and begged the executioner to spare her father. He offered to pardon the condemned man if she agreed to drink a glass of blood from the previous beheading. Which is what she did. You can read her epitaph on the tomb: *[Victim of filial love she only lived to console and succour the unfortunate. Her wounded heart could only be healed by death. Her reward was in heaven.]*

Although her body rests in Avignon, her heart is in an urn at the chapel of Les Invalides in Paris, where her father was governor. This story inspired Victor Hugo who, in La mort de Mademoiselle de Sombreuil (Odes II, IX), ventured into somewhat morbid imagery:

[The unfortunate girl … / Felt, with vain terrors
Freezing in her pale veins / A blood that was not her own.]

In plot 11 lies the British philosopher and economist John Stuart Mill, founder of utilitarianism, who preferred to be buried at Avignon where his wife had died suddenly, rather than at his Westminster home. His epitaph, in English, is very surprising and very moving. The memorial stone, in French, recalls that Mill devoted his entire life to the emancipation of women, thinking that giving them the right to vote would kindle their interest in politics and make them aware of their responsibilities.

Strolling around the paths of the cemetery, in the serene shade of the trees, you might meet a three-wheeled contraption, running on a lawnmower engine and carrying sprinklers to scatter a little water around the curves and angles of the plots. This is driven by Régis Mathieu, brother of the singer Mireille, who shares the work of the family business located at the main entrance to the cemetery. You'll also meet Mireille's mother there, who still holds the reins in the family. For news of Mireille's continuing success … abroad: www.mireille-mathieu.com

ST BÉNÉZET

The statue of St Bénézet is at first-floor level, in a niche, at the corner of rue de la Bourse and place des Corps Saints, opposite the Célestins cloister.
To find it, go round to the right of the tourist office. Place des Corps Saints is just behind.

> ***A voice from heaven ordered the bridge to be built***

Visiting Avignon without seeing the bridge is like visiting Rome and not seeing the Pope. This bridge is indisputably symbolic as everyone has sung (and danced) sous le pont d'Avignon. Remember that the bridge was first built by St Bénézet in the 12th century. Swept away on several occasions by floods of the Rhône, it was finally abandoned in the 17th century. It is now reduced to a section jutting out into the river with no more than four of its twenty-two original arches.

For those wanting to know what St Bénézet looked like, as the builder of the bridge that bears his name, his statuette is waiting, bridge in hand, in a niche in the wall at the corner of rue de la Bourse and place des Corps Saints.

Wrongly designated "saint" (he was never canonized), St Bénézet seems not to be the stuff of legend but to have actually existed, as borne out by an ancient parchment containing two texts. One relates the story of Bénézet, followed by an appeal to the generosity of the faithful to pay for the bridge. The other is a collection of witness statements to support his canonization.

In 1177, the young Bénézet (the name means "little Benoît"), watching over his mother's sheep at Burzet (Vivarais*), heard a voice from the heavens addressing him: *"I am Jesus Christ and I want you to leave your mother's sheep to go and build a bridge over the Rhône for me ..."* The child, who had never left his village, protested his ignorance of roads and bridges ... Be that as it may, an angel disguised as a pilgrim accompanied him to the banks of the Rhône and the little Benoît went to find the bishop, who was delivering a sermon. The bishop sent him to the provost who set him the challenge of lifting a stone that 30 men couldn't move. Bénézet lifted the stone, carried it and laid it down beside the river, in the place where he knew he had to build the bridge. The provost, conscious of the supernatural nature of this happening, came to Bénézet's aid and supplied him with men and money, so that he could fulfill his architectural destiny.

Bénézet died in 1184 without seeing his bridge completed. His remains were preserved in the Saint-Nicolas chapel, on the bridge itself, until 1674, when they were transferred to the Célestins convent, where you can see his statue today. Since the desecration of the convent in 1791, very little of his remains have survived, and these relics are kept in the cathedral of Notre-Dame-des-Doms in Avignon.

*Ancient mountainous province centred on the town of Viviers (Viviers-sur-Rhône) and corresponding approximately to the Ardèche département.

SIGHTS NEARBY

AN ANALEMMATIC SUNDIAL 4

In Avignon's beautiful Doms garden overlooking the Palais des Papes on one side and the Rhône on the other, a curious monument on the ground catches the eye. It is an "analemmatic" sundial that can use the shadow cast by a person. You can therefore find out what time it is by standing in the appropriate place on the date scale. The time is read from the dial by noting where your shadow crosses hour points laid out on the ellipse. It isn't especially accurate but the learning curve can't fail.

LA CHAPELLERIE MOURET 5

20, rue des Marchands, 84000 Avignon
• Tel: 04 90 85 39 38 • Fax: 04 90 86 37 31
• http://www.chapelier.com

Founded in 1860, the Mouret hat shop is listed as a historic monument for its original wooden façade and its Louis XVI interior. As soon as you cross the threshold of the shop, you feel you should be wearing a hat. You have both the impression of going back in time and an irresistible desire to try on one of the numerous top-quality hats on display.
Four types of hat are offered: "The Great Outdoors", which takes you back to the classic adventure films with the incontrovertible Australian hat à la Crocodile Dundee or Indiana Jones; "France Forever", with boaters like those worn by Maurice Chevalier or characters in a Monet canvas; the "Legendary Panama", including the prestigious Borsalino style, and "Flavours of Provence", such as the black broad-brimmed felt hat worn by the Provençal poet Frédéric Mistral that can be used for walking or riding; and lastly, the real Marseillaise cap, indispensable for a game of pétanque or a glass of pastis ... in synthetic fiber for summer and wool for winter.

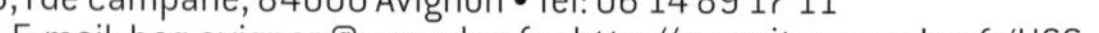

LIGHTING BY HÉLÈNE CARAYON GIORGIS 6

3, rue Campane, 84000 Avignon • Tel: 06 14 89 17 11
• E-mail: hcg.avignon@wanadoo.fr • http://monsite.wanadoo.fr/HCG

TV and cinema set designer and effervescent Parisienne, Hélène Carayon came to Avignon to open an amazing lighting shop where her motto is recycling. She fixes a light bulb and a conical lampshade to a comical, retro vacuum cleaner, uses cake moulds to diffuse light through a transparent glass lemon squeezer, or cycling accessories to support unusual bulbs ... Into the bargain, her smile lights up the place most agreeably ...

OFFICE DE TOURISME D'AVIGNON
41, cours Jean Jaurès - BP 8 - 84000 Avignon cedex 1 • Tel: 04 32 74 32 74
Fax: 04 90 82 95 03 • E-mail: information@ot-avignon.fr • http://www.ot-avignon.fr

SAN MIGUEL RESIDENCE

7

• Rue Ninon Vallin, 84000 Avignon
Access behind the ramparts between the Magnanen and Limbert gates at the south side of the town.

"Sawn stone, shattered stone, a crust of rough stone"... the architect used materials that blended with the town ramparts

The Résidence San Miguel is a group of luxury offices and accommodation built between 1968 and 1988. The successful integration of contemporary buildings with the 14th-century ramparts earned the residence the "20th-Century Heritage" designation from the Ministry of Culture.

Max Bourgoin, an architect involved in the reconstruction of the Vaucluse département after the Second World War, over some 30 years was responsible for thousands of homes and public buildings, mainly schools. In the early 1960s, following the reorganization of his offices and splitting up with his associate, he launched a second career which would interest him in integrating his work with existing buildings.

The real-estate project of the Résidence San Miguel came into being through the strength of will of the architect himself who, together with his wife, acquired the land adjacent to the ramparts. He was thus the sole person responsible for the design of this residence where he intended to live himself, and he wanted no financial or conceptual restrictions because he was both the main contractor and chief architect.

The result is spectacular, as any number of passers-by on the surrounding roads outside the ramparts have noted the residence without realizing how modern it is. The perfect integration of the project with the adjacent ramparts has the authoritative stamp of the architect's vision.

The height of the buildings respects that of the crenels of the battlements, the distance to the road respects the alignments, and, around an interior courtyard, the components blend in with the street intra muros, mixing parking spaces, underground entrances for vehicles and open gates in case passers-by would like to examine the buildings more closely.

To recreate the materials used in the ramparts, Max Bourgoin worked on the "skin" of the buildings using graffiti, ornament or decoration. In his specifications, he stipulated: *"sawn stone, shattered stone, a crust of rough stone, bricks, etc."* He wanted to live here and did not neglect a single aspect of construction, to the point that he sometimes took up a workman's tools on site to get physically involved himself.

SAINT-GENS HERMITAGE 8

• 84210 Le Beaucet
Access by the A7 motorway taking the Cavaillon exit. Continue towards Carpentras, then follow signs for Pernes-les-Fontaines and Saint-Didier, Le Beaucet and Ermitage de Saint-Gens.

The saint caused two springs to burst forth, one with water, and the other with white wine

In the depths of a valley, an unexpected church awaits the visitor: the Hermitage of Saint-Gens pays tribute to an enigmatic saint, whose life and work justify a spectacular pilgrimage which is still flourishing today.

Born in the 12th century, the young man objected to the arranged marriage that his parents wanted to force on him. At the age of 15 he didn't feel ready to wed, but he had above all become conscious of the quasi-pagan devotion of his contemporaries. While he was against the cult of St Raphael, the rainmaker, he was hoist on his own petard in declaring that sort of thing to be completely inane, and he added that he would send them a drought. And so it happened. It was so serious that, after two years without a drop of water, Gens was sanctified the day when, tapping the soil of his natal Monteux with his stick, he brought on the rain.

Living as a hermit with a cow, he tamed an attacking wolf with a single gesture and used it to pull a cart. Hence the common representation of the saint accompanied by a cow and a wolf on a leash, leading it to drink at the spring that became known as the wolf fountain.

A while later, when drought was again causing misery, the exasperated residents came to ask St Gens to intervene. He caused two springs to erupt, one of water and the other of white wine. It's no wonder that the first to dry up was the most alcoholic ...

A devastating storm finally carried off the hermit, whose body was later found some distance away. Today the pilgrimage takes place every 16 May, the anniversary of the saint's death.

Young people (you'll need to be young) leave Monteux (his birthplace) to travel by night, around midnight, the 15 km or so between the two places. They complete their vigil and return the way they came. The Revolution, which mocked most religious customs, didn't succeed in dampening the power of the myth of St Gens: the statue was hidden under a sack so that the pilgrimage could take place. Today, you can see pennants, ex-votos, wax figures of the saint, statues, wolves and cows in the church. Outside, the wolf fountain, resurgence of the miraculous spring, is overlooked by a little temple where a hand is enthroned. Alongside, the (sacred) cow and the wolf, eyes riveted on the hand that trains and nourishes it. Just below runs the spring water, the water of life, reflecting two faces contemplating the passing of time.

THE CAMILLE CLAUDEL MEMORIAL

• Centre Hospitalier de Montfavet - 2, avenue de la Pinède, BP 92 84143 Montfavet cedex • Tel: 04 90 03 90 00 • http://www.hopital-montfavet.com • The sculpture stands in front of the main entrance to the hospital. The commune of Montfavet is 5 km south-east of Avignon. **To get there,** take the motorway in the direction of Marseille then follow the signs to Montfavet at one of the roundabouts on the left. The hospital is indicated from the outskirts of Montfavet.

"From 1915 to 1943, the artist never left the Montfavet asylum

In front of the psychiatric hospital at Montfavet there stands a sculpture that very few people notice, created by Martine Droit, a reminder that the French sculptor Camille Claudel was committed in what was then an asylum until her death in 1943.

The work is in two parts: a block of onyx from which rise four horns, and a stele bearing the names of all those who contributing to erecting this tribute to the artist.

The sister of the celebrated French writer Paul Claudel, Camille was born at Fère-en-Tardenois on 8 December 1864. The family moved to Nogent-sur-Seine, where her father was appointed registrar. She met the sculptor Boucher and, a year later, made a bust of her brother Paul. At the age of 17, sure of her artistic calling, she settled in Paris and launched a career as a sculptor. Two years after this she met Auguste Rodin, whose student, model and mistress she would become. This was a prolific time for her, producing works such as Sakountala, a bust of Rodin, La valse [The Waltz] and Le Dieu envolé [The God in flight]. Camille Claudel, the 1988 film by Bruno Nuytten, relates this period of the artist's life in detail, with Isabelle Adjani playing Camille and Gérard Depardieu playing Rodin. This relationship of passion lasted until the sculptor's liaison with Rose Beuret put an end to it.

Camille Claudel, whose work had been greatly influenced by Rodin, then took things into her own hands and found another lease of life in which she succeeded in creating her most admired works. Having worked in plaster, bronze and marble, she tackled onyx in a Japanese-inspired style. Her masterpieces that can be seen at the Rodin museum are *L'Âge mûr* [The Mature Age], *Les Causeuses* [The Gossips] and *La Vague* [The Wave].

In 1906, Camille Claudel was 42 and beginning to show the first signs of insanity. She was committed to Ville-Evrard in 1913, at her mother's request and upon the decision of the family's doctor, to have her *"mental alienation"* treated. Because of the war, she was evacuated to the Montfavet asylum in 1915 and there she remained until her death on 19 October 1943.

The actor and singer Serge Reggiani has dedicated a splendid song to the unfortunate artist, entitled *Camille*: *"Oh! Monsieur Rodin, the fire, the fire, I want to be able to seal it in stone!"*.

THE RAT BALL

Cathédrale Saint-Siffrein
Place du Général-de-Gaulle
84200 Carpentras

Sculpted above the Porte Juive in the Cathedral of Saint-Siffrein, Carpentras, is a strange ball with a dozen rats running over it.

“The ball was perhaps a reminder that church attendance was the best protection against the plague

Taking the place of two earlier buildings (7th and 12th centuries), the cathedral was begun in 1405 under the Avignon papacy of Benoît XIII (Pedro de Luna), completed in 1519 and consecrated in 1531. The Southern Gothic cathedral has a side door in the flamboyant style known as the “Jewish Portal”. It was by this door, close to the ghetto, that Jews who wished to convert to Roman Catholicism had to enter. Remember that it was because Carpentras was papal territory that the Jews expelled from France in the 13th century were able to take refuge there and build one of the oldest and probably one of the most beautiful synagogues in France. The synagogue was built in 1367, at which time there were 45 Jewish families in Carpentras. In 1779, they received authorization to extend the synagogue, but the bishop reproached them for wanting to build higher than his cathedral. Listed as a historic monument, the present synagogue dates from 1784 when some 750 Jewish families lived at Carpentras.

Located above the Porte Juive, the boule aux rats has elicited any number of interpretations, from the most fantastic to the very likely. Thus, the etymology or topography of Carpentras is sometimes called upon: Latin carpere = browse, nibble; ras = rat …

Perhaps it also represents something to do with the plague, which claimed so many victims in Comtat (Venaissin), despite the Plague Wall (see page 239): epidemics of typhus and plague (the Black Death, so called because of the colour its victims turned), killed 150,000 people in the region in the 14th century. The boulo di gari (Provençal for “rat ball”) would have been set up as a reminder that assiduous attendance at church was the best vaccine against the disease …

There are three other boules aux rats in France, at Saint-Germain-l’Auxerrois in Paris, Le Mans cathedral, and the church of Saint-Jacques de Meulan in Yvelines département, Île-de-France.

St Siffrein, patron saint of Carpentras to whom the cathedral is dedicated, was bishop of the town in the 7th century. He was trained at Lerins and his life is studded with resounding miracles. His cult is still celebrated with great solemnity.

The relics of St Siffrein came to Carpentras around 1220, following the Crusades. He is “preserved” in a magnificent reliquary by the Lyon goldsmith Armand Caillat (1872).

LE MUSÉE DE LA VIEILLE ÉCOLE 11

• Mairie des Valayans - Les Valayans, 84210 Pernes-les-Fontaines
• Tel: 04 90 62 07 28 • Open from 1 June to 30 September, Saturdays, Sundays and public holidays, 10.00–12.00 and 15.00–19.00. Outside these hours, group or individual visits can be booked.
• Admission free.

"The only thing missing is a few dunces at the back of the class...

At Valayans, a hamlet in the commune of Pernes-les-Fontaines, an association organized an exhibition in 1995 on "School as it used to be", to commemorate 100 years of state schooling. In order to best reconstitute the classroom, a trio of volunteers searched through the archives, attics and cellars of local residents and administrative offices. In the light of the incredible riches they found and the unexpected success of their venture, it was decided to make this a permanent initiative. Thus was born the Musée de la Vieille École, whose "first term" was summer 2001.

Set up in the precincts of the town hall annex, the classroom might make the youngest visitors sit up but will come as a particular shock to the oldest ones: it isn't just a reconstitution but a reconstruction using the authentic pieces of furniture and equipment of state schooling of a century ago.

So you'll find oak desks, pottery inkwells with violet ink, steel-nibbed pens, books and manuals, slate, pencil box and paper of bygone days. On the walls, geography maps with obsolete frontiers, the Declaration of the Rights of Man and educational posters on the history of anatomy. The only thing missing is a few dunces at the back of the class ...

Of course there is also the master's desk on a platform and the blackboard where, as if by chance, a dripping tap problem has been left chalked up ...

In a corner, mannequins display the smocks worn by the children of Pernes who formed part of the "scholar's batallions" set up in 1882 for "gymnastic and military service".

The adjoining room recreates the teacher's home, with 28 exercise books to correct for the following day. Opposite, the corner of the kitchen table where the schoolchild did his homework and learned his lessons. Alongside, on a chair, the clothes ready for the coming day are waiting: the black smock that doesn't show ink stains and the socks knitted by maman. Nearby, the satchel with books ready for school, covered with cloth by the parents to make them last for several years.

At the entrance you're welcomed by the volunteer founders of the museum and by some memories of the past in Pernes, including an impressive wooden ruler with a copper scale that was used to measure former pupils.

OFFICE DE TOURISME DE PERNES-LES-FONTAINES
Place Gabriel-Moutte , 84210 Pernes-les-Fontaines
• Tel: 04 90 61 31 04 • Fax: 04 90 61 33 23 • e-mail : ot-pernes@wanadoo.fr
• Good website: http://www.ville-pernes-les-fontaines.fr

MUSÉE MÉMOIRE DE LA RN7

• Château Simian, 84420 Piolenc
• Tel: 04 90 29 57 89 • http://www.memoirenationale7.org
See also the website dedicated to the route: http://www.nationale7.org

"I prefer the road that leads, driving my car or hitching a ride, to the southern shores"

Since 2003 there has been a "Memory of the N7" museum alongside the Route Nationale 7, at Piolenc (Vaucluse), which offers a nostalgic evocation of the famous route. Located in a wine-producing estate, Château Simian, the museum is signposted from the village of Piolenc.

The RN7, which links Paris to the Côte d'Azur, had its hour of glory before the motorway took over. Nostalgia enthusiasts and drivers allergic to motorway tolls still use this symbolic axis.

[Of all the roads in France and Europe / I prefer the one that leads
Driving my car or hitching a ride, / To the southern shores.]

It was in 1955 that Charles Trenet composed the song *On est heureux Nationale 7*, the ambiance and lyrics of which were perfectly in tune with the times. Taking a car from Paris to Provence in the 1950s was a veritable expedition. The route went through towns and villages and an entire economy grew up alongside this blessed tarmac. Service stations, restaurants, souvenir shops, local specialities and road signs that you'll find today in second-hand shops and even antique shops.

Now, the modernized Route Nationale 7 still goes through Provence and has the inestimable advantage of being free. Hence it is packed with lorries. At the roadside, modern archaeology is not without its charm. Signs for disused petrol stations now overlook fruit and vegetable sellers, bakeries with wood-buring ovens and other diverse money-making activities in the car parks.

The milestones with their red semicircle are still there, but the material has changed, plastic having replaced stone and metal. Ceramic signs are becoming rare and, if you look carefully, you can find traces of the ancient imperial name of the route, as at Aix-en-Provence at the junction of cours Sextius and boulevard de la République.

From time to time following the Roman roads, this major axis between Paris and the Mediterranean, taking in both the Nationale 7 and the Nationale 6, was designated "La Route Bleue" [The Blue Road] at the beginning of the 20th century.

ÉCOMUSÉE DES APPEAUX ET DE LA FAUNE ⑬

• Place Neuve, 84210 Saint-Didier
• Tel: 04 90 66 13 13 • Fax: 04 90 66 64 32 • http://www.appeaux-raymond.com

• Open from Tuesday to Friday 9.00–12.00 and 15.00–18.00. Saturdays, Sundays and public holidays 15.00–18.00. Closed Monday.
• Admission €3.50, free for children under 12 accompanied by an adult.

> ***One of only five birdcall makers in the entire world***

The Saint-Didier ecomuseum of bird-calls and wildlife was created by Bernard Raymond, great grandson of Théodore Raymond, founder of the birdcalls "industry" in 1868. Instruments reproducing animal sounds, mostly birdsong, these decoys allowed hunters to attract their prey and line them up in their gunsights, although it's true that wildlife photographers have now become the most widespread users.

In the 19th century, production was very limited: Théodore spent most of his time researching new calls and perfecting his instruments, leaving the production process until later.

The earliest birdcalls were made from humble materials, unimaginable today: olive or cherry stones, small pieces of wood from pine cones or bark, the ends of goose or chicken feathers, scraps of metal, all held together with gum resin. Some of them were just an empty snail shell in which a neat round hole had been drilled, held together with sticking plaster. Others were a simple strip of well-scraped reed.

All these natural objects gathered in the countryside had a disadvantage: they were living materials and thus rather over-sensitive to humidity and temperature, not working well in changeable weather. Often, too, moisture from the user's mouth soon rendered them useless. Today, four generations of Raymonds have solved these problems and the calls work whatever the weather …

The museum is captivating because it was set up by a captivated man. The guided tour is divided into four parts: discovery of wildlife in its natural habitat (animals representative of the main species of the region); showcases of instruments from a bygone age; the workshop; and the high point of the visit, the demonstration.

While the wildlife slides are being shown, Bernard Raymond plays his instruments to let you hear the likeness between the natural and the reproduced sound of the calls. His jovial personality and ready anecdotes make this an enchantment for children and even for adults, who rarely leave without buying some birdcalls. As it happens there are only five producers of these instruments in the world …

Vaison-la-Romaine
Buis-les-Baronnies
Malaucène
Mont Ventoux
Carpentras
Pernes-les-Fontaines
Venasque
Sault
Mormoiron
Gorges de la Nesque
84
Plateau de Vaucluse
Abbaye de Sénanque
Gordes
Village des Bories
La fontaine de Vaucluse
L'Isle-sur-la-Sorgue
Roussillon
Apt
Cavaillon
Oppède-le-Vieux
Ménerbes
Bonnieux
Lourmarin
Cadenet
Cucuron
Pertuis
Parc Naturel Régional du Luberon
Montagne du Luberon
Grand Luberon
Mourre Nègre
Céreste
Simiane-la-Rotonde
Abbaye de Silvacane
La Roque-d'Anthéron
Salon-de-Provence
13
Aix-en-Provence
Istres
Étang de Berre
Martigues
Marignane
Vitrolles
Gardanne
L'Estaque
Allauch
1
2
3
4
5
6
7
8
9
10
11
12
13
14
15
16
17
18
19
20

LUBERON

THE EXTRAORDINARY MUSEUM OF GEORGES MAZOYER

1

- Rue du Vieux Moulin, 84240 Ansouis
- Open every afternoon 14.00–19.00 (18.00 in winter)
- Admission: €3.50, reduced rates for children, groups and students
- Tel/Fax: 04 90 09 82 64

A deep-sea diving enthusiast, Georges Metoyer has put all his finds on display in this museum

Don't miss Georges Mazoyer's "extraordinary museum" in the superb village of Ansouis, dominated by its chateau. Scattered about the grounds, the 11 monumental sculptures of marine and prehistoric animals that populated this place several million years ago, when 800 m of water covered the Luberon region, can be seen from some distance. The museum itself is in a 15th-century building that Georges Mazoyer spent 20 years restoring. Born in Marseille in 1925, he was a keen deep-sea diver. Combing the world's oceans, he brought his finds together in this museum together with pictures he has painted over the years. All this is perhaps not "extraordinary" but it certainly captivates children, who are reluctant to leave the "coral grotto", a reconstituted underwater cave lit by a multicoloured glass window. There is also a painting workshop, a Provençal kitchen, a fossil collection, shells and corals, amphorae and well-honed anecdotes from the family of the late Georges Mazoyer: the shell in the shape of an ice-cream cone that should never be grasped from below because its 4 cm sting can cause heart failure (there's no known antidote); or the fugu, a fish that has to be cooked by experts for fear of poisoning the unwary consumer.

OFFICE DE TOURISME D'ANSOUIS
Place du Château, 84240 Ansouis • Tel: 04 90 09 86 98 • Fax: 04 90 09 86 98

THE "PARADISE" OF LÉOPOLD TRUC ❷

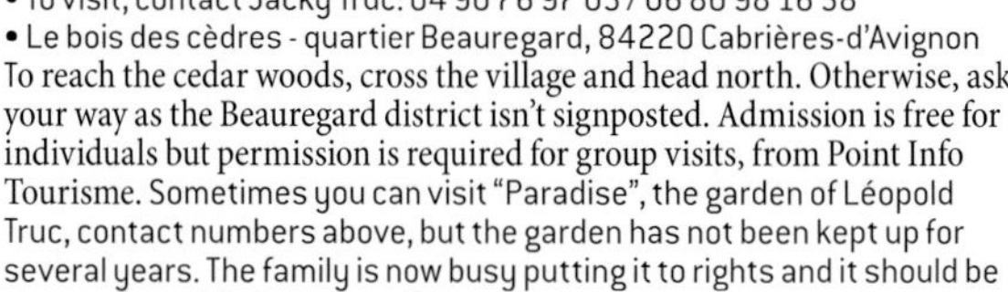

• Quartier la Plantade, 84220 Cabrières-d'Avignon
• To visit, contact Jacky Truc: 04 90 76 97 03 / 06 80 98 16 58
• Le bois des cèdres - quartier Beauregard, 84220 Cabrières-d'Avignon
To reach the cedar woods, cross the village and head north. Otherwise, ask your way as the Beauregard district isn't signposted. Admission is free for individuals but permission is required for group visits, from Point Info Tourisme. Sometimes you can visit "Paradise", the garden of Léopold Truc, contact numbers above, but the garden has not been kept up for several years. The family is now busy putting it to rights and it should be open to the public in the near future.

> ***A naive artist creates a bit of heaven in the Lubéron countryside***

In 1945, when Provence was liberated from the Nazi occupation and the Second World War ended, an immense exuberance was in the air and, at Cabrières d'Avignon, some members of the commune decided to develop the so-called "cedar woods", a municipal property in the Beauregard district, where they could hold events. A primitive stone dance floor was constructed, with a covered space for the band, barbecue ovens resembling the furnaces of Rustrel (a nearby village which had had metal workings), and a whole range of tables, chairs and benches surrounding the area. Today the site is still accessible and used for festivities. People come to picnic and tourists following the silk-spinners path (see Plague Wall) are glad to stop a while there.

Léopold Truc, an agriculturalist from Cabrières, born in 1912, took part in laying out the site. He found his vocation in integrating unexpected elements into nature and threw himself into the creation of "Paradise" on a patch of his land.

Although he designed his garden as a circular tour, with an entrance and an exit, as if he saw himself welcoming visitors later, he in fact only showed it to friends and curious passers-by who had heard of it.

The garden motifs or sculptures are made from concrete decorated with pottery shards or ceramics, recalling the inimitable "roadside inspiration" style (from the title of a work by the French writer Jacques Lacarrière, Les Inspirés du bord des routes). The naive artist and rural postman Ferdinand Cheval, known as Le Facteur Cheval, and the house of the "painter woman" inevitably come to mind (see Pont-de-l'Étoile, page 71). Several "buildings" can be visited. First the central building which he said was his own house (in fact he lived elsewhere), an old borie (drystone hut) that he had done up, a tower the summit of which could be reached by a narrow stairway, and finally a hide for hunters. Designs are traced on the ground in scallop shells, a common sight in the garden.

POINT INFO TOURISME - MAIRIE DE CABRIÈRES-D'AVIGNON
Cours Jean-Giono, 84220 Cabrières-d'Avignon • Tel: 04 90 76 71 42

THE SAINTS' BEDROOM AT THE CHÂTEAU D'ANSOUIS

3

- 84240 Ansouis
- Open 14.30–18.00
Closed Tuesday except in July, August and September
Closed from Hallow'een to Easter
- Tel: 04 90 09 82 70 • Fax: 04 90 09 94 83
- Admission: €6

An exemplary marriage: he became a saint, while she took a vow of silence...

At the beginning of the 14th century, Charles II ("The Lame"), king of Naples, arranged a marriage to further his political ambitions. This involved a union between Elzéar of Sabran, Count of Ariano, Baron of Ansouis and Cucuron, and Delphine of Signes, who was then in a convent having taken a vow of chastity. She accepted the marriage arrangement on condition that her future spouse made a similar vow …

The marital chamber of the Chateau d'Ansouis thus became known as the "Saints' Bedroom" – no need for a bed for a couple whose marriage was formalized but not consummated (the bed that's there now was installed at a later date).

Elzéar died shortly afterwards at Paris. When he was visited by a priest during his last illness, he asked that the truth about his union be made public in order to set an example to ordinary people. Delphine then chose to live in the greatest simplicity, making a further vow – that of silence. She lived to a great age and was noted for miracles and other wonders, as well as visions. She asked the pope to recognize the holiness of her husband, which was done. Clement VI canonized Elzéar. Delphine too was beatified and elevated to the status of "blessed".

The Château d'Ansouis was undamaged by the French Revolution and the Sabran family, Elzéar's descendants, still own and live in it. The well-known pianist Gersende de Sabran hails from this thousand-year-old lineage.

BEATIFIED OR CANONIZED?

Roman Catholics who have led an exemplary and remarkable life can be honoured in several ways. The first step is beatification, which gives the status of "blessed". Certain of the most deserving blesseds can then be canonized, i.e. elevated to sainthood. At the recent death of Pope Jean-Paul II the crowd clearly expressed its opinion – *"Santo subito"* [instant sainthood], the people cried, indicating that the beatification stage was a waste of time for this pope and that direct canonization was in order.

The Congregation for the Causes of Saints, one of the nine congregations of the Roman Curia, oversees the processes of beatification and canonization and judges whether the candidature can be submitted to the supreme pontiff. Note that, during the canonization process, the promoter of the faith is known as the "devil's advocate".

MUR DE LA PESTE

THE PLAGUE WALL

4

- Point Info Tourisme - Mairie de Cabrières d'Avignon
- Cours Jean Giono, 84220 Cabrières d'Avignon
- Tel: 04 90 76 79 43

The "Plague Wall" walk starts from Cabrières d'Avignon tourist office, where you can pick up a leaflet describing the circuit along the walls with information on the plague. The circular route itself is 4.4 km in addition to the 1.3 km from Point Info to the start. Allow around two hours in all.
A guide by Denis Lacaille and Danièle Larcena, La ligne dans le paysage, promenades géographiques dans les monts de Vaucluse autour du Mur de la Peste, suggests three of the most attractive walks around the walls. See also by the same authors: *La Muraille de la Peste*, Éditions Les Alpes de Lumière, No. 114, September 1993. Available in bookshops or from the author: La Cornette, 84800 Saumane, tel: 04 90 20 71 82; e-mail: piersecvaucluse@wanadoo.fr. In less than five months

On a depuis belle lurette oublié ce qu'il délimite
Et que ce fut le grand terrain domanial de l'épidémie
[Long since have we forgotten what it marks out
And that this was the grand domain of the epidemic]
Louis Aragon, Prose du bonheur d'Elsa

On 14 May 1720, the Grand Saint-Antoine, a ship on its way from Tripoli, Syria and Cyprus, brought the plague to Marseille. Dormant for a while, the deadly disease then ran wild – 15 deaths rue de l'Echelle 26 July, 100 deaths per day at the beginning of August, 1,000 per day at the end of the month …

> ***From March to July 1721, a 25-kilometre long wall was built***

In Provence panic reigned, and everything was done to stop those fleeing from Marseille from reaching those villages still spared the sickness. In these circumstances France asked the State of Avignon and the Comtat-Venaissin (see box), both papel enclaves, to construct the Plague Wall (or muraille de ligne, as it was originally known) to creat a cordon sanitaire to stop the epidemic spreading from Provence.

Antoine d'Allemand, an architect from Carpentras, set to work to design a drystone wall 6 feet (1.95 m) high and 2 feet (0.65 m) wide. Work began in March 1721 and each village was obliged to send a contingent of workmen, who had to bring their own tools (hammer, plumbline, spade, pick). But the work fell behind, the communities showing little enthusiasm for supplying "wall-makers". So the authorities decided to reorganize the building site and each village was allotted a precise section of the wall to build. Moreover, the workers were on piecework … paid by the length of wall completed rather than by the day. By the end of July the wall was finished and a thousand soldiers posted to control this new frontier.

The walking tour that starts from Cabrières d'Avignon follows the wall for almost 2 km. In places the structure has crumbled and in general is scarcely

wider than 1.2 m. The purpose of the wall was not in any case to stop any forays but to slow down those who tried to get past, giving the soldiers time to intercept them. There are several sentry-points on the wall: horseshoe-shaped and unvaulted, positioned 2.5 m from the wall and opening towards it. In several places there are also guardhouses where the soldiers slept.

At the end of the path along the wall, a cistern and a signpost for walkers mark the route back to the village. The rest of the walk is a pleasant descent along a path known as le chemin des fileuses, from the time when silkworms were cultivated in Provence. The mills of Gordes having burned down, the spinner-girls had to seek work elsewhere, notably at Fontaine-de-Vaucluse, 10 km on foot, and this path offered them a considerable shortcut.

COMTAT-VENAISSIN

Belonging to the counts of Toulouse, the Comtat-Venaissin came under the control of the king of France in 1271, then was ceded to the pope in 1274. Popes were installed at Avignon from 1309 until 1377, when they returned to Rome, but the Comtat remained under papal authority until 1791. The former Comtat-Venaissin forms part of the département of Vaucluse, between the Rhône, Mont Ventoux and the River Durance. It takes in the towns of Cavaillon and Carpentras. The word "Venaissin" comes from Vénasque, the first capital.

ATTENTION

Access to the ranges of the massif depends on the weather conditions. It is essential to consult Point Info before setting out.

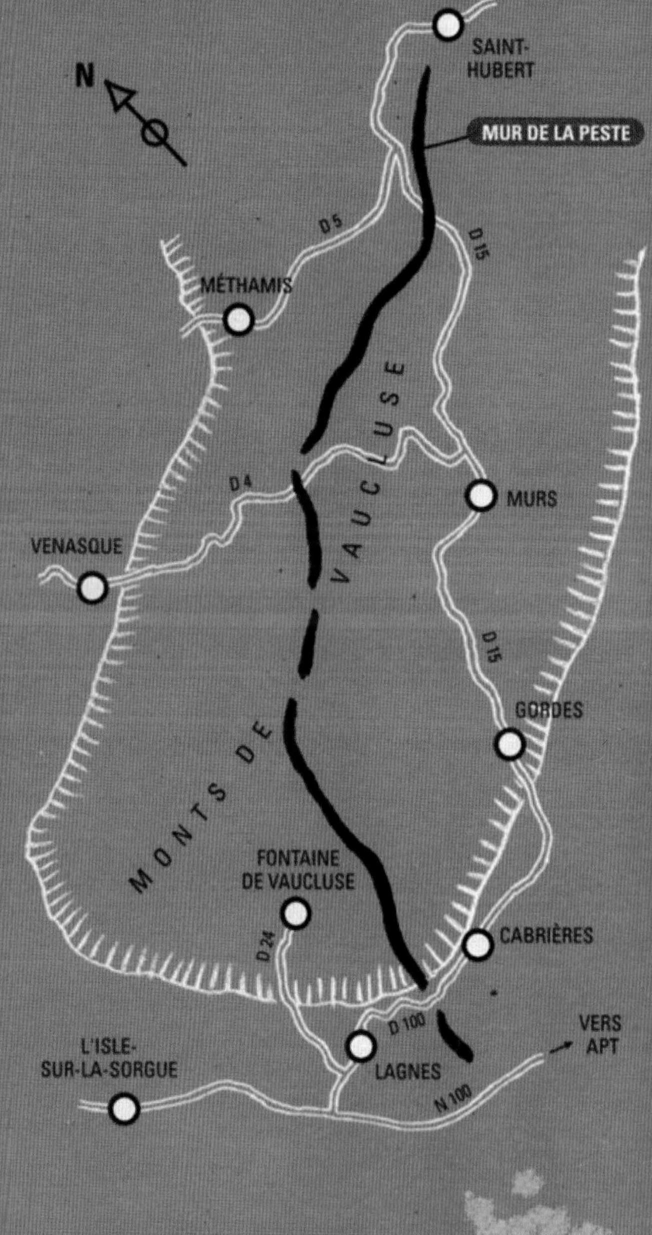

N
SAINT-HUBERT
MUR DE LA PESTE
D 5
D 15
MÉTHAMIS
MONTS DE VAUCLUSE
D 4
MURS
VENASQUE
D 15
GORDES
FONTAINE DE VAUCLUSE
CABRIÈRES
D 24
D 100
VERS APT
L'ISLE-SUR-LA-SORGUE
LAGNES
N 100
AVIGNON
APT

THE STATUE OF THE PETIT TAMBOUR

5

• Place du Tambour d'Arcole, 84160 Cadenet

> *While Napoleon crossed the Arcole bridge on foot and under fire, a lone drummer boy swam to the far shore*

A small but glorious episode in the history of France was recorded by André Estienne, born at Cadenet, who was a drummer in the Napoleonic army. The bronze statue of the drummer boy for which the village is celebrated stands in the main square. Signed by the sculptor Amy, it was erected in 1894.

Contrary to accepted belief, the French word tambour does not refer to the instrument itself but the soldier-musician responsible for beating time on his caisse ("crate"). The idea that drummers were children is also a myth, although there were certain exceptions. Children couldn't join a regiment until they were 16, and the drummer boy of Cadenet was 19 at the time of the events described.

These took place during the battle of Arcole on 15 November 1796. It was impossible to cross the Arcole bridge under Austrian fire. Bonaparte therefore went over alone on foot, carrying his standard. At least that is how Antoine-Jean Gros was to represent it in the symbolic painting Le général Bonaparte au pont d'Arcole. Legend has it that the drummer of Arcole also crossed the river, swimming across alone, and once he reached the other bank beat his drum and thus made the enemy believe that they'd been ambushed from the rear.

Recently another monument has been erected at Cadenet, a base without a statue (but they're working on it), which has been the talk of the village. On this marble column at the southern entrance to the village, its base encircled by a wicker panel, phrases are written in Provençal recalling the story of the young drummer. Its merit is to compare the evolution of modes of expression through the figurative, expressive, convincing and ever-changing style of the bronze statue, in a more modern way, less "readable" although written down, a sign of the village wish to innovate.

OFFICE DE TOURISME DE CADENET
Place du Tambour-d'Arcole, 84160 Cadenet • Tel: 04 90 68 38 21
• Fax: 04 90 68 24 49 • e-mail : ot-cadenet@axit.fr.

THE DRAGONS OF SAINT-VÉRAN CATHEDRAL ❻

84305 Cavaillon
• Admission free
• From 1 October to 31 March: every day except Saturday and Sunday, 9.00–12.00 and 14.00–17.00
From 1 April to 30 September: every day except Saturday and Sunday, 8.30–12.00 and 14.00–18.00

A dragon-slaying bishop

In Cavaillon's cathedral of Saint-Véran, dragons are everywhere: on a painting behind the main altar, in plain wood on the throne, in gilded wood in the first chapel to the left and finally on a painting by the French classical painter Mignard (1657) representing St Véran and the dragon in that same chapel. Unfortunately, moving the main altar has meant that the tabernacle now hides an important part of the picture: the part that shows the dragon. The painting has thus become unreadable and difficult to understand.

Véran, bishop of Cavaillon at the end of the 6th century and patron of the town, was a dragon-slayer. Despite this rather boastful claim, he does seem to have existed, having met Gregory of Tours who was visiting the various Christian traditions in France, as well as frequenting kings of the time such as Guntram and Childebert II. He performed miracles, healed the sick with the sign of the cross, and when he died was buried in the church of Fontaine-de-Vaucluse, where his sarcophagus remains today. The saint's relics were transferred to Cavaillon cathedral in 1321 in the presence of the poet Petrarch.

The dragon was in fact a monstrous snake (colubro in Provençal) that devastated the region. Véran caught it, chained it up and wounded it, but it had enough strength to fly off and landed in the Alps, on a village that was to become the highest commune in Europe: Saint-Véran. Curiously it's the name of the bishop that has persisted, although he never went to Saint-Véran. Collobrières, a village in the neighbouring département of Var, also saw the colubro.

The heritage officer at the cathedral, Florence Bastian, will answer all your questions kindly and competently. She'll help you to make sense of the monument and its rich decoration: at the right of the entrance stands a macabre group frozen in terror. This is the mausoleum of the Marquis de Sade, the ecclesiastic with the sulfurous name, dragged to his death by a hyper-realistic skeleton that threatens to give children nightmares.

On the sundial carved into one of the walls of the cathedral, this Latin phrase can be read, a play on the words ora and hora: *Hora ne te fallat ora,* which means "*Pray, so as not to be surprised at the hour of your death*". Charming but effective.

The tourist office in Cavaillon offers children a tour of the town suited to their age. Among the stages in this play-oriented tour is Cavaillon cathedral, where children are asked to count the number of dragons they can see ... a curious quest in a church, but their keen eyes will be well rewarded as dragons are legion in this holy place.

OFFICE DE TOURISME DE CAVAILLON
Place François-Tourel, BP 176, 84305 Cavaillon Cedex • Tel: 04 90 71 32 01
• Fax: 04 90 71 42 99 • e-mail : O.T.cavaillon@wanadoo.fr

COMMUNAUTÉ NOTRE-DAME-DE-LUMIÈRE 7

• Lumières, 84220 Goult • Tel: 04 90 72 25 05
Alongside the RN100 between Avignon and Forcalquier, near the village of Goult

The healing abilities of the Black Virgin have never been refuted

The convent of Pères Oblats de Marie Immaculée, at Notre-Dame-de-Lumière, is one of the most remarkable sights of the Luberon.

On entering the church you'll find, immediately to the left, a glazed door with an intercom leading to another world impossible to imagine from the roadside. If Notre-Dame-de-Lumière takes its name from the Limergue stream that runs nearby, shining apparitions in the 17th century led to confusion between the original name and the description of what was officially classed as a series of miracles. Several versions exist of these supernatural events. It's said that, sometimes, a procession of lights can be seen. It's also said that Antoine of Nantes, known as Jalleton, a partially paralysed sexagenarian from Goult, was loitering around the ruins of the ancient chapel when he saw a child smiling at him. He was immediately healed and the child disappeared. He had the present church built on that very spot, funded by the money that flooded in from all quarters in the hope that this shrine would represent a genuine insurance policy against sickness.

In the same vein, and around the same time, a shepherd saw a statuette of the Black Virgin in a burning bush. This was set in a suitable position in the church and explains today's exceptional profusion of votive offerings on the walls (you'll need binoculars as they are placed high up to deter thieves). The Black Virgin only stands 46 cm tall and is not in fact black but dark brown, the colour of the pear-tree root from which she was carved. At the back of the base can be seen a small round reliquary, which contains four relics: a piece from the veil and dress of the Holy Virgin, as well as fragments from her house in Nazareth and from her tomb.

Although this place is less well-known than some shrines to miracles, it seems that belief in the ability of this Black Virgin to achieve unexplained cures cannot be denied. You've only to see the faithful, having openly put their hands in their pockets, fill the collection boxes in the crypt to understand that the supernatural is still a powerful force in Lumière/Limergue.

A shop outside the church offers souvenirs and religious texts and, above, the pretty chapel of St Michel, which seems to have been constructed in the beak of a stone eagle, contemplates the Luberon.

THE ANTHROPOMORPHIC TOMBS 

OF THE PRIEURÉ DE CARLUC

Access: follow signs from the RN100, 2.5 km east of Céreste

A place of silence, contemplation, and serenity

Near Céreste, between Apt and Forcalquier, Carluc Priory is a haven of peace and serenity, consisting of a church, the priory ruins and a necropolis dating from the earliest days of Christianity hewn in the rock. It's original in that certain tombs are anthropomorphic (taking the form of the body), something unique in France.

The name Carluc, apparently of Indo-European origin, refers to the rock and to water, for a spring that never fails explains the human and religious presence at the site. It's one of those places that imposes silence, contemplation and serenity, in which the greenery around the church brings to mind the work of the French landscape painter Hubert Robert.

It was probably around the 4th century BC that the monks from the abbey of Saint-Victor at Marseille set up a place of Christian worship at Carluc. It's said to have been a former Druid site and, as a leaflet from the tourist office explains, *"once you've been there you'll understand why"*. The presence of such a reliable spring, on the other hand, leaves no doubt that the site had been occupied for a very long time, as well as the fact that it's only a Roman mile (1,481 m) from the Via Domitia which passed through Céreste, linking Rome to Provence.

The chapels and living quarters hewn into the rock are the most extraordinary part of the site. Reached by underground tunnels, past alleys bordered with sarcophagi in stone hollows, some of them are anthropomorphic and probably house eminent people, supporting the idea that Carluc was a pilgrimage centre.

After the barbarian invasions, which left Provence exhausted, the site was given new life under the patronage of Montmajour Abbey and, in the 11th century, Carluc Priory was founded. It consisted of three chapels joined by a cloister whose vaults covered the necropolis. After the Wars of Religion, the buildings were abandoned and sold as national heritage at the time of the French Revolution.

The "Alpes de Lumière" association has taken on the task of bringing Carluc out of oblivion and working towards its restoration. At present, guided visits are temporarily suspended while the restoration work goes ahead and security measures are put in place.

OFFICE DE TOURISME DE CÉRESTE
Place de la République, 04280 Céreste • Tel/Fax: 04 92 79 09 84
• e-mail : otcereste@wanadoo.fr • www.cereste.fr

THE TRADITION OF THE POPLAR OF CUCURON

> *Every year since the plague of 1720, a poplar taller than the belltower is planted in front of the church*

At Cucuron, a village near Lourmarin, the local people keep up an remarkable tradition: each year between May and August they stand a poplar tree in front of the church to fulfil a vow made at the end of the plague epidemic in 1720.

Spreading north from Marseille, the plague struck the village in October 1720 and took almost 1,000 victims in a month. The epidemic ran its course after a solemn procession during which the people committed themselves to a perpetual vow to St Tulle, patron of the village. This involved making the same pilgrimage each year and placing a tree that was higher than the belltower in front of the church.

From then on, on the first Saturday after 21 May, the men of the village go out and chop down a tree, bodily carrying it (with the help of some wooden beams) as far as the church. A child in traditional costume is seated on the trunk, as a symbol of tolerance, known as the Enseigne (ensign). The crowd applauds and after various manipulations the tree is raised before the church, where it remains until 15 August.

Cucuron is a strange place name, which some think comes from the words of Julius Caesar on seeing the townspeople flee before him: "Cur currunt?" Why are they running? In fact Cucuron comes from Cuques, meaning height, a common name in Provence.

OFFICE DE TOURISME DE CUCURON
Rue Léonce-Brieugne, 84160 Cucuron • Tel: 04 90 77 28 37 • Fax: 04 90 77 17 00

SIGHTS NEARBY

MUSÉE MARC DEYDIER

Rue de l'Église, 84160 Cucuron • Tel: 04 90 77 25 02
• Fax: 04 90 77 26 15• Open every day except Tuesday • Admission free

Lawyer, archaeologist, photographer and pundit, Marc Deydier was an true man of the Third Republic (1815–1940). His souvenirs and collections have been brought together in this pretty museum, which in addition presents the fruit of archaeological digs in the Gallo-Roman villa of Viely. Note especially the graffito on painted plaster representing with amazing accuracy a Roman trading ship.

THE CEMETERY OF SAINT-PANCRACE

11

Access from Grambois: take the RD33 in the direction of Vitrolles (in Vaucluse, not Vitrolles in Bouches-du-Rhône). After passing the Château de Pradines and a farm on the right, you can park in an open space to the left. Retracing your steps, now on your left, there is a track marked by an electricity transformer on the right. The way is barred and several notices warn that this is private property and access is strictly prohibited. A track (suitable for traffic) leads those allowed to use it to the site in 10 minutes. The cemetery is just behind Saint-Pancrace chapel. Another notice points out that a hermit lives there and requests silence Ɛ

«the most bucolic, surrealistic, unexpected, surprising and improbable cemetery in Provence»

In a private property of the commune of Grambois, attached to Saint–Pancrace chapel, lies the most bucolic, surrealistic, unexpected, surprising and improbable cemetery in Provence.

The bad news concerning Saint-Pancrace and the private rural cemetery of Grambois is that the owner of the Chateau de Pradines, also in charge of the chapel, is against anyone visiting the chapel and cemetery. The good news is that very soon he will no doubt be helping to solve the unemployment problem by creating a job for a hermit-watchman to convince potential visitors to make themselves scarce.

We should acknowledge all the same that he didn't stop us from crossing his land and even let us take photos on condition they were not for publication. In short, with a responsible attitude and perfect discretion, the site may be accessible. But this is only theoretical and the situation may change at any moment …

If Saint-Pancrace chapel, which dates from the 14th century, is closed, you can still see three frescoes through the grille, in the inner courtyard. They were painted by three different artists in 1912, at the height of the Fauve period in France, for the then lord of the manor, Douglas Fitch. One of these frescoes, l'Adoration des Rois (Adoration of the Kings), is by Pierre Girieud, a pioneer of modern art born in Paris (rue de Marseille, strangely enough) to a Provençal family. A close look at the background of the work reveals some details that aren't quite "religiously correct", such as naked porters, bathers frightening one of the horses and, right at the back, a depiction of the chapel. The two other frescoes are by Alfred Lombard (La Prédication du Christ – Christ Preaching) and Georges Dufrenoy (La Descente de Croix – Descent from the Cross). These three artists used the methods of the great Italian fresco painters, which explains the excellent state of conservation of their works despite being exposed to the elements.

But the highlight of the site is of course the cemetery. This is in an extraordinarily peaceful spot, below a forest of yews in which an immense pyramid

"Here lies she who had too many virtues for the earth"

(6 m high) commands the view – the sepulchre of Joséphine Honorine Bec who died in 1819 aged 28. Her inconsolable husband had her buried seated on a throne, attired in her finest clothes and most beautiful jewellery. It is even said that he had an tunnel dug between the chapel and the tomb in order to come and visit her. On three sides of the pyramid can be read epitaphs and poems. Here is an extract:

Ci-gît qui pour la terre, avait trop de vertus,
Le ciel en fut jaloux, le ciel nous la ravie (sic),
Ses charmes ont péri, mais son âme affranchie,
est au sein de son Dieu, ah! ne la pleurez plus.
[Here lies she who had too many virtues for the earth,
The sky was jealous of her, the sky snatched her from us,
Her charms have perished, but her liberated soul
is in the bosom of her God, ah! cry for her no more.]

At the side of the pyramid is the tomb of her daughter, Clémence Bec, who married a rich American merchant, Douglas Fitch, who had come to Marseille on business in 1921. He stayed on for love of Clémence but died at the age of 49. Clémence then remarried, with the Marseillais poet and academic Joseph Autran, and the Château de Pradines became a literary centre. Clémence Bec wanted to prove her love to her two husbands and asked to be interred at Saint-Pancrace in the tomb of Douglas Fitch. She also asked that her heart be laid to rest in the tomb of Joseph Autran at La Malle, Bouc-Bel-Air, near Aix en Provence.

In Grambois, a very attractive perched village, Yves Robert filmed scenes from Pagnol's La Gloire de mon Père [My Father's Honour].

SYNDICAT D'INITIATIVE DE GRAMBOIS
Rue de la Mairie, 84240 Grambois • Tel: 04 90 77 96 29 • Fax: 04 90 77 94 68

THE SIRENE OBSERVATORY 

- Z.L. 12, D 34, 84400 Lagarde d'Apt
- Tel (after 14.00): 04 90 75 04 17 • Fax: 08 26 07 27 99
- E-mail: sirene@obs-sirene.com • http://www.obs-sirene.com
- Discovery evenings, beginners or advanced courses, by appointment only. Consult the website or phone for dates of events and festivals.
- Latitude: 44°00'00" N - Longitude: 05°29'13" E - Altitude: 1,100 m

"An astronomical observatory installed in a former nuclear missile silo

In 1965, General de Gaulle decided to install part of the French nuclear deterrent force on the Plateau d'Albion. Over 785 hectares, 27 silos were constructed to receive missiles (although only 18 came into service). After some 30 years the site was abandoned. Most of the silos were covered over and left to oblivion after of course being relieved of their weapons. Some gave rise to projects such as a local café or the Laboratoire Souterrain Bas Bruit [Underground Low Noise Laboratory]. The most original project is SIRENE (SIlo REhabilité pour Nuits Etoilées), a private astronomical observatory.

The idea of Frédéric Bardin, a dedicated astronomer from the Optics Laboratoire at Marseille Observatory, was to use one of the silos as an astronomical observation platform to give introductory sessions and further training. Work started in 2000. Besides easy access by road, the site, whose altitude of 1,100 m takes it above the layer of pollution, benefits from one of the clearest skies in France, not to mention the protective statute acquired by the armed forces for another 30 years against property development and thus against encroaching light pollution.

The military presence is still very obvious: the technical building on the ground has been used for welcoming visitors and for information services, but the most spectacular sight is the door of the silo that formerly contained the missile, still in place today. The concrete-filled steel door weighs 140 tonnes. In peacetime, it was opened twice a year for maintenance and to change the missile. For that to happen two keys had to be brought together, each kept by a representative of two different ministries – Interior and Defence. In the case of a nuclear attack, it would only take 23 seconds from the moment the presidential order was given to launch a missile, which from a depth of 30 m would pulverize everything in its path, including the buildings above ground – which is why these facilities were for single use only.

Obviously it is at night that SIRENE comes into its own. During observations, the roofs of two domes roll back and telescopes aim at the stars, the planets or the moon. The main thing is to wrap up warmly because even in summer the nights are cold. By day, you can observe the sun or familiarize yourself with astronomical imaging.

MUSÉE DU TIRE-BOUCHON 

- Domaine de la Citadelle, 84560 Ménerbes
- Tel: 04 90 72 41 58 • Fax: 04 90 72 41 59
- Open every day

1 April to 31 October: 10.00–12.00 and 14.00–19.00, 1 November to 31 March: 10.00–12.00 and 14.00–17.00 except Sundays and public holidays

- Admission: 4 (free for under-15s)
- E-mail: domainedelacitadelle@wanadoo.fr
- http://www.domaine-citadelle.com

A museum with a twist...

Yves Rousset-Rouard, mayor of Ménerbes and owner of the wine-producing estate of La Citadelle, where you can visit the corkscrew museum, is particularly known as the producer of successful films such as Les Bronzés (French Fried Vacation), Le Père Noël est une ordure [Father Christmas is Rubbish] and Emmanuelle. If the idea of a corkscrew museum seems a little strange, you'll soon be won over by the superb presentation, the clear commentaries and the 1,200 immaculate exhibits of unexpected diversity. Some models have trademarks: le presto, le rapide, l'ultrarapide, with single or double lever, with blades, brush, spiral, protective "cage", etc. Of course there is the Swiss pocket-knife with its umpteenth built-in tool, the corkscrew. Finally, don't miss the erotic display case. Kitsch but amusing.

SIGHTS NEARBY

SCULPTURES BY MALACHIER 14

Chemin du Château, 84480 Lacoste

On the road to the chateau you pass one of the last works still on the site by Louis Malachier, miller and sculptor from Lacoste who practically lived in the quarries at the end of the 19th century. This naive amateur sculptor one day journeyed to Paris, which was a revelation to him. Not only did he raise a stone Eiffel Tower in front of his house, he also sculpted a multitude of personalities, saints, ordinary folk and animals. These works standing in his garden delighted dealers and antiquarians who stopped by and filled the boots of their cars.

A little further on, a private road leads to the quarries. Visiting these white stone cathedrals, today disused, is unfortunately prohibited for obvious safety reasons. You can however go there in summer, because one of the quarries hosts the Lacoste festival productions.

At the end of the track lies the chateau of the Marquis de Sade. This huge site has been under restoration for some years now. Pierre (meaning "stone", a coincidence so close to the quarries?) Cardin owns the property. The famous marquis lived in the chateau and it was there that he sought refuge from the constabulary following the scandalous orgy he had organized with prostitutes in Marseille. The chateau served as model for his work *Les 120 jours de Sodome* (120 Days of Sodom).

SATOR
AREPO
TENET
OPERA
ROTAS

THE MAGIC SQUARE OF OPPÈDE

In the main square at the entrance to the village, in front of the courtyard of the "Echauguette" restaurant, turn left and carry straight on as far as the side street entered by a sharp bend to the left.

"A palindrome so perfect it's driven people mad

At Oppède, a perched village on the borders of the Luberon, a mysterious magic square offers a perfect palindrome.

Oppède le Vieux is one of those places that you'll immediately love or hate. Houses dating from the 12th century, a 13th-century chateau, its setting on the northern border of the Luberon mountains makes it an impregnable fortified village, at least from the south. A deserted fortress, as few people have managed to live there, which explains why most houses have not been restored despite the attractions of the Luberon for which Peter Mayle's books (A Year in Provence, etc.) bear much of the responsibility.

Consuelo de Saint Exupery, wife of the author of Le Petit Prince, took refuge in Oppède in 1940 with a number of artists and architects, with the intention of preparing to pass on her knowledge, but the German invasion interrupted her plans. She left in 1942 to join her husband Antoine in New York with a promise to write an account of the experiences of the village. Her book, soberly entitled Oppède, was published by Gallimard in 1947.

The small and nameless street where the magic square is to be found is narrow with hardly enough space to take a picture. Never mind, it's the physical contact that counts. Nevertheless as the square is on the wall of a private house, you'll have to be discreet and above all avoid making a noise at the door at siesta time.

The square itself is a fantastic play on Latin words:

S A T O R
A R E P O
T E N E T
O P E R A
R O T A S

It can be read backwards or forwards, downwards or upwards, from right to left or left to right, and a possible translation is "The sower Arepo holds the wheels at work". This is a perfect palindrome that can be found in a couple of dozen places in Europe, including Pompeii, where archaeologists have found two examples. Needless to say that it has driven some people mad. Entire books have been written about it, but the mystery remains.

OFFICE DE TOURISME INTERCOMMUNAL DU CANTON DE BONNIEUX
7, place Carnot, 84480 Bonnieux • Tel: 04 90 75 91 90
• Fax: 04 90 75 92 94 • e-mail : ot-bonnieux@axit.fr

THE BLAST FURNACES OF RUSTREL

• Le Colorado - Quartier Saint Peyre, 84400 Rustrel

Industrial saga

Rustrel, particularly noted for its ochre cliffs known as the "Colorado provençal", went through an ebullient period of industrial development in iron and steel-making in the 19th century, of which spectacular traces remain.

From Rustrel, take the road to Apt and follow the signs to "Camping du Colorado". Access to the site is rather delicate as co-ownership plots overlap. You'll need to be discreet and pleasant towards the residents, some of whom will let you through with no problem.

The site is amazing: a collapsed building has served as support for bizarre dwellings giving onto the two immense blast furnaces still standing, now classed as historic monuments. Parasols around an open-air swimming pool adds to the incongruity of the scene. Then follow the Maîtres de Forge path leading to Notre-Dame-des-Anges chapel above the village and the belvedere.

In 1832, a foreman from the ironworks took part in the pilgrimage to Notre-Dame-des-Anges chapel. He noticed that iron-bearing minerals were rising to the surface at the side of the path. Shortly afterwards the iron and steel adventure began in Rustrel, with script and actors worthy of a summer sitcom on television. First of all was the rivalry between an entrepreneur and a solicitor who threw themselves into a race to acquire land, followed by the bankruptcy of the businessman before the manufacturing plant was built. Next appeared Pauline Jaricot, a rich heiress, who bailed him out of prison and bought the still unfinished factory for a considerable sum. A passionate supporter of *"Christian socialism"*, she came to Rustrel with the avowed intention of setting up a *"establishment where virtuous workers and their families can enjoy the advantages of work carefully organized and fairly paid"*. She died two years later, ruined.

The venture was in fact bound to fail because it relied on out-of-date technology and poor-quality minerals. Finally, the train to Avignon, which would have allowed the steel to be transported cheaply was only inaugurated 10 years after the definitive closure of the plant in 1887.

In the village, just behind the grocery store, a discreet metal cross reminds us that metallurgy is a dangerous activity: on 6 May 1849 a cast of molten metal exploded, killing two workers.

SIGHTS NEARBY

CHAMBRES D'HÔTE DE LA FORGE

Claude et Dominique Berger-Ceccaldi, Notre-Dame-des-Anges 84400 Rustrel • Tel: 04 90 04 92 22 • www.laforge.com.fr

Artist's home in an iron foundry. Swimming pool, Provençal decor.

A JOSEPH TALON
Lou rabassié
Père de la
trufficulture

THE STATUE OF THE RABASSIER*

18

• Place Gambetta, 84490 Saint-Saturnin-les-Apt

Joseph Talon, inventor of "trufficulture"

Many a visitor to Saint-Saturnin-les-Apt has thought that the statue in front of the little garden right of Place Gambetta is that of a boules player. But if you look closer, it isn't a petanque ball but a truffle that Joseph Talon is weighing in his right hand. "Weighing" in every sense, for the truffle is real black gold. If its value rose after the 2003 heatwave to €450 per kilo in Carpentras market, it seems to be nearer €700 today.

An illiterate peasant born between 1755 and 1760, Joseph Talon is thought to be the inventor of truffle cultivation. He simply had the idea of planting the acorns that he'd picked up below oak trees where truffles were hidden. During the Revolution, while others were chopping off heads, Joseph was planting acorns with visible success, judging by the quantity of truffles harvested in 1792 and 1793.

Today things are very different because the agricultural landscape has itself hugely evolved through the abandonment of natural truffle grounds (in favour of vines) and massive forest clearance. At the end of the 19th century, Vaucluse produced around 400 tonnes of truffles each year; before the Second World War 1,500 tonnes, and today … some 18 tonnes.

As for Joseph Talon, he was posthumously honoured through the intermediary of his grandson, who was awarded the mérite agricole in 1899. The statue you see in Place Gambetta was unveiled on 9 November 1986 and recalls the ingenuity of the man who contributed so much to the development of these regional riches.

Take care while walking in the region – to maintain good relations with the locals, you're advised never to poke around with your feet under an oak tree and never to let a dog snuffle around it …

Apart from the statue, the village is worth a stroll around to appreciate a historical curiosity: it was divided into two until the 18th century, for although the east side was French the west side belonged to the papacy. Without there being any real logic to this strange observation, all the historic buildings of the village, with their beautiful doors, stand on the right-hand side going up the main street. With one notable exception, the finest porch with a balcony supported by two atlantes (columns in the form of male figures) is on the left.

***Rabassier:** Provençal for "truffle gatherer" (rabasso = truffle).

GRAFFITI AT THE CHÂTEAU DE LOURMARIN 19

• BP 23, 84160 Lourmarin • Tel: 04 90 68 15 23 • Fax: 04 90 68 25 19
• E-mail: chateaudelourmarin@wanadoo.fr
• http://www.chateau-de-lourmarin.com
The graffiti, in private rooms, can only be visited by appointment. The figurines of the frieze of the main staircase are accessible for as long as you care to linger, during the traditional tour of the chateau.

The Gypsy's curse

A number of strange details regularly escape the hurried visitor to the Château de Lourmarin. The "Gypsies' graffiti" is perhaps the most notable of these little-known curiosities.

The chateau in Lourmarin, a typical Luberon village, has two main sections: the old chateau which dates from the 15th century, and the Renaissance wing, built from 1537. In 1801, Pierre de Girard, inventor of the flax-spinning machine, acquired the property. The million francs offered to the inventor by Napoleon I (but never paid), would bring about the financial ruin of the landowner. Until the early 20th century the chateau was passed from hand to hand and squatted. It even seems that the ruined sections had been used by Gypsies on pilgrimage to Les Saintes-Maries-de-la-Mer.

It was to just these "travellers" that was once attributed the famous graffiti of the chateau, representing a boat thought to be that of the Holy Marys coming over from Palestine; a cross the texture of which recalls a palm tree; circles that evoke the sun; five-pointed stars and the mysterious word "ARMENY". The curse weighing down the successive owners of the chateau is even attributed to this graffiti: the very last private owner, Robert Laurent-Vibert, president of Pétrole Hahn, who had bought the property in 1920, was killed in a motor accident in 1925 as he left Lourmarin to return to Lyon. According to Guide de *la Provence mystérieuse* (Éditions Tchou), the graffiti is in fact a drawing signed by a member of the Armeny family, Armenians living in Marseille, who marked their passage thus. As it happens there is a street of that name in Marseille: rue Armeny.

Another strange aspect of the chateau is the main staircase, a masterpiece of academic architecture. Concentrating on the upper frieze as you go up, you'll also notice a progression of sculptures, like flipping through a strip cartoon: a scallop shell followed by a pilgrim's purse, a mason's compass, coats of arms, a man leaning over and – seen from behind, two particular parts of the male anatomy supported by wings …

Finally, a mysterious warning is written on the lintel of the cellar door. In Gothic letters, it reads: *"Drink and take your leave – 1513"*.

OFFICE DE TOURISME DE LOURMARIN
9, avenue Philippe-de-Girard, 84160 Lourmarin • Tel: 04 90 68 10 77
• Fax:04 90 68 10 77 • e-mail : ot-lourmarin@axit.fr

THE SCULPTURE OF THE "MOURVELOUS"

Roc du donjon, 84300 Les Taillades

> ***Snotty but marvellous...***

The village of Les Taillades, a few kilometres from Cavaillon, consists of a few dwellings scattered around a stone quarry. The church at the summit blends in with the stones and the donjon, below, seems to be an extension of an island spared by the stonemasons. The place is sufficiently out of the ordinary, in all its acoustic magnificence, to host performances from the Avignon festival.

Although the donjon, or dungeon, does not shelter a dragon, you won't escape the curious gaze of "Mourvelous". Sculpted at the foot of the donjon, this figure which at first sight resembles a face, is open to many other interpretations and it's easy to see in it anything that your imagination might come up with – a bishop's mitre, a sacrificial offering, a cross clasped to the chest, someone picking their nose ...

If the origin of this sculpture is unknown, it in fact represents the bishop of Cavaillon, Saint Véran (see page 244), seeing his favourite dragon off to the Alps (to create the highest commune in Europe: Saint-Véran) via Les Taillades, which indicates that the colubro, the giant snake that devastated the region, passed through the village. The name *"Mourvelous"*, from the Provençal mourveou (snotty), comes from the fact that delinquents were exposed to public condemnation on that spot, particularly from being spat on.

OFFICE DE TOURISME
Place de la Mairie, BP 401, 84308 Les Taillades Cedex
• Tel: 04 90 71 09 98 • Fax: 04 90 71 99 01

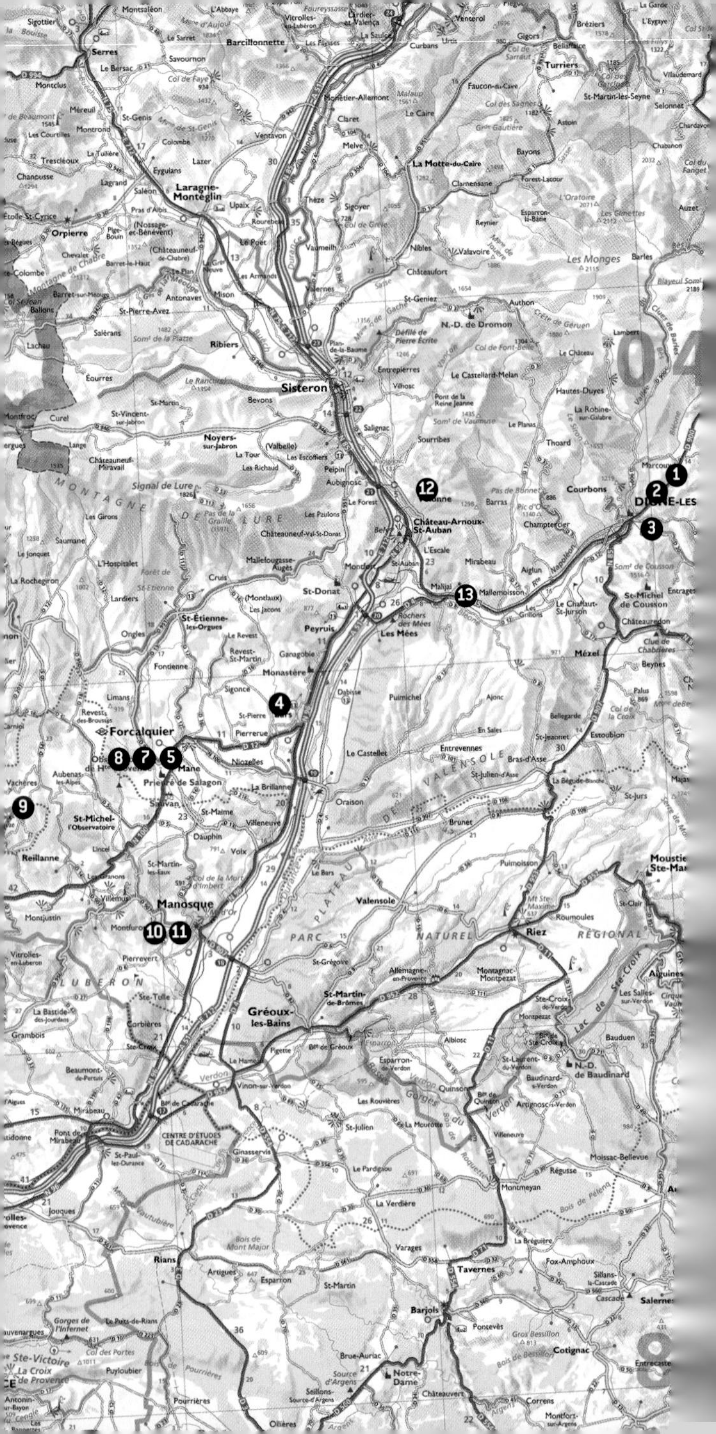

Serres
Montclus
Barcillonnette
Venterol
Turriers
Laragne-Montéglin
Orpierre
La Motte-du-Caire
Les Monges
Barles
Sisteron
N.-D. de Dromon
Défilé de Pierre Écrite
Noyers-sur-Jabron
Montagne de Lure
Signal de Lure
Château-Arnoux-St-Auban
Courbons
Digne-les
St-Donat
Les Mées
Rochers des Mées
Peyruis
Mallemoisson
St-Michel de Cousson
Mézel
Ganagobie
Monastère
Forcalquier
Mane
Prieuré de Salagon
St-Michel-l'Observatoire
Reillanne
Plateau de Valensole
Valensole
Riez
Parc Naturel Régional
Manosque
Luberon
Gréoux-les-Bains
St-Martin-de-Brômes
Lac de Ste-Croix
Moustiers-Ste-Marie
N.-D. de Baudinard
Gorges du Verdon
Vinon-sur-Verdon
Centre d'Études de Cadarache
Mirabeau
Rians
Tavernes
Barjols
Cotignac
Notre-Dame
Ste-Victoire
Gorges de l'Infernet
Col des Portes
04
1
2
3
4
5
7
8
9
10
11
12
13

HAUTE-PROVENCE

FOSSILIZED ICHTHYSAURUS ❶

IN THE RÉSERVE GÉOLOGIQUE DE HAUTE PROVENCE

- Parc Saint-Benoit, 04005 Digne-les-Bains
- Tel: 04 92 36 70 70
- E-mail: contact@resgeol04.org

8 km from Digne-les-Bains by the RD900a in the direction of Barles. Car park to the left of the road is 2 km from the turn-off to Robine-le-Forest.

A fascinating prehistoric relic

Not far from Digne-les-Bains, you can walk to the site where a fossilized ichthyosaurus, a prehistoric reptile that resembles a large swordfish, is preserved in the very place that it was discovered. This symbolic and fascinating route shows all the geological richness of the département, proving that exploitation of this heritage was a good idea.

Allow about an hour for the walk, which includes a 200 m slope to reach the exceptional site of the ichthyosaurus. The route is marked out (in yellow) and looks more like a well-maintained avenue than a track. Climb up the Bélier ravine on the left bank of the stream and, at the waterfall (where the flow varies with the season), cross over the bridge to the right bank. After four bends in the path you reach the Col du Jas, from where you head down again to the palaeontological site. Return by the same route.

The fossil, discovered in the late 1970s, is displayed in a glass case. The Robine-le-Forest ichthyosaurus is one of the main reasons for the creation of the Réserve Géologique de Haute Provence, to preserve the exceptional palaeontological heritage. Since 1984, the 185 million-year-old fossilized skeleton has been exhibited in situ, a European first.

The ichthyosaurus is a marine reptile, a great predator of fish and molluscs such as ammonites, belemnites and nautiluses. The name comes from the Greek ikhthus (fish) and sauros (lizard), as although it looks like a fish it belongs to the reptile family. The shape of its body is similar to a dolphin or shark and its four limbs, transformed into paddles, its dorsal fin and tail would have allowed great speed of movement. It could reach 15 m in length.

This walking trek is described in the guide Digne-les-Bains et ses environs à pied, available at the Digne-les-Bains tourist office

SIGHTS NEARBY

LA DALLE AUX AMMONITES ❷

On the same route (RD900a), leaving Digne-les-Bains, a car park on the left lets you stop and see the "ammonite stone", richly encrusted with some 1,500 fossils. Even for non-specialists, the density of ammonites is really impressive. This phenomenon is probably due to the accumulation of empty shells washed in by the tides of 150 million years ago. Ammonites are snail-shaped marine cephalopods, thousands of species of which have been identified, that abruptly disappeared 65 million years ago.

THE STARS OF SAINT VINCENT

• Musée Gassendi, 64, boulevard Gassendi, 04000 Digne-les-Bains
• Tel: 04 92 31 45 29 • http://www.musee-gassendi.org
Still making jewellery the traditional way with the étoiles de Saint-Vincent (Stars of St Vincent): Bijouterie Commeiras, 39, boulevard Gassendi 04000 Digne-les-Bains • Tel: 04 92 31 34 27

Fossils mounted as jewellery are worn as emblems of local pride

In AD 340, Christianity was brought to Haute Provence by Vincent, a goldsmith and stonemason who renounced his wealth to be part of the epic new religion. Following a meteor shower, he noticed that strange stones seemed to have fallen from the sky. Vincent had in fact discovered fossilized marine invertebrates known as crinoids (from the Greek krinoeides, lily-like), the ancestors of starfish and sea-urchins that lived from the Palaeozoic era some 600 million years ago. Their tentacles floating in the depths of the ocean were composed of five-branched segments which, once separated, really do bring stars to mind.

Shortly after his discovery, Vincent, now a bishop, was asked a favour by a young woman from Digne whose beau had been imprisoned by the local lord of the manor. He would get him freed by offering the lord's wife a jewel made from stars ... these little grey stars, less than a centimetre across (from 2–12 mm), contrast so well with gold or silver that they seem to have been made to set off the precious metals.

1,500 years later, in 1826, Antoine Colomb was born at Digne. His jeweller father soon had him learn the trade. A keen walker and nature lover, Antoine was to set the little fossils found in the hill above Digne, opportunely called St Vincent's Hill.

This stone star, imbued with the aura of so many millions of years, became the diamond of Digne, in tune with a region disinclined to flaunt fictitious or ostentatious wealth.

In the 19th century, when the people of Barcelonette went to seek their fortune in Mexico, the people of Digne, also scattered around the world, recognized one another by the jewels gracing the necks, arms or fingers of their wives. There was also a range of designs for men, with tiepins and cufflinks.

Today this very unusual jewellery can be seen at the Musée Gassendi and Bijouterie Commeiras on boulevard Gassendi.

CURIOUS STREET NAMES

Digne-les-Bains has several very unusual street names: rue Pied de Cocu evokes against all expectations the call of the cuckoo and rue Prête à Partir, alongside the Bléone (the river that waters the town), is a reminder that the townspeople always had a bag packed in case they had to leave quickly in a flood ...

RURAL GÎTES OF LA GRAND'TERRE

• RN96, 04700 Lurs • Tel: 06 82 08 02 61
€300–€400 per week depending on the season
• Photographs and details available on http://www.abritel.fr
(enter "Lurs" in the field "Recherche spécifique, par ville")
Access by the A51 motorway in the direction of Sisteron.
Leave the motorway at La Brillanne (exit 19, after Manosque), take the RN96 in the direction of Sisteron. From the junction with the RD12, travel 3 km further north to reach the "Grand'Terre".

Sleep at the scene of the most famous crime in postwar France

The new owners of La Grand'Terre make no bones about it, their holiday let is a "historic" place. It is in fact the farm of the Dominici family, who were at the centre of one of the most celebrated criminal affairs of the 20th century, the first human-interest story with full media coverage.

During the night of 4–5 August 1952, Sir Jack Drummond, his wife Lady Ann, and their little girl Elizabeth were assassinated at Lurs, near the house of the Dominici family. After years of legal proceedings and contradictory inquiries, Gaston Dominici, the "grandad" of the family aged 76, was denounced by his sons Clovis and Gustave and sentenced to death. He was later pardoned by General de Gaulle.

The people of Provence and the English tourists are all familiar with the details of the affair and the layout of the site, the precise place where this English family had pitched their tent, the track leading from the main road and the little bridge over the railway line where the child was finished off. This incident had extraordinary repercussions, concerning as it did a rural drama taking place not long after the war with the main parts played by romantic characters: an austere and withdrawn peasant from the Basses-Alpes département surrounded by an uncommunicative family on the one hand, and on the other an unknown English family in which the father had been recruited by the British secret services during the Second World War. This is why so many hypotheses were put forward during the proceedings. The trial took place at Digne-les-Bains, which came under Basses-Alpes jurisdiction (thanks to civil servants' intolerance of pejorative remarks, the département has since been renamed Alpes-de-Haute-Provence). The Drummond family is buried in the magnificent cemetery of Forcalquier.

Today, dozens of "tourists" still stop here and try to exorcise the visions of horror that have haunted an entire Anglo-French generation. To prove it, the cross at the corner of the bridge where the child was killed is covered in flowers and decorated with morbid soft toys.

THE SAINT-MICHEL FOUNTAIN

• Place Saint-Michel, 04300 Forcalquier

> ***The sculpture in fact represents a child playing a game called "fart in the face"***

Saint Michael's fountain in Forcalquier, apparently perfectly classical in style, conceals a little gem of medieval urban eroticism that's worth a visit.

Forcalquier has sometimes been compared with Saint-Rémy-de-Provence because of the number of northern Europeans who can be seen strolling around or who've settled there, but also because of the quality of its market, held on Mondays, and which makes you want to live in this privileged spot all the year round. This town, all curves and gentle slopes (except for the citadelle) has a special charm, and it's a great pleasure to lose yourself in the streets of the old quarter. You'll soon come to the Place Saint-Michel, just above the cathedral of Notre-Dame du Bourguet.

St Michael's fountain stands in the square, where it was constructed in 1521. At the time it was no mean feat to bring water from the nearest source, 3 km from the town. The fountain itself is still there but its octagonal basin was replaced in 1912 with an ordinary round one and its ornamental spire, whose sculptures were damaged by the passage of time, was replaced with a copy in 1976. The original is in a museum. At the top of the spire, St Michael strikes down the dragon. Look more closely at the fountain and you'll also see four sculptures, original ones this time, around the base of the spire between the water jets. One of these is unmissable, depicting as it does two characters head to tail, so to speak, in a position not usually found in a public place. According to Patrick Ollivier-Elliott (author of Pays de Lure, Forcalquier, Manosque, carnet d'un voyageur attentif, Éditions Edisud), it shows a children's game from past times known as "fart in the face" ... no need to say more, the sculpture speaks for itself!

SIGHTS NEARBY

LIBRAIRIE LE BLEUET ❻
Place Saint Just, 04150 Banon • Tel: 04 92 73 25 85
• Opening hours: 9.15–20.00, every day

One of the biggest book shops in France in a rural village of 880 inhabitants? This was the challenge met by Joël Gattefossé: after starting out in 1990, in 2000 he bought the adjoining house and in 2004 the barn next door. During all this time people were watching what he was doing. Local readers, then those from Marseille or Nice, were attracted not only by the choice and size of his stock, but also by the thoughtful layout, the warm welcome in extended opening hours and an indefinable something that made people want to be part of the Bleuet adventure. Today, 70,000 titles and 100,000 other works are in stock, 364 days per year (closed 1 January only).

THE FORCALQUIER CEMETERY

• Avenue Fontauris, 04300 Forcalquier
From the tourist office, take the road to the right of the town hall and follow the signs. You can reach the cemetery on foot in about 15 minutes.

The most beautiful cemetery in France?

Often referred to as the most beautiful in France, the listed cemetery of Forcalquier is worth a hundred visits, not only for its beauty but for some of its more unusual residents …

The distinctive feature of the cemetery is its yew trees, cleverly pruned in angular shapes, but especially artistically pierced with "doors" of greenery that break down the gloomy impression that long rows of tombs generally produce. Here, the plots are lawns bordered with yew, like a kind of natural chapel where the graves seem to have found their natural setting.

Although there is no documentation of the beginning of this initiative in funerary arborescence, it's said that it was a kindly gardener who thought of composing this fresco of plants at the end of the 19th century. At the entrance to the site the yews predominate, while as far as you can see there are restanques (low drystone walls) from which the occasional isolated borie rises.

At the main gate, turn right and look in the second row for the tomb of Professor Edmond Henry, the first surgeon to carry out a successful heart transplant in France, at Marseille. The most moving thing about it the grave is the plaque placed on it, which reads: *À celui qui m'a redonné la vie. ("To him who gave me back my life.") Emmanuel Vitria.* This Marseillais, known as "Bicou", was in fact the first Frenchman to benefit from this legendary operation, in 1968. He was thus able to live another 19 years, whereas he had been condemned to an early death.

Close to the far wall towards the right, the tomb of the Bouche family rises above the green hedge. It carries a curious epitaph:

"During their existence they endured many adversities, injustices and unfortunate tribulations. Then the last serene breath of their life went into the sublime and mysterious vastness … Reason and the family tradition meant they were devoted to pure liberalism, which was their creed. Free from servility, they bowed before no grasping or intrusive influences. They had to suffer the vile arrogance of opposition to their fleeting success. They ignored them. They remained faithful to democracy ceaselessly growing in the just assertion of their rights." There is a special mention below for Eugène Bouche, died 1895: *"With regret at not having been able to enjoy for long the Republican institutions, the glorification of France and the good fortune of having come from a civilized people."*

THE GÎTE OF LES BORIES DU SERRE

- Impasse des Restanque, 04300 Forcalquier
- Tel: 04 92 75 23 72 • E-mail: jp.vander@tiscali.fr
- http://boriesduserre.free.fr/
- Rates from €550 to €1,100 per week according to season
Weekends (off-season only) €240

Sleep in a borie

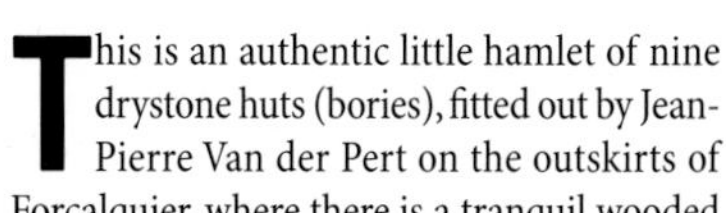

This is an authentic little hamlet of nine drystone huts (bories), fitted out by Jean-Pierre Van der Pert on the outskirts of Forcalquier, where there is a tranquil wooded park beside a beautiful swimming pool. Having inherited land on which stood three age-old bories, he had the idea of rethinking the interior of these huts to provide all mod cons. The huts that he later built to complete his holiday rental accommodation were identical to the ancient ones on the outside, although the latest construction techniques were used.

Although these dwellings have undoubted external charm, you'll have to go inside and stay there a while to fully appreciate them. The interior layout is really very well thought out and the domed roof, seen from inside, has a very special feeling. You'll also be surprised by the size of the living space, which is much larger than you might think. The "typical" borie (if such exists) comprises an entrance/living area opening onto a kitchen corner, two adjoining bedrooms and a mezzanine for extra sleeping space. Enough to put up a family.

THE MYSTERY OF THE BORIES

Should you say "un" borie or "une" borie" in French? For the Larousse dictionary, borie is feminine, like une maison (house). These drystone huts with no jointing, mortar or bonding, are built from the inside so their shape sometimes defies the laws of gravity. The roof is conceived on the "house of cards" principle, which means that no stone can be placed at random. The first bories were Neolithic, but those existing today date from the 17th, 18th and even 19th centuries.

Many hypotheses were put forward concerning bories at the end of the 20th century. Some people think they are simply "garden sheds" where the peasants stored their tools and which served as occasional shelters. Homes of persecuted Vaudois (Protestant Christian group founded in the 12th century), refuges for the inhabitants of towns and villages infected by the plague, remains of strongholds of the Gauls and, to be really far-fetched, second homes for extra-terrestrials ε

To find out more about these domed huts, go and visit the famous "Village des Bories" near Gordes (Vaucluse), which has dozens of them, some specializing as bread ovens, stables or wine-presses.

VILLAGES DES BORIES
84220 Gordes • Open every day from 9.00 until sunset
• Tel: 04 90 72 03 48 • www.gordes-village.com

MUSÉE DE VACHÈRES

9

• 04110 Vachères • Tel: 04 92 75 67 21 • Mairie: 04 92 75 62 15
• Opening hours: 1 May to 30 September: 10.00–12.00 and 15.00–18.00
1 October to 30 April: 14.00–17.00 by appointment

Where did the prehistoric gazelles go?

In the 1970s, the territory of Vachères was visited and excavated by a new type of trader – retailers of fossils and minerals. They enhanced the value, so to speak, of this rich palaeontological site of the Oligocene lakes dating back 35 million years. There, below the village, lie thousands of fossilized plants, animals and especially fish, including the famous *Dapalis macrurus,* the star of mineral and fossil shops for almost two decades. At the time, you only had to give a few banknotes to the peasant owners of this land to extract, in a day, as many as 200 to 300 fossilized fish with spectacularly detailed bones and cartilage.

The recently restored Vachères museum displays specimens taken from this exception fossil bed.

The high point of the collection is the *Bachiterium,* a primitive "gazelle" now extinct, an ancestor of modern ruminants. This unique specimen was found by one of the new excavators who were living on the fruits of their discoveries. He was called Siméon Loggia, wore a beard and long hair, lived at Draguignan and came to Vachères for the season, just as archaeologists stay at the site of a dig. The specimen, the only one of its kind, was sold for a small fortune to a German collector who, finding himself in financial difficulties some time later, resold it to the local commune for a price said to be "quite high" … Since the time when unregulated digs were tolerated, the site has been included in the natural geological reserve and there is no longer any question of collecting from it.

THE WARRIOR OF VACHÈRES

In the mid-19th century, a coachman exasperated by the bump in the road that his team of horses stumbled over each time they passed decided to dig out the protruding object. He discovered a stone statue representing, larger than life-size, a warrior from the time of Augustus (who reigned around the time of the birth of Christ). The body was covered by a coat of mail, he carried a broadsword and his chain was typically Gaulish. This masterpiece was taken away from the village, which retains only a (very fine) copy that can be seen in the museum. The original now belongs to the Musée Calvet in Avignon and is displayed at the entrance to the lapidary collection of this celebrated Vaucluse town.